FREE
MARKET
REVOLUTION

HOW AYN RAND'S IDEAS
CAN END BIG GOVERNMENT

FREE
MARKET
REVOLUTION

HOW AYN RAND'S IDEAS
CAN END BIG GOVERNMENT

YARON BROOK AND DON WATKINS

palgrave
macmillan

FREE MARKET REVOLUTION
Copyright © Ayn Rand Institute, 2012.
All rights reserved.

First published in 2012 by PALGRAVE MACMILLAN® in the United States—a division of St. Martin's Press LLC, 175 Fifth Avenue, New York, NY 10010.

Where this book is distributed in the UK, Europe and the rest of the world, this is by Palgrave Macmillan, a division of Macmillan Publishers Limited, registered in England, company number 785998, of Houndmills, Basingstoke, Hampshire RG21 6XS.

Palgrave Macmillan is the global academic imprint of the above companies and has companies and representatives throughout the world.

Palgrave® and Macmillan® are registered trademarks in the United States, the United Kingdom, Europe and other countries.

ISBN: 978-1-137-27838-8

Library of Congress Cataloging-in-Publication Data for the hardcover

Brook, Yaron.
    Free market revolution : how Ayn Rand's ideas can end big government / by Yaron Brook and Don Watkins.
        p.   cm.
    Includes index.
    ISBN 978-0-230-34169-2
    1. Free enterprise. 2. Capitalism. 3. Self-interest. 4. Rand, Ayn. I. Watkins, Don, 1982– II. Title.
HB95.B76   2012
330.12'2—dc23

                                                                    2012002899

A catalogue record of the book is available from the British Library.

Design by Letra Libre Inc.

First edition: September 2013

10 9 8 7 6 5 4 3 2 1

Printed in the United States of America.

Note: Some material from chapter 1 has appeared in a somewhat different form in the journal *The Objective Standard*. Material from chapters 7, 9, and 12 has appeared in a somewhat different form in the authors' Forbes.com column, *The Objectivist*.

CONTENTS

To Revital Brook and Kate Watkins—
for your unwavering support and infinite patience

PREFACE TO THE PAPERBACK

FREE MARKET REVOLUTION IS AN INSTRUCTION MANUAL for fighting Big Government. It lays out what the free market is, how it works, and why it is profoundly moral. If you read and understand the principles in this book, you will have the tools you need to wage the war of ideas, seize the moral high ground, and help stop the growth of the state in our time.

America desperately needs new ideas. Since the reelection of Barack Obama, the right has been in tatters—directionless and demoralized. "The Republican Party is in trouble," write Michael Gerson and Peter Wehner in *Commentary* magazine. "In the wake of the presidential election, everybody has said so, and everybody is right."[1]

There is always soul searching in the wake of an election defeat, but this is something more. Syndicated columnist Rich Lowry puts it this way: "It is not just the winter of Republican discontent. It will in all likelihood be the spring, summer and fall, as well. And more seasons yet after that. The national party is leaderless and nearly issue-less."[2]

There is a real sense on the right that no one knows what to do, that the Tea Party has failed, that the country is lost. The number one question we hear whenever we speak is: "What's the use? Isn't it hopeless?"

The fight for freedom is not hopeless. What is hopeless is the political right as it presently exists.

What have we seen since Obama's reelection? The GOP rolled over on tax hikes for high-income Americans, and top-ranking Republicans spent the early part of the year decrying *cuts* in government spending. In 2010,

Republicans had gained control of the House on the promise to cut the growth of the state—it took less than an election cycle for that commitment to fizzle out.

That collapse did not come as a surprise to readers of *Free Market Revolution*.

No, we did not predict the outcome of the 2012 election. What we did predict was that, without a fundamental shift in Americans' thinking, the state would keep growing *regardless* of who won the election.

The events of the last year have only confirmed our diagnosis: that the state keeps expanding because of deeply entrenched ideas hostile to freedom and capitalism.

So the bad news is that the mainstream cannot save us. But here's the good news: the mainstream can be changed. How? By changing people's *ideas*. Ideas shape policy, and ideas can be reshaped. America was created on the basis of new ideas—and if it is to be saved, it will only be through ideas.

What does a battle of ideas look like?

It starts with taking a definite stand. It means rejecting the Republican establishment's pattern of praising free markets with worn-out slogans while endorsing every major restriction on economic freedom the left dreams up. It means defending a truly free market—one in which the government's only job is to protect the individual's rights to life, liberty, property, and the pursuit of happiness against violation by force or fraud.

But that is only the first step. A battle of ideas requires that you be philosophically armed to the teeth—that you know your case, and that you know your opponents' case and are able to demolish it.

Above all, it requires that in every battle or skirmish, you *control the moral high ground.*

This country was founded by men who owned the moral high ground. The Founding Fathers declared their independence from Great Britain on *moral* grounds: on the principle that each individual has a right to pursue his own happiness. On that basis they established the freest nation in history.

But for over a century, the left has dominated the moral high ground in the debate over economic policy. The right has been reduced to evasion, apology, and helpless 'me too'-ing.

All of that needs to change—and you're holding in your hands the knowledge that can help change it.

Can we succeed? Yes, but only if we act. The greatest danger we face in the near term is passivity, and the greatest cause of passivity is cynicism—a cynicism that says ideas don't matter, and that it's too late to save this country.

Cynicism and surrender are easy. What's much, much harder is to fight even when the odds are against you. The Founding Fathers, in order to vindicate their rights, had to face the mightiest military on earth at the risk of their own lives. All that's required of us is the courage to speak out in defense of freedom. Can any of us honestly say that burden is too great?

Don Watkins and Yaron Brook
Irvine, California, March 2013

ACKNOWLEDGMENTS

ONE REASON JAMES MADISON INITIALLY DID NOT WANT TO include a bill of rights in the Constitution was because he worried that by naming *some* rights the government could not infringe upon, people would draw the conclusion that these were the *only* rights the government could not infringe upon. We can sympathize. In acknowledging those who made this book possible, we are left with the desire to include our own Ninth Amendment: *The failure to include someone in these acknowledgments should not be construed to deny or disparage his contribution.*

Our debts to history's great thinkers run deep, and, for the record, this book would not exist but for the achievements of men like Aristotle, John Locke, Adam Smith, the Founding Fathers, and Ludwig von Mises.

Our greatest intellectual debt is, of course, to Ayn Rand. Her philosophy has shaped virtually every aspect of our work and our lives. We hope this book does her justice.

It would be impossible to name every Rand scholar whose work we have profited from, but we would be remiss not to tip our hats to Andrew Bernstein, Harry Binswanger, Eric Daniels, Eric Dennis, Allan Gotthelf, John David Lewis, Gregory Salmieri, Rob Tarr, C. Bradley Thompson, and Darryl Wright. In particular we want to recognize Tara Smith for her work on Rand's virtues, Peter Schwartz for his many lectures on Rand's analysis of altruism, and Robert Mayhew for editing a series of outstanding books on Ayn Rand's fiction. All of these individuals have contributed to our understanding of Ayn Rand's ideas, and we draw on their work throughout this book.

We have also benefited from the work of a number of non-Objectivist economists and economic commentators including Peter Boettke, Russell Roberts, Peter Schiff, George Selgin, Thomas Sowell, William Voegeli, Lawrence H. White, and George Will, among many others.

We would like especially to thank our colleagues at the Ayn Rand Institute. Your contributions, direct and indirect, were invaluable. Particular thanks go to Angela Dietrich, who performed the unenviable task of creating time for Yaron to work on this project; Richard E. Ralston, who helped guide us through the publication process; Rituparna Basu, who assisted with research and fact checking; Donna Montrezza, who skillfully proofread the entire manuscript; and Elan Journo and the entire Policy team, who helped us develop our thinking on these issues over the years.

We owe a special debt of gratitude to Onkar Ghate. From day one, Onkar helped guide this project and went above and beyond editing the final manuscript under the pressure of a grueling deadline. But even that understates his contribution. There is simply no way to quantify how much we have learned from him over the years: about capitalism, about philosophy, about how to think and to write. Thank you, Onkar, for all that you have done.

Two other individuals assisted in editing this book (although the standard disclaimer applies: any errors are our own). Michael Berliner helped us sharpen many of our arguments (and, occasionally, our grammar). Leonard Peikoff graciously offered his comments on several of the chapters, improving them immensely—to say nothing of his enormous and unparalleled contribution to our understanding of Ayn Rand's philosophy through his books and lectures.

From Yaron: I would like to personally thank Leonard Peikoff for being a teacher and a mentor to me over many years: His advice and feedback have been crucial to my intellectual development and achievements. And none of this would have been possible without the patience, understanding, and love of Revital, Niv, and Edaan Brook, who remained supportive and encouraging in spite of long working hours and frequent absences from home. Thank you for making the world a place worth saving.

From Don: I would like to thank Lisa VanDamme, Chad Morris, Kyle Steele, Adam Edmonsond, Damon DeBusk, Rob Watkins, and Don and Sandy Watkins for their encouragement and support. My deepest gratitude goes to my wife, Kate Watkins, and my friend and mentor Alex Epstein. Kate made this work possible in a thousand ways, not the least of which was by patiently tolerating my intolerable work schedule. Alex: Here is a down payment on a debt that can never fully be repaid.

Finally, we would both like to thank the Ayn Rand Institute's supporters. This project would not have been possible without your generosity.

FREE
MARKET
REVOLUTION

HOW AYN RAND'S IDEAS
CAN END BIG GOVERNMENT

INTRODUCTION

IN 2007, AYN RAND'S NOVEL *ATLAS SHRUGGED* SOLD 185,000 copies, an all-time record for the book. Fifty years after it was first published, readers were still captivated by *Atlas*'s unforgettable characters, its gripping plot, and its challenging ideas. We at the Ayn Rand Institute were elated but not entirely surprised. Thanks in part to our efforts, sales of *Atlas Shrugged* have been growing since Rand's death in 1982. But even we did not expect what came next.

In late 2008, as the economy experienced a devastating financial crisis followed by an avalanche of government intervention, sales of *Atlas Shrugged* skyrocketed. By the end of the year, it would sell more than 200,000 copies. In 2009, that number would reach half a million. In a world where 98 percent of new books sell fewer than 1,000 copies and the typical best seller doesn't break 100,000, *Atlas Shrugged* was a phenomenon.

And it wasn't just book sales. Referring to *Atlas*, bloggers debated whether it was time to "Go Galt." Tea Party activists carried signs declaring "Ayn Rand Was Right." Pundits, TV hosts, talk radio personalities, and even politicians were praising Rand and recommending her books. Ayn Rand was everywhere.

Why were people turning en masse to an author who had been dead for more than a quarter century? On one level it was the striking parallels between *Atlas Shrugged* and present-day America. *Atlas* describes a world hit by economic ruin, a world where every problem is blamed on "greedy" businessmen, and where the "solution" is invariably to cede more power to the state. After eight years of Bush and eight minutes of Obama, it sounded all too familiar.

The deeper reason, however, was that Americans were looking for answers. What had gone wrong? Was it too much greed or perhaps too much government? Had the state grown too big? How could it be limited to its proper purpose? What *is* the proper purpose of government? What should be *my* purpose as an individual? Is it right to pursue wealth, success, and happiness—or is that selfish and immoral? Can I even trust my own mind in such complex issues, or should I listen to some authority, such as my teacher, my minister, Glenn Beck, or Jon Stewart?

Rand provides challenging new answers to just these questions. Her answers defy convention, but that is part of their appeal. It was a conventional path, after all, that led to economic meltdown and an ever-expanding government. A growing number of Americans were ready to hear Rand's message: that many of our standard views about morality, politics, economics, and life are *corrupt* and need to be thrown out. (Some people mistakenly believed that Rand's ideas *were* mainstream and in fact helped shape the economic policies that created the financial crisis. As we show in chapter 4, this wasn't even close to true.)

Rand, however, is not primarily a critic. She does not simply censure the mainstream—she defines and fights for a revolutionary ideal to replace it: a new philosophy of individualism. "My philosophy, in essence, is the concept of man as a heroic being, with his own happiness as the moral purpose of his life, with productive achievement as his noblest activity, and reason as his only absolute."[1]

This book is written from the perspective of Ayn Rand's philosophy, and all of the philosophic ideas in it are hers. (This is true even in the many cases where we don't reference her directly.) But the focus of the book is not Rand's philosophy as a whole but one element of it: her moral defense of free markets. We aim to show how the ideas of *Atlas Shrugged* help explain today's political and economic world and provide the intellectual ammunition to take down Big Government.

"Big Government," by the way, is not our favorite term. The problem with government today is not its size per se but its role in the economy and in our lives. The problem is what government *does*: Instead of performing the delimited function the Founders assigned it—protecting individual rights—the government intervenes in our lives in countless ways, restricting our freedom, redistributing our wealth, and erecting barriers to our pursuit of happiness. Yes, it *is* too big, but it's too big because it is no longer limited by the principles of the Declaration of Independence. If it was up to us, we would label the threat "Statist Government." But "Big Government," as inexact as it is, does suggest the essential idea: The Founders' vision of limited government has been replaced by an *unlimited* government, and something has to be done to restore those limits.

This book is written in the conviction that those limits cannot be restored until Americans understand and reject the *ideas* that cause government to grow. Although many of us claim to want smaller government, we keep electing politicians who openly tell us that they intend to make government bigger. We don't like the idea of Big Government, but many of us do like the individual handouts, subsidies, regulations, and government favors that it entails. We think these are necessary, good, and noble. When a politician does try to cut government, popular support for his efforts almost always erodes in the face of charges that he is cruel, hardhearted, mean-spirited.

To change the trajectory of the country, we have to change the way we look at free markets. This is what we call the Free Market Revolution. It is a revolution in the way people think about markets and about the central activity that takes place on them: the self-interested pursuit of profit. It is the moral attack on self-interest and the profit motive that has led us farther and farther away from the profit system, and only a moral defense of self-interest and the profit motive can save us.

We are not the first to observe that behind the growth of the state lies a moral attack on the free market. A number of recent works have tried to argue that capitalism *is* a moral system, but for reasons very different from ours.[2] Free markets, they say, need not celebrate self-interest. Self-interest can be tolerated without being glorified. Capitalism—so long as it is tempered by appropriate levels of regulation and wealth redistribution—is good despite being fueled by man's "lower motives"; good, because it raises up the poor, because it promotes hard work and other "bourgeois" virtues; good because, despite its flaws, the alternatives are worse. As economist Deirdre McCloskey puts it in *The Bourgeois Virtues*, a work touted as a powerful moral defense of capitalism, "markets and the bourgeois life are not always bad for the human spirit."[3]

If the best that capitalism's defenders can muster is that vice sometimes, somehow, leads to good, that capitalism is "not always bad for the human spirit," that a free market is to be embraced because it is less awful than a socialist dictatorship, is it any wonder that government's power over the market has been growing, decade after decade?

If we are going to succeed in ending Big Government, we have to recognize that a halfhearted defense of free markets is worse than no defense at all. We have to recognize that capitalism—full, unregulated, uncontrolled, laissez-faire capitalism—is not simply "less bad" than any alternative: It is the only moral economic system in history. And, further, that it is moral not because it helps the poor or teaches us to be good citizens but because it enables the individual to make the most of his *own* life—to exercise his mind, take risks, make money, pursue and achieve his own happiness.

This is the Free Market Revolution: It is the idea that economic freedom can flourish only in an America that celebrates *selfishness*—the individual's pursuit of his rational, long-term self-interest—as a virtue.

PART I
THE PROBLEM

ONE
THE INCREDIBLE
UNSHRINKING GOVERNMENT

I T HAS BEEN CALLED "THE RANT HEARD ROUND THE WORLD." After a month of nonstop bailouts and stimulus packages, the Obama administration had announced a new bailout plan, this one designed to rescue underwater homeowners. On February 19, 2009, CNBC's Business News Network editor Rick Santelli blared from the floor of the Chicago Mercantile Exchange, "The government is promoting bad behavior. . . . We're thinking of having a Chicago Tea Party. . . . All you capitalists who want to show up on Lake Michigan, I'm going to start organizing."[1]

On April 15, 2009, cities all over the country witnessed the first large-scale Tea Party protests, as an estimated 268,000 Americans showed up at more than two hundred different locations.[2] And that was only the beginning. The protests continued, peaking on September 12, 2009, when, by some estimates, more than 100,000 Americans marched on Washington, D.C.[3]

What were they protesting? Their signs said it all:

- Don't spread the wealth; spread my work ethic
- Free Markets, Not Free Loaders!
- HONK . . . If I'm paying your mortgage
- I Am Not Your ATM
- If Dependence Is Your Idea Of HOPE, You Can Keep The CHANGE
- If You Think Health Care Is Expensive Now, Wait Until It's Free

- Liberty Is All the Stimulus We Need
- Obamanomics: Chains You Can Believe In
- Stop Punishing Success; Stop Rewarding Failure
- You Can't Multiply Wealth by Dividing It
- Your Mortgage Is NOT My Problem

The protesters were fed up with Big Government. "My thing with government is: smaller is better," said Jack Rice, a Tea Party activist and disillusioned Obama voter. "And so in that regard, [the government] taking control of health care and health insurance is just going to make government bigger. I don't think that they will do a very good job."[4]

Rice was not alone. As much as a quarter of the electorate has declared its support for the Tea Parties.[5] They are perhaps the most tangible sign of the widespread alarm at the rapid growth of government over the last few years.

In an October 2008 piece titled "Big Government Ahead," *New York Times* columnist David Brooks predicted that the financial crisis would help the Democrats win the presidency and expand their control over Congress. What would follow, he said, would be a flood of new spending, coming in four streams: bailouts, more stimulus packages, Keynesian-style government spending, and a new government health care plan. "When you add it all up," concluded Brooks, "we're not talking about a deficit that is 5 percent of G.D.P., but something much, much, much larger."[6]

It doesn't happen often, but David Brooks was right. Since 2008, Americans have had to weather a parade of "stimulus" spending sprees, bailouts, regulatory shackles, and the passage of ObamaCare. The sheer numbers are chilling. A total of $862 billion on the stimulus, $30 billion expansion in the State Children's Health Insurance Program (SCHIP), and a 2011 budget that approached $4 trillion.[7] As for the deficit, it exploded from 3.21 percent of GDP in 2008 (itself an unusually high number) to more than 8 percent in 2011.[8]

In the long run, the picture looks even worse. In 2010, the president released his long-term budget, which called for $45 trillion in spending over the next decade, trillions in new taxes, and a public debt that amounts to 90 percent of GDP, double today's level. "President Obama would add more to the national debt than every other President in American history from George Washington through George W. Bush *combined*," one report concludes.[9] Meanwhile, Obama has done nothing to address the looming entitlement crisis and the $66 trillion in unfunded liabilities we face.[10]

The growth of state spending and state controls under Obama is disturbing, to say the least. But that growth didn't start with President 44. George W. Bush not only championed what was then the largest expansion of government regulatory power since the New Deal (Sarbanes-Oxley) and the largest expansion of the entitlement state since the Great Society (the prescription drug benefit), he managed to increase government spending by *50 percent* in eight years. Bush has the distinction of being the first president to propose a $2 trillion budget (2002) *and* the first to propose a $3 trillion budget (2008). (We didn't get our first $1 trillion budget until Reagan.) But the trend toward greater government control over the economy didn't start with Bush either.

The American economic system is often referred to as *free market capitalism*. But for the last hundred years, and in particular since FDR's New Deal, America's market has been hindered by an elaborate web of government restrictions, interventions, controls, and wealth redistribution programs. Our once-free market has been replaced with a burgeoning regulatory-entitlement state.

In a 2010 town hall meeting, Congressman Pete Stark candidly admitted, "The federal government, yes, can do most anything in this country."[11] It doesn't take a James Madison scholar to conclude that that is not what the Founding Fathers had in mind. The growth of government power—at the federal, state, and local levels—over the last century represents a break with our tradition of limited government, the very tradition that has made America the most prosperous nation in history.

THE WEALTH OF FREE NATIONS

In a memorable interview on *Late Night with Conan O'Brien*, comedian Louis C.K. observed that most of us take for granted the West's abundance. "[W]e live in an amazing, amazing world and it's wasted on the crappiest generation of just spoiled idiots that don't care." Telephones, he noted, had gone from rotary devices that would ring endlessly unless answered to mobile devices with voicemail. "Flying is the worst," C.K. added.

We describe our flight experiences as if they are horror stories, ignoring how remarkable it is that we *can* fly. "People say there's delays on flights. Delays? Really? New York to California in *five* hours. That used to take thirty years! And plus you would die on the way."[12]

America, and the West more broadly, is fabulously wealthy—not only compared to the rest of the world today but compared to any other civilization in history. The poorest Americans live better than the average Haitian—and in many ways better than even the wealthy elite did a few centuries ago.

Although C.K. didn't mention it, what makes possible today's "amazing, amazing world" is *economic freedom*—or, more precisely, the extent to which we've *had* economic freedom.

"Economic freedom" refers to people's ability to engage in production and voluntary exchange without government barriers. Although no nation has ever had complete economic freedom (the United States came the closest during the nineteenth century), on the whole, less government intrusion into the economy is associated with a higher standard of living.

Look at the world before capitalism. The medieval world was marked by unremitting famine, plague, and poverty. If you wanted to have a midlife crisis, you would have been well advised to do so when you were fifteen: Half the population never saw thirty. In the few cities of the period, animal and human waste filled the streets, and vermin were everywhere. Drinking water was so filthy that most people drank beer instead. The English would "drink no water, unless at certain times upon religious score, or by way of doing penance," Sir John Fortescue noted in the fifteenth century.[13]

As late as the seventeenth and eighteenth centuries, vast swaths of the population were barely subsisting. From sunup to sundown people worked—arduous, grueling, backbreaking work. Forget tractors—most farmers (which was almost everybody) lacked even horses. Children worked as well, or they starved.

Then something changed. A famous graph based on the research of economist Angus Maddison marks this astonishing moment: It shows centuries of an unchanging standard of living that hovered just above the level of starvation, like the EKG of a lifeless patient—and then, without warning, a sudden spike, as if the patient had been brought back to life with a shot of adrenaline (see figure 1.1). That spike coincides perfectly

FIGURE 1.1 WORLD PER CAPITA GDP

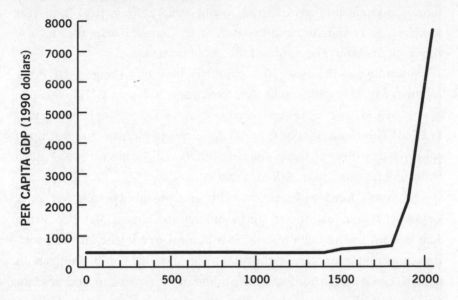

with the birth of free market capitalism in the late eighteenth and nineteenth centuries.[14]

Today, citizens of capitalist countries live about twice as long as our ancestors (and more than 50 percent longer than our Third World contemporaries).[15] Many of the diseases that once ravaged mankind have been eliminated. If we do need medical attention, a vast array of medical technology can help diagnose and treat us—and we have access to anesthesia to help us through once-painful treatments. We have access to so much cheap, tasty food that the greatest danger we face is not starvation but obesity. Most of our "poor" own cars, and 30 percent of them own two. Gadgets like dishwashers, laundry machines, and gas-powered lawn mowers free up our time, allowing us to pursue the kinds of hobbies and leisure activities that didn't exist two hundred years ago. Then, only the wealthy few had access to great art and music. Today, they're a mouse-click away. Then, there was no such thing as a vacation. Today, luxurious Caribbean cruise ships are teeming with blue-collar workers. Then, there were no amusement parks, movie theaters, sports stadiums, or shopping malls. Today, we have so many pleasurable distractions that people pay to "get away from it all."[16]

The power of capitalist freedom is confirmed when we compare more economically free countries to ones that are less free. Each year the Heritage Foundation and the *Wall Street Journal* release the *Index of Economic Freedom*. The results of the *Index* are striking.[17]

According to the *Index,* free countries have on average a GDP per capita of $40,253, while moderately free countries have a GDP per capita of only $15,541 and repressed countries have a GDP per capita of a paltry $3,926.[18] This means that by the time the average American pours a cup of coffee, chats with a colleague, and checks his email, he has earned as much as his unfree counterpart will earn that entire day.

Economic freedom leads to wealth and prosperity—and yet we're losing it. To take just one rough barometer, the United States fell from 80.6 percent free in 2008 to only 76.3 percent free in the latest *Index.*[19] Unsurprisingly, economic commentators have started complaining about today's "Great Stagnation" and the decline of the American middle class. As economic freedom withers, our rate of economic growth declines, threatening our ability to live longer, more prosperous, increasingly enjoyable lives.

Thankfully, many Americans are determined not to end up like Italy or Greece and are rebelling against the attacks on economic freedom. But will this rebellion succeed? What can be done to reverse the trend of growing government power? *Can* anything be done?

One place to look for an answer is history. What happened the last time Americans rebelled against Big Government?

WHY THE LAST SWING TO THE RIGHT FAILED

You may have heard the American political landscape compared to a pendulum: Sometimes we swing to the left, other times we swing to the right, but never do we veer too far from a fixed center. Not true. The reality is that the "center" keeps moving—every step back from Big Government is canceled out by two giant leaps forward. But there have, nevertheless, been steps back.

The most recent was the swing to the right that came at the end of the 1970s. If we want to assess today's rebellion against Big Government, that swing is a phenomenon well worth examining.

The swing to the right has often been portrayed as a time when the country embraced capitalism. In reality, all it did was reject some of the disastrous policies of the left. The 1960s and 1970s were a time of incredible growth in government power. It was during this era that we established the massive entitlement state of the so-called Great Society, launching Medicaid and Medicare and greatly expanding sundry welfare programs. Government interference in the economy exploded: Industry was heavily regulated, from how much airlines could charge and what destinations they could service, to the routes trucking companies could use and how much they were allowed to charge for freight, to the commissions that stockbrokers could charge. The Federal Reserve dictated not only the interest rates at which banks could borrow from one another, as it does today, but also the interest rates that banks could pay on savings accounts.

As a consequence, inflation was rampant, in double digits for much of the 1970s. American industry struggled and became less competitive. The stock market, as measured by the Dow Jones Industrials, was basically flat from 1965 to 1982.[20] Economic growth was nonexistent, with repeated recessions and high unemployment during the 1970s. And because the combination of inflation, stagnation, and unemployment was a phenomenon unanticipated by mainstream economists, a new term was coined: stagflation.[21]

Jimmy Carter expressed the bleakness of the time in his famous "malaise" speech, claiming that America was suffering from "a crisis in confidence."

> Human identity is no longer defined by what one does, but by what one owns. But we've discovered that owning things and consuming things does not satisfy our longing for meaning. We've learned that piling up material goods cannot fill the emptiness of lives which have no confidence or purpose.[22]

The message? Stop desiring progress. Stop desiring prosperity. Stop aiming at productive achievement. Lower your expectations and try to find meaning in pursuing something other than your own happiness.

But instead of sharing Carter's sense of defeat, Americans rebelled. It began with a tax revolt. In 1978, California voters passed Proposition 13, a severe limit on property taxes, by a margin of 2 to 1. It "started a peasants' revolt that swept across the country," write journalists John Micklethwait and Adrian Wooldridge. "It reminded Americans that their country was founded by a tax revolt, and that politicians were the public's servants, not its masters."[23]

Then came the presidency of Ronald Reagan. Reagan was elected under a banner of smaller government. "It is time to check and reverse the growth of government," he told Americans. The country was facing a crisis, and the problems were "parallel and . . . proportionate to the intervention and intrusion in our lives that result from unnecessary and excessive growth in government."[24]

The rhetoric was inspiring. But Reagan's actual efforts to limit government were disappointingly feeble. His administration and conservative legislators repealed only some of the disastrous interventions strangling the economy. They lessened our crushing tax burden, rolled back a few of the most crippling regulations, undid some of the most destructive controls, and helped curb inflation—the effect of which was to help the economy. But Reagan failed to undo any significant elements of the New Deal or Great Society. Indeed, the entitlement state *grew* during his tenure— even though America had grown incredibly *richer* during that time.[25] Far from ending Big Government, the best that can be said about Reagan is that in some ways he slowed down our march toward it.

The next and last chance to capitalize on the swing to the right came in 1994, when, for the first time in almost half a century, Republicans took control of the House, sweeping into power on the promise to reduce the size of government. The mastermind of this victory, newly crowned House Speaker Newt Gingrich, spoke boldly of Republicans' goals: "This is a genuine revolution. We're going to rethink every element of the federal government. We're going to close down several federal departments."[26]

It didn't happen. The class of '94 did make an attempt to roll back the interventionist state, but as we shall see it encountered three walls of impenetrable resistance: opposition from colleagues in government, opposition from the American people, and the complete lack of a moral spine.

FARM SUBSIDIES

The '94 Republicans actually succeeded in passing a measure that would have significantly slashed future farm subsidies; the change lasted for about a minute. As historian John Samples notes, they were able to succeed at first because "the budget was tight, and deficits seemed to matter to the public." Meanwhile, farmers at the time were prospering. But two years after the Agriculture Improvements and Reform Act was passed, "the world had changed, and Congress could not make good on its 1996 intentions. Farm prices were low, and farmers were struggling. The federal budget had turned toward surplus, which allowed Congress to avoid tough choices."[27] In other words, Congress had been able to trim farm subsidies not because of a commitment to free market principles ("no subsidies for anyone for any reason") but because a budgetary emergency seemed to warrant drastic action. When conditions changed, back came massive farm subsidies.

SCHIP

As we'll see in a moment, the House Republicans tried and failed to curtail the expansion of Medicare and Medicaid. But they also *expanded* government intervention in medicine, passing the State Children's Health Insurance Program, which funneled billions to parents whose children did not qualify for Medicaid. Republican Senator Orrin Hatch cosponsored the bill with Democratic Senator Ted Kennedy, in an attempt to prove that the Republican Party "does not hate children." According to the *New York Times,* Hatch "added that 'as a nation, as a society, we have a moral responsibility' to provide coverage for the most vulnerable children."[28] No one missed the implication: Opposing government handouts was a moral crime motivated by hatred for the intended beneficiaries—not a love of freedom and limited government.

THE BUDGET BATTLE

The defining moment for the class of '94 was the showdown with President Clinton over the budget. The House budget for fiscal year 1996 included reductions in projected welfare spending ($82 billion), Medicare spending ($270 billion), and Medicaid spending ($163 billion). Clinton vetoed the bill, and, without a budget, the government was forced to shut down for a time. The conflict dragged on, with a second shutdown shortly after the first.

It was do-or-die time—time for the right to make its case to the American people for cutting government. It failed. As conservative William Kristol put it, "The budget battle played into the two great Republican vulnerabilities: that we are the party of the rich and the meanspirited."[29] Republicans could not answer those charges, and once they lost the battle of public opinion, they waved the white flag. The fight over the '96 budget was, according to a freshman House member, "a disaster ... the momentum of 1994 came to an end."[30] Writing in 2000, one commentator noted that "the combined budgets of the 95 major programs that the ['94 Republicans] promised to eliminate have increased by 13%."[31]

"The era of Big Government is over," President Clinton had said in 1996. It wasn't true—well, depending on the meaning of the word "is"— but it was notable that Clinton felt compelled to say so. By 2000, however, Americans had elected a "compassionate conservative" who announced "We've had enough of the stale debate between Big Government and indifferent Government"—and then proceeded to expand the size of government like no president since Lyndon Johnson.[32]

The swing to the right was aimed at avoiding economic catastrophe— it was a pragmatic lurch away from Big Government, not a principled turn toward limited government. Confronted with the prospect of economic collapse, Americans temporarily put aside concerns about favoring "the rich" or being "meanspirited" for the sake of changing the direction in which the country was heading. But those concerns soon resurfaced, and the swing to the right came to an end.

CONCLUSION: THE SITUATION TODAY

Today, Americans are facing a new emergency—a faltering economy, a coming entitlement crisis, and the rapid disintegration of economic freedom under Obama. The alarming expansion of the regulatory-entitlement state offers a glimpse of a future wherein government taxes away much of our wealth, controls most of our economic choices, and cripples our well-being. The question is: Will today's Tea Party revolt get the job done—or will it, like the last revolt, wither and die?

The results to date have fallen short of spectacular. Consider the opening salvo of the war between the new Republican House and the Obama administration—2011's budget battle. Paul Ryan, a favorite among Tea Partiers, put forward a plan that claimed to make historic cuts in the size of government. The left predictably denounced the plan as an attack on "the poor," but in truth the Ryan plan didn't even cut spending—it merely grew it at a slower rate than Obama's plan. It increased Medicaid spending, for instance, from $275 billion in 2011 to $305 billion in 2021 and saw Medicare spending soar from $563 billion to $953 billion.[33] And even that was too controversial for most of Ryan's colleagues. They denounced it as a radical attack on Medicare.[34]

Some revolution.

Under the influence of a number of Tea Party–affiliated Congressmen, the Republicans have started to show a little more backbone, opposing attempts by Democrats to raise taxes. But to date they have done precisely nothing to cut government power. To truly limit government will require something more than refusing to raise taxes: namely, a powerful, principled, uncompromising defense of a clearly defined positive agenda.

And herein lies the problem the Tea Party rebellion faces: For all its virtues, it is a rebellion that does not know what it stands for or even fully what it is rebelling against. While many Tea Partiers are alarmed by the growth of government, when it comes to identifying what specific regulations should be repealed and what specific government programs and agencies should be abolished, they have little to say.

When they claim to want to roll back the government, what is it they want to roll back? Do they want to repeal Dodd-Frank or Sarbanes-Oxley? Abolish the Department of Energy, the Department of Education, or the Department of Agriculture? Eliminate the Federal Reserve and return to a gold standard? The Environmental Protection Agency, the Food and Drug Administration, or the Federal Communications Commission? Do they want to phase out Medicare, Medicaid, and Social Security? The Tea Party is not a monolith, and you can no doubt find some who would endorse all of these proposals. But if the Tea Party is to become a pro-freedom *movement* and not simply a rebellion, it needs to define and defend an agenda that would answer these questions in a principled, pro-freedom manner. At present that seems unlikely. Who can forget the demand of some Tea Partiers to "keep your government hands off my Medicare"?[35] Even ObamaCare, the symbol of Obama's Big

Government agenda, polls extremely well when its elements are considered individually.[36]

While today's rebellion is a positive sign, it is not enough to be against "Big Government" or for "smaller government." It is not enough to say you support the principles of the Declaration of Independence or fidelity to the Constitution or free enterprise or capitalism. The question is: What does "Big Government" mean? What should the role of government be? How do the principles of the Declaration and the Constitution apply to issues like Social Security, Medicare, financial regulation, or the Federal Reserve? What is capitalism? Does it work? Is it moral? Without a clear, positive, *specific* agenda—and a solid defense of that agenda—today's rebellion cannot achieve meaningful or lasting success.

But to develop such an agenda, we first need to solve a puzzle. Why, if economic freedom has proven itself time and time again to be the engine of prosperity, do we keep moving toward Big Government? Why is a pro-freedom agenda so hard to come by and to defend? Why, no matter the rhetoric, no matter the mood of the electorate, no matter how much the weight of Big Government pulls down economic progress, do we get more regulations, more government spending, less economic freedom?

The answer might surprise you. It has to do with something we don't often talk about in explicit terms. It has to do with *morality*.

TWO
WHY GOVERNMENT GROWS

I N HIS BOOK *THE HEALING OF AMERICA: A GLOBAL QUEST FOR Better, Cheaper, and Fairer Health Care*, T. R. Reid notes how Taiwan and Sweden were able to implement socialized health care despite opposition:

> Both countries decided that society has an ethical obligation—as a mat-
> ter of justice, of fairness, of solidarity—to assure everybody has access
> to medical care when it's needed. The advocates of reform in both coun-
> tries clarified and emphasized that moral issue much more than the nuts
> and bolts of the proposed reform plans. As a result, the national debate
> was waged around ideals like "equal treatment for everybody," "we're all
> in this together," and "fundamental rights" rather than on the commer-
> cial implications for the health care industry.[1]

"We are all in this together," said President Obama in his health care speech to Congress. In America, when "fortune turns against one of us, others are there to lend a helping hand," but "sometimes government has to step in to help deliver on that promise."[2]

Some on the left criticized Obama for not making even more hay of the moral argument in his push for ObamaCare. After all, while polls showed that few could swallow the idea that a massive new health entitle-ment would lower medical costs, virtually everyone granted that "society" had a duty to insure the uninsured. Everyone agreed that doctors, hospi-tals, and health insurance companies had a duty to serve a person in need regardless of his ability to pay—and that there was something vaguely indecent about profiting from the sick. And once the government guaranteed health care to someone, virtually everyone agreed that to revoke that guarantee would be a moral crime. As one Newsvine.com commenter put it, mocking the notion that ObamaCare could be repealed:

> How are you going to take insurance away from a child with a pre-existing condition who now, for the first time ever, has it? Do you just tear up the policy and say, "tough luck, kid"? . . . [H]ow about the adults with pre-existing conditions who have finally gotten access to high-risk pools? . . . [H]ow are you going to take away insurance from the 23-year-old child who has yet to find a "real" job and now remains on mom and dad's plan?[3]

Need, this line of reasoning went, is as good as gold. If people need health care, they are by that very fact entitled to it, and society's job is to make sure they get it. To deny them the health care they need would be cruel, mean-spirited, immoral, *selfish.*

If morality explains why ensuring the needs of the sick was treated as a categorical imperative, it also explains the vicious attacks waged by ObamaCare supporters on health insurance companies and even doctors. "Villains" was Nancy Pelosi's characterization of the health insurance industry.[4] President Obama was more generous, suggesting only that they were not honest.[5] Doctors, meanwhile, were accused by Obama of performing unnecessary tests and even unnecessary *surgeries* in order to selfishly line their pockets.

> [Y]ou come in and you've got a bad sore throat, or your child has a bad sore throat, or has repeated sore throats, the doctor may look at the reimbursement system and say to himself, "You know what? I make a lot more money if I take this kid's tonsils out."[6]

Health insurance companies and doctors, the logic goes, are motivated by profit, by greed, by *selfishness.* As a result, they cannot be trusted.

Underlying the push for ObamaCare was a single idea, an idea that almost everyone accepts, and almost nobody questions: the evil of selfishness.

The basic argument of our book is that this near-universal conviction provides the central reason why government power grows. Free (or freer) markets, despite their unmatched record for improving human life, are widely viewed as fundamentally greed-driven, materialistic, selfish, immoral. This moral outlook shapes people's understanding and evaluation of how individuals act under economic freedom. It is what determines the economic policies they advocate. It is what leads people to condemn anyone who advocates economic freedom as cruel and "mean-spirited." And it is chiefly responsible for today's Big Government.[7]

THE LEAST CONTROVERSIAL IDEA

Politically, America began to veer sharply from its free market roots around the end of the nineteenth century, with the ascension of the Progressive movement. It was the Progressives who were responsible for the first major restrictions on American capitalism, namely the creation of the Interstate Commerce Commission, which regulated the railroads, and the Sherman Antitrust Act, which allowed the government to break up large companies. Although on the surface these efforts were directed at the "practical" effects of capitalism, Progressives saw capitalism's allegedly destructive effects as resulting from an underlying problem. Capitalism, they held, was deeply immoral.

"The existing competitive system is thoroughly selfish," wrote Progressive Josiah Strong.[8] Leading Progressive Herbert Croly agreed. The American system, he said, needed to temper "the influence of selfish acquisitive motives," adding that

> the promise of American life is to be fulfilled not merely by a maximum amount of economic freedom but by a certain measure of discipline; not merely by the abundant satisfaction of individual desires but by a large measure of individual subordination and self-denial.[9]

Theodore Roosevelt condemned as selfish the advocates of private property rights and insisted that "every man holds his property subject to the general right of the community to regulate its use to whatever degree the public welfare may require it."[10]

Markets, the Progressives argued, were saturated with self-interest. And about this, they were right. The central activity of a market is the self-interested pursuit of profit. The chef cooks your meal not because he's your servant but because he gets paid. And the trucker who delivers the meat to the restaurant isn't doing it a favor but is exchanging his time and effort for a check. And so on for the cattle rancher who sells the restaurant its meat, the banker who provides the rancher a loan, the scientist who discovers new drugs for raising healthy cows, and the philosopher who defines and teaches the methods of scientific inquiry.

Free markets are about individuals trying to better their *own* lives. There is no central authority dictating what jobs or products society "needs." There is no national mission that binds individuals and directs their choices. People choose jobs that they find fulfilling, they work for their own success, and they spend their paychecks on themselves, their friends, their families.

Take Disneyland, for instance. It's teeming with people pursuing their own profit. Disney operates the Happiest Place on Earth in hopes of making it the most profitable theme park on earth. The aspiring actor who plays Mickey puts smiles on children's faces in order to put dollars in his wallet and a reference on his résumé. The family waiting in line for Space Mountain isn't there to "stimulate the economy" but to have some fun. That's to say nothing of the investors who buy Disney stock in order to increase their wealth, or the marketers who give away mouse-ear hats in order to attract future visitors, or the retired popcorn vendor who works part time just so he can enjoy the delightful atmosphere.

Economic freedom, in short, *means* the freedom to be self-interested. Under capitalism, people aim to produce more, to consume more, to continually increase their standard of living, for themselves. "The principles of 'more' are everywhere," writes a modern critic of capitalism. "'More' is embedded in the behavior of every business enterprise and the principles of marketing, in the self-interested decisions of every investor and consumer."[11]

This relentless pursuit of "more" by profit-seeking individuals outraged the Progressives. To them, the capitalist system was driven by an immoral motive—one that, in their view, predictably, led to an immoral result: a materialistic society in which some people reaped huge rewards while others struggled to survive. Capitalism, they argued, unleashes and rewards self-interest and its economic concomitant, the profit motive. It is, therefore, vicious at its very core. This is the moral outlook that has motivated virtually every critic of capitalism.

That was certainly true of capitalism's most notorious critic, Karl Marx. Marx didn't hate capitalism because he thought it couldn't work. Instead, he developed and embraced anticapitalist economic theories because of his deep-seated *moral* opposition to capitalism.

As historian Jerry Z. Muller shows in *The Mind and the Market: Capitalism in Western Thought,* while Marx claimed that people's ideas are rationalizations for their class interests, Marx's own economic views were rationalizations for his moral fury. From the start, writes Muller, Marx was motivated by a profound dislike of capitalism on ethical grounds. "Self-interest was the fundamental basis of bourgeois society. And that, Marx thought, made bourgeois society morally abhorrent."[12]

So began Marx's search for economic views that would undermine the classical economists' defense of free markets. The cornerstone of Marxian economics, for instance, is the labor theory of value—the idea that the value of goods produced is a function of the physical labor that went in to producing them. To Marx, the labor theory implied that profit earned by businessmen (who after all don't physically build the goods that come out of their factories) is inherently unjust and exploitive—a stinging indictment of the "profit system." Writes Muller, "When Marx first came upon the labor theory of value, his response to it was 'Eureka.'" Marx "picked it up and adhered to it because of his assumption that the making of money by money was unjust."[13] This explains why Marx stubbornly "clung to the labor theory of value after it had been abandoned by virtually all economists."[14]

Daniel Yergin and Joseph Stanislaw summarize the anticapitalist mentality this way:

Capitalism was considered morally objectionable. . . . [T]here was skepticism and outright disbelief in the idea that the individual's pursuit of what Adam Smith defined as self-interest would add up, in aggregate, to the benefit of "all." No, the sum was injustice and inequality, the few benefiting from the sweat of the many. The concept of profit itself was morally distasteful.[15]

Something needed to be done to curb the free market and its rampant greed and immorality, critics argued. In America, the decisive split from capitalism was FDR's New Deal. After he helped transform America's economy into a regulatory-entitlement state, FDR told Congress that the New Deal had "established a new relationship between Government and people. . . . Government became the representative and the trustee" not of the individual and his inalienable rights but "of the public interest."[16]

In Europe, meanwhile, totalitarian leaders argued that curbing capitalism wasn't enough. The immorality of self-interest and the profit motive had to be eliminated altogether.

You must, said Benito Mussolini, accept "a life in which the individual, through the denial of himself, through the sacrifice of his own private interests . . . realizes that completely spiritual existence in which his value as a man lies."[17]

Marx had trenchantly condemned one of capitalism's most distinctive features, the protection of private property rights:

> The practical application of man's right of liberty is man's right to *private property*. . . . The right of man to private property is, therefore, the right to enjoy one's property and to dispose of it at one's discretion *(à son gré)*, without regard to other men, independently of society, the right of self-interest.[18]

Instead of protecting the right of self-interest, Marx declared, the state must enforce the principle "From each according to his ability to each according to his need."[19] Lenin and Stalin would go on to enforce that principle at the point of a gun.

> This state of mind, which subordinates the interests of the ego to the conservation of the community, is really the first premise of every truly human culture. . . . The basic attitude from which such activity arises, we call—to distinguish it from egoism and selfishness—idealism. By this

we understand only the individual's capacity to make sacrifices for the community, for his fellow men.

So said Hitler, who then proceeded to sacrifice millions of individuals for the German community.[20] According to Nazi leader Joseph Goebbels, "To be a socialist is to submit the I to the thou; socialism is sacrificing the individual to the whole."[21]

Of course we assume that President Obama was not intentionally invoking Goebbels when he said that we "need to think in terms of 'thou' and not just 'I.'"[22] And we assume this because the evil of selfishness is perhaps the least controversial idea in our culture. From the time we're very young, it is drilled into us by our parents, our teachers, our religious leaders, our political leaders. Books, television, newspapers, movies, the Internet are filled with proclamations to not be selfish, to think of others first.

In elementary school, we're told to share our toys. In high school, we are forced to perform community service. In college, we are reminded not to focus too much on our own lives: "You must bend down and let someone else stand on your shoulders so that they can see a brighter future," Michelle Obama told University of California at Merced graduates before going on to invoke one of her favorite quotes: "Service is the rent we pay for living."[23] (She did not say what should happen to those who refuse to pay their rent.)

In politics, no speech is complete without a reminder of our duty to sacrifice: We must "reaffirm that fundamental belief—I am my brother's keeper, I am my sister's keeper—that makes us one people, and one nation," says Obama.[24] "Faith, purpose greater than self, and willingness to sacrifice are part of what makes America, America," says Mitt Romney.[25] You must "seek a common good beyond your comfort," George W. Bush tells us.[26]

Today's universal demand for sacrifice has its roots in the realm of religion and philosophy. The Old Testament commands, "Be openhanded toward your brothers and toward the poor and needy in your land."[27] The New Testament counsels, "Give to everyone who asks you, and if anyone takes what belongs to you, do not demand it back."[28] Saint Paul declares,

"Do nothing out of selfish ambition or vain conceit. Rather, in humility value others above yourselves."[29] Pride, writes Augustine, "builds up the city of Babylon."[30] Aquinas calls self-love "the beginning of every evil."[31] The word "Islam" actually means "submission."

And philosophers? From Plato to Rousseau, to Hegel, to Dewey, to Rawls, to Singer, most philosophers have preached the duty of sacrifice in one form or another. The most influential modern philosopher, Immanuel Kant, went so far as to say that if you derive any benefit whatsoever from an action—even the warm feeling of having done a good deed—your action is without moral merit.[32]

THE ARGUMENT FROM GREED AND
THE ARGUMENT FROM NEED

How does this moral perspective translate into more and more power placed into the hands of government? To answer that, we have to realize that Americans haven't chosen between complete capitalism and complete socialism. They've chosen particular policies that restrict *some* economic freedoms or redistribute *some* wealth. It is the sum of these choices that is responsible for today's trend of increasing government control.

Here, then, is the answer to the question of why government grows: Although Americans generally claim to favor economic freedom, they distrust and disapprove of self-interest. As a consequence, when critics blame the self-interest unleashed by capitalism for particular problems and point to government intervention in the name of the "public interest" as the solution, Americans nod their heads in agreement. Regulation by regulation, tax by tax, program by program, they surrender economic freedom in favor of government control.

The process follows two tracks. One starts with the conviction that greedy profit seekers are a potentially destructive force and concludes they have to be reined in by government controls. The other starts with the conviction that a person's need entitles him to others' wealth and concludes that government must redistribute wealth to fulfill that need. We call these arguments the Argument from Greed and the Argument from Need.[33]

THE ARGUMENT FROM GREED

For most of America's early history, businesses generally operated without government interference. So long as they respected individual rights, they were largely free to produce and trade.

By 2008, however, more than one hundred regulatory agencies were enforcing tens of thousands of rules at the federal level alone; the *Federal Register,* which lists regulatory rules, hovered around 75,000 pages and took up—people have measured it—about thirty feet of bookshelf space.[34] (Although critics of capitalism claim regulations were being gutted during the Bush years, the number of *Register* pages exploded—as did the amount spent by federal regulatory agencies and the number of people employed by those agencies.[35])

Even in the era before Obama, the federal government regulated every inch of the ground, water, and sky. Consider some of the alphabet agencies that controlled and that continue to control our economic affairs:

Administration for Children and Families (ACF)
Agency for Healthcare Research and Quality (AHRQ)
Agricultural Marketing Service
Agricultural Research Service
Alcohol and Tobacco Tax and Trade Bureau
Alcohol, Tobacco, Firearms, and Explosives
Bureau of Economic Analysis (BEA)
Bureau of Industry and Security
Bureau of International Labor
Bureau of Labor Statistics (BLS)
Bureau of Land Management (BLM)
Bureau of Public Debt
Bureau of Reclamation
Bureau of Transportation Statistics
Center for Nutrition Policy and Promotion
Centers for Medicare & Medicaid Services
Community Planning and Development

Cooperative State Research, Education and Extension
Economic Development Administration
Economic Research Service
Economic, Business, and Agricultural Affairs
Economics and Statistics Administration
Elementary and Secondary Education
Employee Benefits Security Administration
Employment and Training Administration (ETA)
Employment Standards Administration
Farm Service Agency
Federal Housing Administration
Federal Railroad Administration
Federal Student Aid
Federal Trade Commission (FTC)
Federal Transit Administration
Financial Management Service (FMS)
Food and Drug Administration (FDA)
Food and Nutrition Service
Food, Nutrition and Consumer Services
Food Safety and Inspection Service
Foreign Agricultural Service
Forest Service Geological Survey (USGS)
Government National Mortgage Association (Ginnie Mae)
Grain Inspection, Packers and Stockyards Administration
Health Care Financing Administration
Health Resources and Services Administration (HRSA)
Indian Health Service (IHS)
Institute of Education Sciences
Internal Revenue Service (IRS)
International Trade Administration (ITA)
Mine Safety and Health Administration
Mineral Management Service
Minority Business Development Agency
National Agricultural Statistics Service
National Highway Traffic Safety Administration
National Institute of Standards and Technology (NIST)
National Marine Fisheries

National Technical Information Service

National Telecommunications and Information Administration

Natural Resources Conservation Service

Occupational Safety & Health Administration (OSHA)

Office of Disability Employment Policy

Office of Enforcement

Office of Fair Housing and Equal Opportunity

Office of Federal Housing Enterprise Oversight

Office of Healthy Homes and Lead Hazard Control

Office of Innovation and Improvement

Office of Intergovernmental and Interagency Affairs

Office of Management

Office of Public and Indian Housing

Office of Safe and Drug-Free Schools

Office of Surface Mining, Reclamation and Enforcement

Office of the Chief Financial Officer

Office of the Chief Information Officer

Office of the Comptroller of the Currency

Office of the Pardon Attorney

Office of Thrift Supervision (OTS)

Pension and Welfare Benefits Administration

Pipeline and Hazardous Materials Safety Administration

Research and Innovative Technology Administration

Risk Management Agency

Rural Business-Cooperative Service

Rural Development

Rural Housing Service

Rural Utilities Service

Saint Lawrence Seaway Development Corporation

Science and Technology Directorate

Securities and Exchange Commission (SEC)

Vocational and Adult Education

Women's Bureau

Some estimates put the annual cost of today's omnipresent regulatory state as high as $1.75 *trillion* a year.[36] But even these estimates don't include the opportunities forgone, the innovations that didn't take place, the discoveries that were not made thanks to government controls—to say nothing of the emotional toll imposed on businessmen forced to spend more time wading through red tape than growing their companies. Regulation "discourages our best entrepreneurs," write John Allison, former CEO of BB&T Corporation, and Ron Johnson, former CEO of Pacur. "By treating entrepreneurs as latent criminals, the regulatory state crushes the creative spirit—and wastes the energy and talents of the job producers and the prosperity producers."[37]

How did we get to this point? How did we go from the freest nation on earth to a highly regulated one? Well, just take a look at how our culture views businessmen.

When Yaron taught at a university, he gave his students an entire semester to name a recent movie in which the hero was a successful businessman. Few of them ever were able to, although a handful of such movies do exist. Nowadays, there's *Iron Man* and we suppose *The Aviator,* if you don't count the fact that Howard Hughes was crazy. But if you want a total nonchallenge, try to name a movie where the *villain* was a businessman—we'll wager there's at least one playing right now.

In 2006, the Business & Media Institute published a study in which it concluded that if you see a businessman on TV, he's as likely to be killing as he is to be *making* a killing.

> [B]usinessmen on TV committed more crimes than any other demographic. . . . According to primetime TV, you are 21 times more likely to be kidnapped or murdered at the hands of a businessman than the mob. Businessmen also committed crimes five times more often than terrorists and four times more often than gangs.[38]

A different study by the Business & Media Institute found that by age eighteen, "the average TV viewer has seen businessmen attempt more than ten thousand murders and countless lesser offenses, all in the name of greed." Asked about Hollywood's obsession with bad guy businessmen, former chairman of NBC Grant Tinker said, "Businessmen deserve what they get. . . . Dammit, there is a lot of villainy in business."[39]

And it's not just Hollywood that hates businessmen. "Few are the businessmen in literature and drama," observes economist Diane Coyle, "and those there are tend to be, like Trollope's Melmotte or Fitzgerald's Gatsby, either flawed characters or outright villains."[40]

These are just some of the symptoms of a widespread cultural phenomenon: Today, businessmen are probably the most vilified group in America. Don recalls watching the *South Park* movie some years ago in a crowded theater. When a cartoon Bill Gates was gratuitously murdered, the audience broke into applause. Although publicly wishing harm on a group of Americans is generally frowned upon, we make an exception for businessmen. Radio host Thom Hartmann, after reflecting on why there are so few people capable of running America's most successful companies, concluded that only sociopaths are capable of being CEOs.[41] National Public Radio's Patt Morrison declared of the CEOs who presided over failed companies during the financial crisis (most of whom were not accused of committing any crime), "I want blood."[42] Columnist Maureen Dowd was a bit more circumspect, asking only for "shackles" and "show trials."[43]

Why have businessmen been so vilified? It's not for any particular evil, real or imagined. It's not because some may have produced shoddy products or defrauded customers. (Political leaders have committed crimes, enslaved nations, even slaughtered millions, and we go on giving them more and more power.) It is, instead, because we view businessmen as in some sense corrupt by their very nature: Businessmen, we think, are *greedy*. They are driven by the selfish pursuit of profit—they have an insatiable desire for "more"—and we equate that with a willingness to lie, cheat, and steal. Businessmen, we conclude, are necessarily heartless, greedy bastards out for themselves, willing to sacrifice the welfare of employees, customers, friends, and orphans if it helps them make a buck.

Just think back to the classic film *It's a Wonderful Life*. The hero is a businessman—an *unsuccessful* businessman, whose goodwill drives him into bankruptcy. Who is the successful businessman? It's crotchety old Mr. Potter, the allegedly selfish banker who revels in destroying everyone around him, who profits (somehow) by denying loans to the creditworthy little guy, and who doesn't hesitate to steal from his competitors and send innocent men to prison. It's a portrait that many Americans seem to find plausible.

Observe, for instance, the reaction to the accounting scandals of 2001–2002. Did Americans conclude that a few individual businessmen committed crimes and should therefore be punished? No. According to the general sentiment, *most* businessmen were greedy shysters. The collapse of Enron and WorldCom wasn't viewed as a tale of how a few individuals at a few companies resorted to crime and self-destructed as a result; it was trumpeted as one more piece of evidence that business in general was corrupt.

The same sentiments were expressed after Bernie Madoff's Ponzi scheme unraveled. Madoff was not simply a criminal who happened to work on Wall Street. He was, in the words of one reporter, "a creature of the world he helped create, a world that was greedy for riskless gain . . . arrogantly certain of success, woefully deluded about what could go wrong, and selfishly indifferent to the damage done to others."[44]

If this is your view of businessmen, whom will you blame when things go bad, and how will you respond? History has made the answer clear.

What caused the Great Depression? It was "the foolishness and greed of the individuals at the helm of this economic system, captains of industry who pursued personal wealth at the expense of workers and the public."[45] What Americans got was the regulatory onslaught of the New Deal.

What caused spiraling health care costs? "Consumers Believe Greed Is the Reason for Rising Health Care Costs";[46] "Health Insurance Industry Exposes Its Insatiable Greed";[47] "'Greed' Inflates Drug Prices, Democrats Say."[48] What Americans got was ObamaCare.

What caused the financial crisis? "Human Greed Lies at Root of Economic Crisis."[49] What Americans got was Dodd-Frank.

"[W]hether it's tulips or credit default swaps," concludes Coyle, "there's nothing new about financial crises or about their causes, greed and selfishness."[50]

In all of these cases, however, a full examination of the facts would reveal that it was government intervention that caused the problems and that economic freedom is the solution. But because of people's view of business—a view based on their notions concerning self-interest and the profit motive—they did not demand a full examination of the facts. The idea that businessmen were the culprits *made sense.* The explanations were convincing despite the lack of specific evidence. They were convincing because they cohered with our deepest views about human nature and morality.

Now, maybe you're thinking that cases like the health care crisis and the financial crisis *do* reveal the destructive effects of greed. We will address these in due course.[51] But first, consider a more straightforward example: Why do we have elevator inspectors? Because we believe that "greedy" businessmen have no qualms about cutting corners to save a few bucks, even if it means letting customers plummet to their deaths. And we call on "public-spirited" regulators to protect us from self-interested businessmen while never thinking to ask: How in the world would an elevator manufacturer expect to make money by killing his customers?

The question is: Why *don't* we ask this? It doesn't take much to realize that food makers like McDonald's have a powerful interest in ensuring the quality of their food—and would go bankrupt if they started poisoning their customers with rotten meat. Why don't we trust McDonald's—and why do we trust the judgment of the faceless bureaucrat who regulates it? The answer is: because we do not trust the profit motive—we do not trust self-interest.

So long as the Argument from Greed holds sway, we will continue to demand more and more restrictions on economic freedom.

THE ARGUMENT FROM NEED

Today, the entitlement state—programs that redistribute wealth in the name of guaranteeing important needs—is vast and includes unemployment benefits, disability benefits, income subsidies, food stamps, Social Security, Medicare, Medicaid, housing subsidies, and public education. More than 60 percent of the federal budget alone goes to fund entitlements.[52] Today, the average American household pays $16,000 a year toward entitlements—*excluding* education—virtually double what we paid a decade ago.[53] From the start of LBJ's war on poverty through 2008, more than $14.3 *trillion* was spent just on means-tested welfare programs.[54]

Accumulation of debt, warned Alexander Hamilton, "is perhaps the NATURAL DISEASE of all Governments. And it is not easy to conceive anything more likely than this to lead to great and convulsive revolutions of Empire."[55] Today, America's national debt is $14 trillion and change—and growing. That's to say nothing of the incredible spending taking place at the state and local levels. All told, government spending constitutes a breathtaking *41 percent* of gross domestic product.[56] And that number is only going to grow: The government currently has unfunded liabilities surpassing *$66 trillion.*[57] That's $66 trillion in expected entitlement payouts over the coming decades for which there is no known revenue source.[58] If nothing is done to scale back the entitlement state, then, according to a report by nonpartisan financial analyst Mary Meeker, "By 2025, entitlements plus net interest payments will absorb all—yes, all—of" government revenues.[59]

How did we get to this point? How did we go from a limited government based on the sacred right to private property to a burgeoning entitlement state?

"When somebody hurts," said George W. Bush, "government has got to move."[60] At the same time that our moral notions about selfishness cause us to support an increasingly powerful regulatory state, we look to government to enact the "proper" moral ideal of selflessness. Wherever there is someone in need, we think something must be done.

Why are we obligated to turn over more than 15 percent of our paycheck to Social Security? To provide for the needs of the elderly, the jobless, and the disabled. Why are we taxed to fund welfare? To meet the needs of the poor. Why does the government dictate a minimum wage and force certain businesses to provide workers' comp? To meet the needs of workers. Why are Americans facing tens of trillions of dollars in unfunded liabilities under Medicare and Medicaid? To meet the needs of the sick.

The widespread conviction that it is our moral duty to sacrifice for the needs of others is what has made need a political entitlement. If you need something someone else has produced, you have a right to it—the person who produced it does not. Bare your sores, get a handout—that's the motto of the entitlement state.

Of course, few Americans would go so far as to say that *anyone* who has *any* need is entitled to have it fulfilled at other people's expense. But that is what's implied by the entitlement state. As a result, although it started out as an effort to provide a small "safety net" for the "truly needy," the entitlement state has grown continuously.

Take Social Security. As historian Walter Trattner observes:

The seed planted by the Social Security Act sprouted in many ways. Not only did subsequent legislation widen the law's coverage and increase its benefits . . . but also, from the agency created to implement the act, the Social Security Board, a new cabinet-level department grew—the Department of Health, Education, and Welfare, established in 1953. Thus . . . the federal government established an agency responsible for the health, education, and social welfare of all its citizens, one that spawned its own bureaucracy whose momentum would be difficult to stop.[61]

Or consider the history of government involvement in health care. In the 1960s, there was a perception that some elderly were not receiving adequate health care. To meet this need, Congress passed Medicare. The same concern was voiced about the poor. To meet their need, Congress passed Medicaid. The same concern was voiced about those too destitute (or too irresponsible) to buy health insurance, and, in the 1980s, Congress passed the Emergency Medical Treatment and Labor Act, forcing emergency rooms to treat anyone who needed medical attention, regardless of his ability to pay. The same concern was voiced about parents who were too well off for Medicaid but who nevertheless supposedly couldn't meet their children's health care needs, and, in the late 1990s, Congress passed the SCHIP. And so on with the Medicare Prescription Drug, Improvement, and Modernization Act and now ObamaCare, which was sold in part by appealing to the "needs" of the uninsured and those with preexisting conditions.

With each new expansion, a new group of "truly needy" emerges, and anyone who opposes further government efforts to come to their aid is denounced as heartless and cruel.

CONCLUSION: A MORAL CRISIS

In his Notre Dame commencement address, President Obama condemned

the imperfections of man—our selfishness, our pride, our stubbornness, our acquisitiveness, our insecurities, our egos; all the cruelties large and small that those of us in the Christian tradition understand to be rooted in original sin. We too often seek advantage over others. We cling to out-worn prejudice and fear those who are unfamiliar. Too many of us view life only through the lens of immediate self-interest and crass material-ism; in which the world is necessarily a zero-sum game. The strong too often dominate the weak, and too many of those with wealth and with power find all manner of justification for their own privilege in the face of poverty and injustice.[62]

This is the moral outlook that is destroying capitalism. In issue after issue, our culture's attitude toward business greed and its commitment to the alleged duty to serve others' need has had a profound effect on our politi-cal policies.

No, (almost) everyone says, we don't want to follow the totalitarians in getting rid of self-interest completely. We recognize that the freedom to better oneself provided by capitalism is crucial to our standard of living. But we want self-interest limited. The solution, we believe, is neither total capitalism nor total socialism, but the mixed economy. We just need to find the right mixture of selfishness and selflessness, of freedom and con-trols, of capitalism and socialism—and that will solve all our problems. And yet what we get instead is an overarching trend away from freedom and toward state control of the economy.

In the 1972 case *U.S. v. 12 200-Ft. Reels of Super 8mm Film,* then Chief Justice Warren Burger noted:

> The seductive plausibility of single steps in a chain of evolutionary de-velopment of a legal rule is often not perceived until a third, fourth, or fifth "logical" extension occurs. Each step, when taken, appeared a rea-sonable step in relation to that which preceded it, although the aggregate or end result is one that would never have been seriously considered in the first instance.[63]

The phenomenon Justice Burger was observing is wider than the devel-opment of legal rules. If we accept the Arguments from Greed and Need, then the state *must* keep growing. If the selfish pursuit of profit is immoral and destructive, then it *should* be eliminated. Although each step away from economic freedom has a "seductive plausibility," we have to come to terms with the fact that those steps unavoidably add up to an "end result that would never have been seriously considered in the first instance."

This is what's required to stop the growth of the state and end Big Government: We will have to see that business "greed" is not to be feared, that "need" is not a mortgage on the wealth and lives of the productive, and that self-interest is not a moral stain on capitalism's soul.

THREE
WITH FRIENDS LIKE THESE . . .

N 1978, CONSERVATIVE LUMINARY IRVING KRISTOL PUB-
lished *Two Cheers for Capitalism*. Why only two cheers? Because,
Kristol explained, while capitalism brought men riches and freedom, it
was tainted by its inherent selfishness.

> Who on earth wants to live in a society in which all—or even a ma-
> jority—of one's fellow citizens are fully engaged in the hot pursuit of
> money, the single-minded pursuit of material self-interest? To put it
> another way: Who wants to live in a society in which selfishness and
> self-seeking are celebrated as primary virtues? Such a society is unfit for
> human habitation; thus sayeth the Old Testament, the New Testament,
> the Koran . . . the medieval theologians, all of modern moral philosophy.[1]

Years later, in a speech billing itself as a moral defense of the free market,
prominent conservative writer Michael Novak chastised Kristol for giving
capitalism two cheers.

> Capitalism is by no means the Kingdom of God. It is a poor and clumsy
> human system. Although one can claim for it that it is better than any of its
> rivals, there is no need to give such a system three cheers. My friend Irving
> Kristol calls his book *Two Cheers for Capitalism*. One cheer is quite enough.[2]

Is it any wonder that economic freedom is disappearing? With champions
like this, you hardly need critics.

FREE MARKETERS VERSUS THE MARKET

Crisis triggers change, but which way a country goes—whether it fights for more freedom or lurches toward tyranny—depends on its governing ideas. When the economy collapsed in the early 1930s, collectivism—the idea that the individual is and should be subordinate to the group—was on the ascendency worldwide, even in America; not coincidentally, we elected FDR, who brought the New Deal. But when crisis hit in the 1970s, America's political direction swung to the right. What had changed?

The major factor was the collapse of collectivism as an intellectual and moral ideal. In the aftermath of World War II, when the devastation that collectivism wreaked across the globe—in Nazi Germany, in Communist Russia, in Fascist Italy, among others—was impossible to ignore or explain away, the pretense that collectivism brings prosperity withered. Although much of the intellectual establishment retained sympathy for collectivism, the crusading spirit that had animated its proponents during the '30s was dead.

Into this vacuum entered other intellectuals, such as Milton Friedman, F. A. Hayek and Ayn Rand. They argued for the superiority of capitalism. By the late 1970s, these thinkers had gained some political traction (Friedman and Hayek were awarded the Nobel Prize in economics during that decade). But, with the exception of Ayn Rand, something crucial was missing from their work. On capitalism's *moral* superiority—on whether capitalism is a *good and just* system—they had nothing new or persuasive to say. In fact, most of these thinkers downplayed or denigrated the significance of morality altogether. To be sure, some in the 1980s spoke of economic prosperity in vaguely moral terms. Reagan, for instance, spoke of a new "morning in America." But neither he nor his supporters could explain why seeking wealth and pursuing your own economic well-being are morally proper.

This, as we've seen, was a fatal shortcoming. But their silence was not the worst of it. Some of capitalism's so-called champions *did* talk about morality—not to defend capitalism but to denigrate it.

"Conservatives and liberals agree on little these days," observes conservative columnist Rich Karlgaard. "But most agree on this: Capitalism . . . is insufficiently moral."[3]

Capitalism, writes economist James Doti,

> is not a pretty sight. Capitalists motivated by greed seek their own gain
> by maximizing profits. The forces of the marketplace, however, convert
> this private vice into public virtue. Thus, living a life based on greed . . .
> can do quite well . . . to better society and benefit our fellow human
> beings.[4]

This was not a particularly inspiring argument. It told men they could
do no better than the imperfect and the immoral, that capitalism was at
odds with idealism, that anyone concerned with promoting man's material welfare had better give up hope of promoting his nobility. "[I]f people
believe that something is evil," notes one commentator, "the response 'But
it works!' doesn't win arguments."[5]

Even those who could swallow the idea that a million vices could add
up to virtue were unable to get very far with this argument. Although it
was plausible in the abstract, its cogency collapsed the moment someone
pointed to real needs that were going unfulfilled or to specific evils supposedly caused by greed. Sure, the critics of capitalism would say, we can't
do away with economic freedom altogether—but what about the mother
who can't afford health insurance for her child? What about the grand-
mother who can't afford her rent? What about the son struggling to pay off
his student loans? What about Enron? What about Madoff? What about
greedy oil companies with their price gouging and their windfall profits?

Economic freedom, as we've seen, was not lost in one fell swoop.
Americans demanded specific entitlement programs and specific regulations to deal with what they saw as specific problems. Whenever they
were faced with a choice between economic freedom and a perceived need
for government intervention, government intervention won out. Leading
conservatives Arthur C. Brooks and Paul Ryan describe the pattern this
way:

> [R]edistribution and statism always win out over limited government
> and private markets.
>
> Why not lift the safety net a few rungs higher up the income lad-
> der? Go ahead, slap a little tariff on some Chinese goods in the name

of protecting a favored industry. More generous pensions for teachers? Hey, it's only a few million tax dollars—and think of the kids, after all.

Individually, these things might sound fine. Multiply them and add them all up, though, and you have a system that most Americans manifestly oppose—one that creates a crushing burden of debt and teaches our children and grandchildren that government is the solution to all our problems.[6]

We baby-stepped our way into Big Government. To break this pattern, free market advocates would have to challenge Americans' view of self-interest; they would have to explain why, even individually, these things *don't* "sound fine." They haven't, because at heart, they agree. As a result, when one goes looking for a moral defense of free markets by capitalism's defenders, what one finds, by and large, are moral *attacks*.

Capitalism is, at its core, the economic system based on the individual's right to seek his own happiness. It is the system where we are left alone to pursue our own dreams, make our own choices, achieve our own potential. That does not sit well with many on the right.

> During the past 30 years [laments *Book of Virtues* author William Bennett], we have witnessed a profound shift in public attitudes. . . . [W]e Americans now place less value on what we owe others as a matter of moral obligation; less value on sacrifice as a moral good, on social conformity, respectability, and observing the rules; less value on correctness and restraint in matters of physical pleasure and sexuality—and correlatively greater value on things like self-expression, individualism, self-realization, and personal choice.[7]

The problem, says legal scholar Robert Bork, is that people take the rights expressed in the Declaration of Independence—above all, the pursuit of happiness—too seriously.[8] "Liberty," former Senator Rick Santorum protests, does not mean the "freedom to be left alone," but "the freedom to attend to one's duties to God, to family, and to neighbors."[9] (What Taliban cleric could disagree?)

Even such an ardent defender of capitalism as Adam Smith believed that free markets would have a deleterious effect on most people, who, he thought, would be reduced to automatons, performing the same few mindless tasks day after day. Although Smith argued that free markets lead self-interested actors to act for the "public good," he was not a fan of self-interest per se and held that in any contest between the welfare of society and self-interested motives, the welfare of society "ought to cast the balance against all other motives."[10] Self-interest did not invalidate a moral action—but it did diminish its moral status. In capitalist societies, therefore, "all the nobler parts of the human character may be, in a great measure, obliterated and extinguished in the great body of the people."[11]

How can a movement that attacks businessmen defend the economic system that lionizes them? How can critics of the profit motive uphold the system of the profit motive? They can't, says Christian conservative George Gilder.

> It just won't do any longer to suggest that businessmen are bad guys, or ambitious dolts, or self-serving money grubbers, and then conclude that if they are given maximum freedom, they will build the new Jerusalem: a good and bountiful society.

He continues:

> To defend capitalism—even to understand it—you have to comprehend that businessmen are not bastards, but the heroes of the modern age—crucial vessels of those generous and creative impulses that give hope to an evermore populous humanity in overcoming its continuing scarcities and conflicts. In a world always divided in part between the givers and the takers, businessmen are among the most persistent and ingenious of donors and all of us who benefit should be thankful.[12]

What, then, of Gilder's own defense of businessmen? Adam Smith had famously argued that the businessman

> intends only his own gain, and he is in this, as in many other cases, led by an invisible hand to promote an end which was no part of his intention. . . . By pursuing his own interest he frequently promotes that of the society more effectually than when he really intends to promote it.[13]

Gilder's defense consists of the wildly implausible claim that businessmen really *do* intend to promote the interests of society rather than their own. Capitalists don't invest in order to reap rewards, says Gilder: They engage in "contests of altruism," providing a "spontaneous flow of gifts" out of a spirit of generosity.[14] As John Stossel might say: Give me a break.

To be sure, say some free market advocates, capitalism is not bereft of all virtue. It does require and encourage certain "bourgeois virtues"— thrift, moderation, honesty, hard work. But, they admit, these are pretty selfish and uninspiring. "[S]uch characteristics are not ennobling," writes essayist Stephen Miller, "not even wholly admirable. The bourgeois virtues—all set in motion by self-interest—are not heroic virtues, not the stuff of great literature."[15]

A moral society, most conclude, requires the government to intervene—people must embrace the regulatory-entitlement state in order to curtail man's selfish, individualistic impulses and spark a collective crusade to supply people's lives with meaning.

Hayek had warned against a "dogmatic laissez-faire attitude." This is not a problem for most of capitalism's alleged champions.[16] As Kristol points out:

> [I]f you believe that man's spiritual life is infinitely more important than his trivial and transient adventures in the marketplace, then you may tolerate a free market for practical reasons, within narrow limits, but you certainly will have no compunctions about overriding it if you think the free market is interfering with more important things.[17]

The right has had no such compunction.

THE RIGHT'S CRUSADE FOR BIG GOVERNMENT

"Wishing to be left alone isn't a governing doctrine," writes *New York Times* conservative columnist David Brooks.[18] If Americans "think of nothing but their narrow self-interest, of their commercial activities, they lose a sense of grand aspiration and noble purpose."[19] Instead of leaving individuals free to focus on their own lives and their own happiness, government must get Americans "to serve a cause larger than self-interest, fuse their own efforts with those from other regions and other walks of life and cultivate a spirit of citizenship."[20]

Brooks himself favors pushing Americans to serve the cause of "American Greatness."[21] He advocates, for instance, mandatory national service, which would take "kids out of the normal self-obsessed world of career and consumption and [orient] them toward service and citizenship." As he elaborates elsewhere, "Today's children . . . would suddenly face drill sergeants reminding them they are nothing without the group."[22]

Others on the right are not so gung ho about state-mandated, militaristic moral indoctrination but agree with Brooks that capitalism is dispensable in the battle for a moral culture. Irving Kristol, for instance, called for a "conservative welfare state";[23] conservative journalist David Frum has too;[24] and George W. Bush famously labeled himself a "compassionate conservative."[25]

The right's approach is simple: Embrace the same collectivist goals as the left, and quibble over the means. *Wall Street Journal* columnist William McGurn praises "American liberals" for "their ability to set goals for our society," noting that even if ObamaCare is repealed, "it's a good bet that Republicans will still have to find a way to meet another goal set by liberals, that of ensuring that Americans with pre-existing medical conditions can get coverage."[26]

Conservatives aren't enemies of Big Government per se, argues McGurn. They share the left's goals but want to find creative programs for *how* to achieve them, programs that minimize cost and bureaucracy. "Even Milton Friedman's proposal for school vouchers . . . is essentially a 'how' argument."[27]

Given the right's attack on self-interest and the profit motive and its endorsement of the regulatory-entitlement state, it's no surprise that when it held power during the last decade, the size and reach of government exploded. Today's mainstream right gave us a protectionist steel tariff. It gave us a prescription drug bill—until ObamaCare, the largest expansion of the entitlement state since LBJ. It gave us the No Child Left Behind bill, which massively increased the federal government's control of education. It gave us Sarbanes-Oxley, a draconian web of new business regulations. It increased government spending by 50 percent in less than eight years. It responded to a financial crisis it helped to create with bailouts and stimulus bills; President Bush justified it with a double lie: "I've abandoned free market principles [as if he had them] to save the free market system [as if there were one]."[28]

Even Ronald Reagan passed substantial tax *increases* following his initial tax cuts, increased government spending, and in many respects grew the size of government.[29]

CONCLUSION: IN SEARCH OF A DEFENSE OF "MORE"

The free market *is* the system of "more"—the system of more wealth, more innovation, more progress. Consumers seek more, businesses seek more, investors seek more. Most people interpret this as the frenzied, irrational, materialistic, immoral pursuit of wealth. It means taking what you can get, indulging in your whims, living at others' expense, with no thought of your neighbor or of the future. Markets, they often conclude, are dangerous, reckless, amoral rat races that need to be reined in through regulation, and purified by wealth redistribution.

To end the growth of government, we need to take the opposite view. We need to defend the pursuit of "more" itself.

Some of capitalism's alleged champions sidestep the issue completely. Others concede that the pursuit of "more" by individuals is an ugly, irrational, immoral process—but the market, they say, transforms it "by an invisible hand" into something that is if not noble, then at least tolerable. This is not a convincing approach, and, unsurprisingly, many of these people expanded the size of government once they got into office.

To stop the growth of the state and place capitalism on a solid foundation, we need to defend the profit motive—and not merely its beneficial social consequences but the pursuit of profit itself. This is why today's alleged free market champions are powerless to stop Big Government. Whatever their virtues, they cannot change people's basic attitudes toward self-interest and the profit motive.

To do that, you need Ayn Rand.

FOUR
THE 2008 HOUSING MELTDOWN
A Crisis That Government Built

O**N OCTOBER 23, 2008, FORMER FEDERAL RESERVE CHAIR-**man Alan Greenspan appeared before Congress. The financial crisis had exploded onto the headlines only a few weeks earlier, and Greenspan's appearance set off a firestorm: Greenspan, the alleged archdefender of capitalism, admitted that the crisis revealed a "flaw" in his free market ideology, thus giving credence to the most popular account of the 2008 housing meltdown—that it illustrates how free markets inevitably fail.[1]

But what Greenspan didn't mention was that the events leading up to the crisis took place on a market that was anything but free—a market where, among other things, the government intervened in order to promote "affordable housing." As Greenspan himself observed in his autobiography, published a year before the credit meltdown:

> I was aware that the [government-backed policy of] loosening of mortgage credit terms for subprime borrowers increased financial risk, and that [government] subsidized home ownership initiatives distort market outcomes. But I believe then, as now, that the benefits of broadened home ownership are worth the risk.[2]

Greenspan didn't always have such faint convictions; his younger self challenged the standard view of an earlier financial crisis popularly attributed to free markets. In his 1966 article "Gold and Economic Freedom,"

Greenspan explained how America's Great Depression was not the result of capitalism but of a credit boom manufactured by the Federal Reserve.

> When business in the United States underwent a mild contraction in 1927, the Federal Reserve created more paper reserves in the hope of forestalling any possible bank reserve shortage. . . . The "Fed" succeeded . . . but it nearly destroyed the economies of the world, in the process. The excess credit which the Fed pumped into the economy spilled over into the stock market—triggering a fantastic speculative boom. Belatedly, Federal Reserve officials attempted to sop up the excess reserves and finally succeeded in breaking the boom. But it was too late: by 1929 the speculative imbalances had become so overwhelming that the attempt precipitated a sharp retrenching and a consequent demoralizing of business confidence. As a result, the American economy collapsed.[3]

It was another credit boom—this one manufactured by Greenspan himself—that set into motion the events that would culminate in the devastating financial crisis of 2008. Economists Steven Horwitz and Peter Boettke summarize the cause of the crisis nicely: It was, they wrote, "a credit-fueled and regulatory-directed housing boom and bust."[4] The Federal Reserve kept interest rates artificially low, flooding the market with cheap money, which eventually created a housing bubble. This bubble was intensified by government housing policy and a highly regulated financial industry able to take on monstrously large amounts of risk (since taxpayers would be liable for most of the losses in case of failure). The bust followed as a matter of course.

This chapter challenges the conventional view that free, unregulated markets were responsible for the financial crisis. Although this is of course an enormously complex issue, and there is room for debate about the details, government intervention is unquestionably the fundamental cause of the crisis. In fact, far from revealing a "flaw" in the free market, the financial crisis eloquently confirms our thesis about why government grows.

In this chapter, we'll sketch some of the evidence that points to this conclusion. Then we'll discuss how our culture's prevalent morality both contributed to the crisis and shaped our response to it.[5]

THE FEDERAL RESERVE SPIKES THE PUNCH

The Federal Reserve is America's central bank. Established in 1913, it regulates other banks, sets key interest rates, acts as a "lender of last resort," and controls the American money supply. Its putative goal is to "provide the nation with a safer, more flexible, and more stable monetary and financial system."[6] But in the Fed's relatively brief history, it has contributed greatly to the crash of 1920, the Great Depression of the 1930s, the inflation and stagflation of the 1970s, the tech bubble of the 1990s—and today's financial crisis.[7]

In the wake of the attacks of September 11, 2001, in an attempt to avoid a recession, Greenspan lowered the interest rate at which banks borrow from and lend to each other, first from 6.25 percent to 1.75 percent, then to 1 percent, where it held for a full year. These were historic lows—for two and a half years rates were lower than the rate of inflation. This meant, in effect, that people were being *paid* to borrow money.

And borrow we did. We borrowed to start new businesses. We borrowed to buy homes. When those homes went up in value, we borrowed against the equity to fill our debt-financed homes with debt-financed TVs, pool tables, marble counters, and stainless steel dishwashers. During the boom years, Americans borrowed and spent so much that our savings rate actually turned *negative*. It seemed to make sense—after all, money was cheap.

"Alan Greenspan needs to create a housing bubble to replace the Nasdaq bubble," cried *New York Times* columnist Paul Krugman in 2002.[8] And that's exactly what Greenspan did. Much of the new cash that flooded into the market as a result of his policies went into real estate, where small fluctuations in interest rates have a huge impact on prices. A $250,000 30-year fixed-rate mortgage at 8 percent, for instance, translates to a monthly payment of $1,834.41, but at 6 percent, the cost plunges to $1,498.88—a difference of more than $300 a month. Greenspan's artificial interest rates meant that more people felt they could afford homes—and those who had homes felt they could afford bigger ones. Home values soared, which attracted more investment in the housing industry, which sent home values even higher, and so on.

But this trend was not sustainable. Home prices couldn't rise forever (nor could interest rates stay low), and once the price rise stopped (or interest rates rose), the bubble would collapse. It was only easy money from Greenspan that permitted housing prices to go on rising for as long as they did.

In a truly free market, there would be no central bank. Interest rates would be determined by the supply of savings and the demand for loans, not by the machinations of an Alan Greenspan. Money would consist of a finite commodity like gold, so the government couldn't create bubbles by printing gobs of cash. This financial crisis was rooted not in a free market but in our *unfree* market.

HOUSING POLICY MADE THINGS WORSE

"Uncle Sam wants you . . . to own a home." That was the message drilled into Americans for decades.[9] Homeownership, we were told, was good for everyone, and the government's job was to make sure as many of us as possible owned homes—regardless of whether we could truly afford one. We can, President Bush said in 2002, "put light where there's darkness, and hope where there's despondency in this country. And part of it is working together as a nation to encourage folks to own their own home."[10]

This was not idle talk. The Department of Housing and Urban Development (HUD), the Federal Housing Administration, the Federal Home Loan Bank, the Federal Housing Finance Board, the Office of Federal Housing Enterprise Oversight, along with Congress and the president all worked to implement this goal.

In a free market, individuals don't ask politicians where they should live—they decide for themselves what living arrangements best suit their needs. They buy if they want to buy, rent if they want to rent, or live with friends or family. Not so in the lead-up to the crisis. Homeowners received all kinds of special tax advantages. Interest payments on mortgage debt were tax deductible. Borrowing against the equity in one's home was also tax deductible—which made owning a home more attractive and encouraged homeowners to take on debt. And starting in 1997, home sellers could make up to $500,000 in profit from selling their primary residence without having to pay capital gains taxes, creating an additional incentive to speculate in real estate.

But those in Washington seeking to increase homeownership still faced a formidable obstacle: Many of the people who didn't own homes couldn't get loans. In the past, when the housing market had been relatively free, profit-minded lenders sought to diligently manage risk, so they required things like a substantial down payment, a strong credit history, and a strict ratio (usually about 1:4) between monthly payments and income.[11]

That kind of profit-minded lending was precisely what the government aimed to eliminate. In order to end the tyranny of sensible underwriting standards, the government put into practice a number of regulations designed to encourage the very nonprime loans that would later come under fire. (This is one reason why it's so farcical to pretend that more regulation was the solution to the crisis: Lowering lending standards was the government's official policy.)

The most flagrant of these was the Community Reinvestment Act. Passed under President Jimmy Carter, the act was resurrected and strengthened under Clinton in order to remedy (now-discredited) allegations of widespread racial discrimination in lending. The CRA forced banks to lend to "underserved" communities, and the only way to carry out this command was to make loans, including home loans, to borrowers who were not creditworthy. Banks had to loosen their lending standards without regard for what this would mean if home prices ever started to decline.

But the chief villains in the push for "affordable housing" were two government-sponsored entities (GSEs), Fannie Mae and Freddie Mac. Officially known as the Federal National Mortgage Association and Federal Home Loan Mortgage Corporation, respectively, Fannie and Freddie were established by the government in order to create a secondary market in mortgages, with the goal of making housing more affordable. Banks could make home loans and then sell these loans to the GSEs, giving the banks the funds to make additional loans.

Although Fannie and Freddie eventually were nominally privatized, they were beneficiaries of a number of government favors and had an implicit guarantee by the U.S. Treasury on their debt. This guarantee enabled them to borrow money at below-market rates and take on enormous amounts of debt with which to buy up mortgages. Freddie Mac wound up leveraged at an astounding ratio of 67.9 to 1 in June 2008; most highly leveraged hedge funds had ratios half that size.[12] This meant that a mere 1½ percent decline in its assets would erase its capital. A ticking time bomb of this size would never be tolerated on a free market. It was possible only because no one fretted about lending money to Fannie and Freddie, thanks to their implied government guarantee.

During the 1990s, under pressure from HUD and Congress, Fannie and Freddie began to expand their "affordable housing" efforts. Then Fannie Mae chairman Franklin Raines vowed to close "America's homeownership gaps" through "underwriting experiments that [redefine] creditworthiness."[13] And redefine they did. According to economist Russell Roberts, by 2005, HUD was requiring that 22 percent of Fannie and Freddie's mortgage purchases be "special affordable" loans, "typically to borrowers with income less than 60 percent of their area's median income." That meant "funding hundreds of billions of dollars worth of loans," including no small number of subprime and other less-than-solid loans.[14]

Congress had been warned about the risks at least as far back as 2003, but such concerns were brushed aside. As Representative Barney Frank put it:

> I believe that we, as the Federal Government, have probably done too little rather than too much to push [Fannie Mae and Freddie Mac] to meet the goals of affordable housing and to set reasonable goals. . . . The more people, in my judgment, exaggerate a threat of safety and soundness, the more people conjure up the possibility of serious financial losses to the Treasury, which I do not see . . . the more pressure there is there, then the less I think we see in terms of affordable housing.[15]

The astonishing results: By early 2008, Fannie and Freddie owned or guaranteed nearly half of the American mortgage market. The not-so-astonishing results: By late 2008, Fannie and Freddie were on the verge of collapse and were taken over by the government. Thus their implicit guarantee became explicit.

FINANCIAL REGULATION MADE THINGS A DISASTER

The housing bubble, fueled by the Federal Reserve's artificially low interest rates and the government's affordable-housing crusade, was exacerbated by a regulated financial system that not only fed the bubble but did so in a way that would transform the economy into a giant house of cards.

Of all the claims made about the financial crisis, none is more prepos-
terous than that the financial industry was a bastion of freedom. While it
is true that some of the particular financial instruments that took center
stage during the crisis were not directly controlled by regulators, the industry itself was *the* most regulated industry in the country.

Consider this: At the national level alone (not counting state regulatory agencies), the U.S. financial system is subject to *eight* different regulatory authorities. They are:

1. U.S. Securities and Exchange Commission (SEC)
2. Financial Industry Regulatory Authority (FINRA)
3. Commodity Futures Trading Commission (CFTC)
4. Federal Reserve (Fed)
5. Federal Deposit Insurance Corporation (FDIC)
6. Office of the Comptroller of the Currency (OCC)
7. National Credit Union Administration (NCUA)
8. Office of Thrift Supervision (OTS)

If you want to take a ride through hell, spend some time perusing the thick
sea of regulations issued by these agencies.[16] If this is a free market, we
can't imagine what a regulated one would look like.

Or consider this: Between 1980 and 2009, for every one instance of
financial "deregulation," there were *four* instances of new financial regulation (see table 4.1).[17]

The truth is that, throughout the 2000s, bankers and financiers had
to get government permission to do almost anything. In a very important
sense, all the supposedly unregulated financial instruments that have been
blamed for the crisis—the mortgage-backed securities, the collateralized
debt obligations, the credit default swaps—*were* regulated: They were instruments that arose in a highly regulated industry and that were created
and traded by actors fully at the mercy of the government. The only reason the government didn't stop the financiers was because it *approved of*
what they were doing: helping to lower the cost of homeownership.

More important, these instruments could never have developed
as they did without the distortions created by decades of government
meddling. Above all, what enabled the financial industry to take on an

TABLE 4.1. THE MYTH OF FINANCIAL DEREGULATION

Year	Regulatory Action	Type of Action
1980	Depository Institutions Deregulation and Monetary Control Act repealed "Regulation Q" ceilings	Deregulation
1980	National Bank Act extended to state banks and savings associations	Regulation
1980	OCC changed national bank charter standards	Regulation
1982	Garn–St. Germain Depository Institutions Act authorized banks to compete with money market funds	Deregulation
1985	OCC changed national bank charter standards, requiring chief executives to be designated before charter approval	Regulation
1986	OCC changed national bank charter standards, requiring institutions to provide statements on formal lending policies and fund-management strategies	Regulation
1986	Guidelines on managing banks' off-balance-sheet exposures	Regulation
1987	Competitive Equality Banking Act, preventing commercial banks from creating nonbanking institutions or selling new insurance, real estate, and securities underwriting services; also expanded FDIC responsibilities	Regulation
1988	Basel I—international convergence of capital measurement and standards	Regulation
1989	Financial Institutions Reform Recovery and Enforcement Act, created OTS, Federal Housing Finance Agency, Savings Association Insurance Fund, Resolution Trust Corporation; increased Fannie Mae and Freddie Mac support of mortgages	Regulation
1991	Federal Deposit Insurance Corporation Improvement Act, allowed the FDIC to borrow directly from the Treasury department, mandated that the FDIC resolve failed banks using the least-costly method available, ordered the FDIC to assess insurance premiums according to risk, and created new capital requirements	Regulation
1994	Amendment to Basel I to broaden recognition of collateral	Regulation
1994	Treatment of credit risk associated with certain off-balance-sheet items	Regulation
1995	Changes made to capital standards of special-purpose vehicles	Regulation
1996	Supervisory guidance for credit derivatives	Regulation
1997	Reverse tying practices repealed, increasing competition between banks and nonbank credit providers	Deregulation

(continues)

TABLE 4.1. (CONTINUED)

Year	Regulatory Action	Type of Action
1999	Repeal of Glass-Steagall removed firewall between commercial and investment banks	Deregulation
2000	Commodity Futures Modernization Act provided legal certainty that derivatives would not be regulated by the CFTC	Deregulation
2001	United States moved further to adopt Basel standards	Regulation
2001	Ratings-based approach applied to asset- and mortgage-backed securities	Regulation
2001	Patriot Act contains financial regulations to crack down on terrorist finance	Regulation
2002	Sarbanes-Oxley	Regulation
2004	Basel II—international convergence of capital measurement and capital standards: a revised framework	Regulation
2004	Some broker-dealers permitted alternative means to compute capital	Regulation
2006	Credit Rating Agency Reform Act of 2006	Regulation
2007	U.S. regulators attempt to further incorporate Basel standards	Regulation
2008	Basel Committee on Banking Supervision consultative document on computing capital	Regulation
2009	Revisions to Basel II market risk framework	Regulation

Source: Steven Horwitz and Peter Boettke, *The House That Uncle Sam Built*. Courtesy of the Foundation for Economic Education.

unprecedented amount of debt were government policies that shielded it from failure.

The best known of these policies was the government's notion that some financial institutions are "too big to fail" and would be bailed out by Washington if they got into trouble. In a free market, risk carries both a potential upside (greater returns) and a potential downside (greater losses). Debt holders are quick to put on the brakes when a company starts taking on unmanageable risk. Why would anyone lend to such a company? Well, with "too big to fail" in place, the question instead became: Why not? More and more, investors minimized the significance of risk because, thanks to the bubble, the returns seemed to be effortlessly high, and, in any case, investors would be shielded by taxpayers from catastrophic downside.[18]

But "too big to fail" was itself an outgrowth of another regulation—namely, deposit insurance, which guarantees that if a bank fails, its depositors will be paid back up to a specified limit ($100,000 before the financial crisis). In other words, deposit insurance is simply a bailout plan for depositors, and it has the same effects that more recent bailouts did.

We would have to deal with many other issues if this were a complete assessment of the financial crisis: the role of the credit agencies; the significance of derivative securities; the behavior of bankers, lenders, and homeowners; and so on. It is the task of economists to sort out exactly what happened and which of the tens of thousands of regulations, controls, and distortions led to the specific actions that caused the financial crisis in 2008. What we can say with certainty is that it could not have been the free market that caused the crisis, since no such market existed, and that therefore the government controls bear fundamental responsibility for the crisis. The government created an economically distorted environment in which making a killing seemed easy and losing one's shirt impossible—an environment that never could have existed in a truly free market.

THE UNLEARNED LESSONS

But the lessons of the financial crisis go deeper. Why did the government intervene in the market in the first place? Why did it manipulate interest rates, regulate voluntary behavior, and create the perverse incentives that brought the economy to its knees? In a word: morality.

Why did we have a Federal Reserve? Because Americans did not trust "greedy" bankers like J. P. Morgan (America's leading banker at the time the Fed was created) to wield power over the financial system—and so they placed incredible, arbitrary powers in the hands of "public servants" like Alan Greenspan.

Why did Alan Greenspan lower interest rates to 1 percent? Because recessions always involve pain and people "needed" a "soft landing."

Why did we have a housing crusade? Because people "needed" housing they couldn't afford, and only the government could force "greedy" lenders to lower their lending standards. George W. Bush, for instance, justified government housing policy by declaring that we "have a responsibility . . .

to promote something greater than ourselves. And to me, that something greater than yourself is to love a neighbor like you'd like to be loved yourself."[19]

Why did the government institute a policy of "too big to fail" and deposit insurance? Because depositors "needed" risk-free banking and protection from "greedy" bankers.

To be sure, all of these policies came ready-made with multiple justifications. But at root, they were put into place to restrain greed and serve need. So, when the crisis hit, there was no real question about how, in essence, Washington would respond.

"Wall Street has betrayed us. They've broken the social contract between capitalism and the average citizen and the worker.... This is a result of excess and greed and corruption. And that's exactly what is plaguing Americans today. And we got to fix it and we've got to update our regulatory system."[20] No, those aren't the words of Barack Obama. The speaker was then-Republican presidential nominee John McCain. It seemed that everyone on Capitol Hill in the fall of 2008 was racing to blame the crisis on capitalism, Wall Street, and "greed"—and, of course, to "solve" the crisis with unprecedented amounts of government intervention.

We have been assured by politicians and pundits across the ideological spectrum that this intervention prevented an economic doomsday. This is not true, although what other options we had in the short term is admittedly a difficult question. Under a system of fiat money (as opposed to a market-based gold standard), bank failures can lead to deflationary credit contractions, like the one we went through during the Great Depression. Once government had created the economic crisis, it faced few good choices in the short run.

However, the long-term solution should certainly have been the gradual freeing up of the American financial industry and the complete dismantling of government housing policy. Not surprisingly, Washington gave us the worst of all worlds. The government blamed economic freedom and the profit motive for our economic troubles and ramped up its economic intervention—making it more arbitrary and unpredictable than ever.

The capstone of the insanity was the regulatory response. In 2010, Congress passed one of the greatest regulatory expansions in American history. The bill, the Dodd-Frank Wall Street Reform and Consumer Protection Act, was named after two of the politicians who had done the most to promote Fannie and Freddie's malignant growth.

CONCLUSION: FREEING THE UNFREE MARKET

For decades, the government has intervened in the economy in the name of curtailing "greed" and serving "need." These policies perverted the market, sparked a housing bubble, and led to the ultimate bust.

But because the conventional view of selfishness remained entrenched, it was not the "public servants" in Washington who took the blame: It was "greedy," profit-seeking businessmen and the "free market." The inevitable expansion of government followed.

The true lesson of the financial crisis is exactly the opposite of what the pundits concluded. The conventional view is that the free market failed. In fact, it was the *unfree* market that failed, and it is *more* freedom that is the solution. But if we're to start moving back toward a free economy, we have to provide the profit motive with a *moral* defense.

What would a moral defense of the profit motive look like?

It would jettison the image of businessmen as greedy exploiters. It would show that most businessmen aren't irrational shysters driven to cut corners and cut throats but producers who earn their living. It would explain why the profit motive leads the businessman to pursue his interests rationally, which means that a productive businessman is not a threat to your interests but an ally. It would show how the selfish pursuit of profit makes people safer, richer, freer, and happier. And it would explain why straitjacketing the profit motive with regulations and controls is morally wrong.

A moral defense of the profit motive would dispense with the notion that need is a moral entitlement—that morality requires surrendering the fruits of your labor to any wound-bearing beggar seeking something for nothing or that it sanctions punishing the successful in order to reward the unsuccessful. And it would explain how government wealth-redistribution schemes are a source of injustice.

A moral defense of the profit motive would have to say that living as a trader, for your own happiness and by your own effort, is *noble*. And it would call for shrinking government to its proper size and function: the protector of the individual's right to pursue his own profit, his own life, and his own happiness.

At the deepest level, a moral defense of the profit motive would have to show that it *is* selfish—and that that is a good thing.

PART II
THE SOLUTION

FIVE
RETHINKING SELFISHNESS

ECEMBER 11, 2008. THE DETAILS WERE UNCLEAR BUT the bottom line was not: Bernie Madoff had carried out the largest Ponzi scheme in history. His investors had lost billions.

One of those investors was the French aristocrat René-Thierry Magon de la Villehuchet, head of the hedge fund Access International Advisors. As the economy started to slow in 2008, de la Villehuchet's company revved up its investment in Madoff's fund, which was one of the few still showing strong returns. By December, de la Villehuchet had invested all of his personal wealth with Madoff, along with 20 percent of his brother's and nearly half of his company's funds. On December 23, shortly after learning that Madoff had been arrested for fraud, de la Villehuchet was found dead of an apparent suicide. His death symbolized the almost inconceivable scale of destruction Madoff had caused.

"How could he do such a thing?" Madoff's victims asked. The answer they were given: Madoff was greedy and selfish. Indeed, Madoff has come to personify selfishness. To be selfish is to be like Madoff: to screw anyone, even family and friends, in order to get more, more, more for me, me, me.

Madoff is just the latest poster boy for the evil of selfishness. Before him there was Kenneth Lay. Before Kenneth Lay there was Charles Keating. And before Charles Keating there was a long line of villains stretching back thousands of years, each embodying the same proposition: To be concerned with one's own interests is cruel, evil, and dangerous.

Of course, if these lowlifes were true representatives of selfishness, who could object to that proposition? No one disputes that they are evil (save for those who dispute that anyone is evil). But historically, another kind of man has been an archetype for selfishness as well: the producer.

THE PRISONER AND THE PRODUCER

For years Apple CEO Steve Jobs had a vision of a single device that would unite a phone, a personal digital assistant, an MP3 player, and the web surfing capability of a computer. But the technical challenges were daunting. How to design an operating system that used up minimal memory but had excellent functionality? How to design a touch screen that wouldn't get scratched in people's pockets? How to keep radiation to safe levels? And how to do it all for a price customers would be willing to pay? "It was a great challenge," said Jobs. "We had a big debate inside the company whether we could do that or not. And that was one where I had to adjudicate it and just say, 'We're going to do it. Let's try.' The smartest software guys were saying they can do it, so let's give them a shot."[1]

One by one, Apple's engineers solved these seemingly impossible problems. But Jobs demanded still more. With the release date looming, he looked at the design of what would become the iPhone and announced to his team, "I just don't love this. I can't convince myself to fall in love with this." Jobs was asking his team to toss out a year's work and start over. "And you know what everybody said?" Jobs later recalled. "Sign us up."

But with only three months left before Jobs was to announce the product at the annual Macworld trade show, the iPhone still did not work. The pressure on Jobs's staff was tremendous. They worked days. They worked nights. They argued, fought, battled, quit, and returned. Said Jobs:

> My job is to not be easy on people. My job is to make them better. My job is to pull things together from different parts of the company and clear the ways and get the resources for the key projects. And to take these great people we have and to push them and make them even better, coming up with more aggressive visions of how it could be.[2]

Jobs was the quintessential producer—someone who devoted his mind and every ounce of his energy to creating material values. The result was the Apple II, the Macintosh, Pixar, the iPod, iTunes, the iPhone, the iPad, and much, much more. Jobs made Apple the world's most valuable company and radically improved the way we live in the process.

But throughout his career, and indeed in the doorstop-size biography published just after his death, Jobs was also routinely derided as selfish. Whatever his virtues, people said, Jobs was primarily concerned with his vision and his company's success—not with the welfare of others. In the wake of his resignation from Apple, shortly before his death, some even rushed to condemn Jobs for focusing his efforts on profit seeking rather than philanthropy. Journalist Andrew Sorkin, for example, penned a missive in the *New York Times* in which he acknowledged that Jobs was a "visionary" and an "innovator" who "clearly never craved money for money's sake and has never been ostentatious with his wealth." Nevertheless, Sorkin complained, "there is no public record of Mr. Jobs giving money to charity."[3] A 2006 column in *Wired* put it more bluntly: Jobs was "nothing more than a greedy capitalist who's amassed an obscene fortune. It's shameful."[4]

In some ways, though, Jobs is the exception that proves the rule. Unique among businessmen, he was admired by many for his unrivaled creativity and passion for making "insanely great" products. If even *he* could not escape charges of "selfishness" and "greed," then what chance have other producers had? Indeed, from Morgan to Rockefeller, to Ford, to Walton, to Gates, virtually no successful businessman has been immune from the accusation that he is selfish.

But here's the trillion-dollar question: Does it really make sense to equate producers like Jobs with criminals like Madoff—to accuse them of the same dark motive and the same moral crime (in spirit, if not in scale)? One creates wealth; the other steals it. One thrives by trading with other people; the other destroys the lives of everyone he touches. One works incredibly hard to build a product or company he can be proud of; the other spends his time trying to cover up the fact that he has nothing to be proud of. In what sense are the two at all similar?

If you moved to a foreign land and you were told that the worst thing you could call someone is a "floober," and that this designation applies to Adolf Hitler, Charles Manson, and Abraham Lincoln, you would probably think, "That's a pretty stupid word." Well, whenever we hear people label destructive monsters like Madoff and benefactors like Jobs "selfish," it strikes us as no less senseless.

It's not that Steve Jobs wasn't selfish. However much his work benefited others, that was never his primary motive, and he did not benefit them at his own expense. (If Jobs's chief goal was to benefit others, he could have sold his notoriously expensive products at a fraction of the price.) While men like Jobs are clearly not indifferent to other people, their driving motive is to profit by creating products *they* think are good. They are obsessed with value creation; the effects on others are secondary to them. "Going to bed at night saying we've done something wonderful," Jobs said, "that's what matters to me."[5] Indeed, Jobs was famous for eschewing focus groups and instead designing products that he and his team loved. As he said of the difference between the übersuccessful iPod and the total flop that was Microsoft's Zune:

> We won because we personally love music. We made the iPod for ourselves, and when you're doing something for yourself, or your best friend or family, you're not going to cheese out. If you don't love something, you're not going to go the extra mile, work the extra weekend, challenge the status quo as much.[6]

If being unselfish meant serving and sacrificing for others—giving up worldly wealth and happiness à la Mother Teresa—then who could deny that Jobs epitomized selfishness?

The real question is: By what standard is *Madoff* supposed to be selfish? Exactly what concern did he ever show for his actual, long-range interests?

Truth be told, we find it hard to think of a less selfish life than Madoff's. For starters, his scheme turned his days into a constant wave of lies and anxiety. As Madoff himself put it:

> It was a nightmare for me. It was *only* a nightmare for me. It's horrible. When I say nightmare, imagine carrying this secret. . . . Look, imagine going home every night not being able to tell your wife, living with this ax over your head, not telling your sons, my brother, seeing them every day in the business and not being able to confide in them.[7]

When Madoff's scheme finally did collapse, he confessed, "I wish they had caught me six years ago, eight years ago."[8]

And what did life look like for Madoff after he had been caught? In the days immediately following his arrest, he and his wife attempted suicide. Today, Madoff lives separated and estranged from his family in prison, surrounded by criminal slime, unable to attend his own son's funeral (a funeral Madoff was probably responsible for: Two years after Madoff was arrested, Mark Madoff hanged himself from the ceiling of his SoHo loft). Bernie Madoff's external life now matches his inner life. A man whose inner demons consumed him is now trapped in an existential nightmare.

If Madoff is surprised by how all this turned out, he shouldn't be. It would not have taken a great deal of thought to realize that all Ponzi schemes eventually crumble, that honesty is the best policy, and that betraying his friends, family, coworkers, and customers is a recipe for low self-esteem and a medium-security prison stay. But *thinking* about his actual interests is precisely what Bernie Madoff did not do.

A PACKAGE DEAL

Make yourself worse off for the sake of others or make others worse off for your own sake: Mother Teresa or Bernie Madoff. That's the moral alternative we've traditionally been offered. How does this apply to the world of business?

Well, it is undeniable that business is a selfish activity and, by extension, that free markets encourage and reward selfish behavior. But it doesn't follow that business is about harming, using, or exploiting others. As we'll argue, what we actually observe when looking at successful markets and companies is not ruthless exploitation but mutually beneficial production and trade: an Apple economy, not a Madoff economy.

Business involves individuals producing wealth in order to make themselves better off. To gain customers, however, businesses have to create valuable products and services, since a trade takes place only when both parties believe they will benefit. Profits are the result not of fraud and exploitation, but of value creation—of producing something more valuable than what was used to create it. The greater the value created, the greater the profit earned.

Business has nothing to do with harming others. Although it would surely be ridiculous to call men like Steve Jobs self-sacrificing altruists, it is equally bizarre—not to mention unjust—to lump them together with self-destructive criminals.

This is why Ayn Rand called the conventional notion of "selfishness" a *package deal:* It groups together things that are crucially different based on superficial similarities.[9] To equate Jobs with Madoff morally because both were "after money" is like equating George Washington and Adolf Hitler morally because both pursued victory in war. Our conventional category of "selfish" is a package deal that leaves us no means of classifying and morally evaluating *traders*—people such as Jobs who neither sacrifice others as Bernie Madoff did nor sacrifice themselves as Mother Teresa did.

CONCLUSION: UNPACKING THE PACKAGE DEAL

In earlier chapters, we've talked about "selfishness" without questioning its meaning. But the fact is, the way we usually use the word "selfish" doesn't make any sense. It leads us to treat magnates as monsters, heroes as hucksters, suicide as self-interested, profitable trade as exploitation.

Bottom line: It's true that Madoff is evil—but not because he was selfish. And it's true that business and free markets are selfish—but not because they unleash Madoffs.

In the next chapter, we're going to sketch Ayn Rand's reconceptualization of "selfishness." What she does is scrap the package deal and start fresh by asking: What *genuinely* promotes a man's long-term best interests? Her unprecedented conclusion is that only a life of *production* is selfish, that one person's pursuit of his self-interest does not conflict with the interests of others—and that *sacrificing others is not actually selfish at all.* She argues that genuine selfishness consists of the rational, principled pursuit of your objective well-being, neither sacrificing yourself to others nor sacrificing others to yourself.

It is in this sense, we'll see, that the profit motive is selfish, and it is this kind of principled, rational behavior that the free market makes possible and rewards.

SIX
THE MORALITY OF SUCCESS

MOST PEOPLE TAKE IT FOR GRANTED THAT MORALITY *means* self-sacrifice. They believe you can be self-interested or you can be moral, but not both. This hasn't always been the case, though.

In ancient Greece, where the science of ethics got its start, morality was not about self-sacrifice. The purpose of ethics, said the Greeks, is to rationally investigate what is good—to investigate the basic choices and character traits that distinguish a successful life from an unsuccessful life. A leading advocate of this pro-self orientation was Aristotle. Aristotle argued that the individual's proper aim is what he called *eudaimonia*, which translates roughly into "happiness" or "flourishing." The ethical man is not someone who surrenders his values, according to Aristotle. He is, rather, the "great-souled man," the man who is "a perfectly good or excellent man" and as a result "deserves the greatest things." And while most popular moralities emphasize the virtue of humility, Aristotle concluded that the great-souled man is justly *proud*—that indeed pride is the "crowning grace . . . of the virtues."[1]

It was Christianity that banished the Aristotelian conception of ethics from the philosophic scene. Instead of praising the great-souled man, Christianity enshrined the poor and the meek. Instead of lionizing pride, it warned that pride goeth before a fall. It elevated service to God above the individual's pursuit of his own welfare and commended obedience to the deity, even if it meant giving up earthly values—even if it meant murdering your own child.[2]

This anti-self approach to morality was later secularized by thinkers like Comte and Kant. Comte said your moral duty was to sacrifice your interests not to God but to Humanity. Kant said your moral duty was to sacrifice your interests to no one—sacrifice as an end in itself.[3]

In the twentieth century, Ayn Rand revived the Aristotelian tradition, making it more rigorous, more consistent, and more scientific. Indeed, Rand did more than that: In our view, she was the first philosopher to provide an objective foundation for ethics.

This is not a book about ethics. For readers interested in learning about Rand's moral theory—including her arguments for *why* her theory is true—we refer you to her works, above all *Atlas Shrugged* (1957), *The Virtue of Selfishness* (1964), and *Philosophy: Who Needs It* (1982).[4] Our goal in this chapter is only to describe her unique view of selfishness. Whether you come to agree with Rand's morality or not, what we aim to show in the rest of the book is that it is rationally self-interested action that proliferates when markets are left free and that markets will not be left free until rationally self-interested action is prized.

IT'S HARD TO BE SELFISH

Here's an idea for our next book: *Don and Yaron's Hedonist Guide to Health*. The basic idea? The key to health is doing whatever you feel like doing. Sit on the couch. Smoke a pack a day. Eat pizza and doughnuts. Wash them down with a Heineken. Just do what you feel like and the result will be health. What do you think?

Most people recognize that what makes a person healthy is not a matter of opinion but a question of fact. Some things are objectively healthy for you and some things aren't. Figuring out which is which requires scientific exploration: careful observation, ongoing experimentation, inductive reasoning, and fierce debate.

Well, just as you can't make yourself healthy eating whatever you feel like, you can't make yourself happy doing whatever you feel like. What promotes your life as a whole is a factual, scientific question: There are objective requirements of a happy and successful life. (The science that investigates those requirements is ethics.) The rationally selfish person is one who does his best to learn what these requirements are and then consistently puts that knowledge into practice.

"The purpose of morality," Rand writes, "is to teach you, not to suffer and die, but to enjoy yourself and live."[5] We need morality to help us make choices that will foster success and happiness.

Nowadays, the word "happiness" conjures a subjective, fleeting state of pleasure or satisfaction. The modern image of a happy person is the free-spirited bohemian or the motivational speaker with the perma-grin. That is not what Rand means by happiness. To be happy, in her view, is to experience a deep, enduring, undiluted joy in living. Like every effect, happiness has a definite cause: the achievement of life-advancing values. Not just food and shelter, but an entire constellation of values that includes work, friendship, love, art, purpose, and self-esteem.

To convey what we mean by "happiness," we can do no better than to borrow Rand's own description of one of her heroes. (The "she" in this passage refers to the heroine of *Atlas Shrugged*, Dagny Taggart.)

> She was looking up at the face of a man who knelt by her side, and she knew that in all the years behind her, this was what she would have given her life to see: a face that bore no mark of pain or fear or guilt. The shape of his mouth was pride, and more: it was as if he took pride in being proud. The angular planes of his cheeks made her think of arrogance, of tension, of scorn—yet the face had none of these qualities, it had their final sum: a look of serene determination and of certainty, and the look of a ruthless innocence which would not seek forgiveness or grant it. It was a face that had nothing to hide or to escape, a face with no fear of being seen or of seeing, so that the first thing she grasped about him was the intense perceptiveness of his eyes—he looked as if his faculty of sight were his best-loved tool and its exercise were a limitless, joyous adventure, as if his eyes imparted a superlative value to himself and to the world—to himself for his ability to see, to the world for being a place so eagerly worth seeing.[6]

This is Ayn Rand's vision of the great-souled man. That kind of attitude toward oneself and life, in her view, is morality's reward—and the true meaning of selfishness. How, then, to achieve it?

PRINCIPLE 1: RATIONALITY

If you want to boil down to a single word Rand's answer to "What do success and happiness require?" the word would be: *thinking*.

In the movie *Cast Away*, Tom Hanks becomes stranded on an uninhabited island. If he's going to stay alive, he needs to act. But the island is relatively barren. What makes the film riveting is the fact that Hanks, like all of us, has no survival instinct: He does not know automatically how to satisfy his needs. He knows he needs to eat, and drink, and find shelter, but he needs to *discover* how to achieve these ends. He must figure out how to open coconuts, how to catch fish, how to build fires, how to remove an infected tooth, or he will die. At every step, what enables Hanks to overcome these obstacles and survive is his continual choice to *think*. Even his need for companionship requires creative thought to fulfill: Hanks memorably draws a face on a volleyball and dubs it "Wilson," after the manufacturer.

The same is true of all of us. Whether we're trying to eke out a living on a desert island or make the most of life in modern America, no human value can be conceived or achieved without thought. Human beings are not physically strong creatures. We don't have claws. We don't have fangs. We're not particularly fast. We rose to the top of the food chain by virtue not of our muscles but of our minds. Every human value—everything that keeps us alive and makes us prosperous—is the product of human reason.

Consider your job. Whether you're an administrative assistant, a car mechanic, a mid-level manager, or an investment banker, what enables you to excel? What determines how productive you are and how much money you earn? It's not your muscles—even athletes know that brute strength is only a small part of what makes them successful. The core of what enables you to achieve your career goals is your knowledge, skills, and judgment. That's true no less of janitors than jet pilots: The difference between a good janitor and a bad one is in large part determined by the former's superior knowledge of how to clean well, quickly, and efficiently. In any field, it's your *mind* that makes you indispensable. As Napoleon Hill put it: "Think and Grow Rich."

It's no exaggeration to say that the history of man is the history of thought fostering survival. Human beings discovered agriculture about ten thousand years ago. Before the agricultural revolution, men lived in roaming tribes, in a hand-to-mouth existence that consisted almost purely of foraging for food. With the development of agriculture, men took control of their own existence. They were able to settle land and to form civilization. No subsequent advance would have been possible without agriculture. But what made agriculture possible?

For one, it required long-range planning: Men had to take actions that wouldn't pay off for months. It required grasping cause and effect: They had to understand what causes food to grow, which in turn required understanding the properties and potentialities of seeds, soil, fertilizer, water, the sun, and more. They had to make tools and weapons, which involved observing what was given in nature and then figuring out ways to alter and rearrange it to serve human purposes.

The Agricultural Revolution and all the benefits that flowed from it were made possible by reason. Reason is the human faculty that identifies and integrates sense experience. Men used their minds to identify and connect facts, grasp cause and effect, plan a long-range course of action, and rearrange nature to meet their needs.

The Industrial Revolution required a similar feat, only this time what men discovered was not isolated spheres of practical knowledge—they discovered that knowledge as such, from the most concrete to the most abstract, could transform human life for the better. It was during the Industrial Revolution that men took the great discoveries of science and math, translated them into dazzling inventions, and found innovative ways to organize men and technology in order to create unprecedented wealth. We are still reaping the rewards.

The idea that today's economy is a "knowledge economy" disguises the fact that *every* economy is at root a knowledge economy; *all* human values depend on rationally acquired knowledge. Reason, in other words, is our basic survival tool, and so rationality is our basic virtue. The motto of a selfish man is "I am, therefore I think."[7]

At the most fundamental level, rationality means facing facts. It means using your mind to understand how the world works and to chart your course through it. The rational person places no consideration above the facts of reality—even if those facts are unpleasant. He is the person who will stand by his own judgment—even when the crowd is going the other way. He is the person who stands by his principles—no matter the short-term cost or discomfort. He recognizes and obeys the law of cause and effect—never trying to get effects without causes or enacting causes without accepting full responsibility for their effects. The rational person recognizes that he can close his eyes to reality but that doing so won't change reality. And he recognizes that if he wants to live in reality, refusing to acknowledge reality is a recipe for disaster.

But rationality doesn't simply mean facing whatever facts happen to come to your attention. It means a commitment to constantly expanding your knowledge and putting it to use in action. Being rational means thinking about how to gain food, shelter, money, information, inspiration. It means thinking about the kinds of people you want to have as employees, colleagues, friends, and lovers (as well as where to find them and how to treat them). It means thinking about what political system your life requires. It means being a thinker, through and through. Thinking, writes Rand,

> does not consist merely of grasping a few simple abstractions, such as "chair," "table," "hot," "cold," and of learning to speak. It consists of a method of using one's consciousness, best designated by the term "conceptualizing." It is not a passive state of registering random impressions. It is an actively sustained process of identifying one's impressions in conceptual terms, of integrating every event and every observation into a conceptual context, of grasping relationships, differences, similarities in one's perceptual material and of abstracting them into new concepts, of drawing inferences, of making deductions, of reaching conclusions, of asking new questions and discovering new answers and expanding one's knowledge into an ever-growing sum. The faculty that directs this process, the faculty that works by means of concepts, is: reason.[8]

Rationality doesn't involve becoming a robot, scorning or suppressing emotions. It means recognizing that emotions are not a source of knowledge: Enjoy your emotions, feel them deeply, but use your mind to understand them. Don't act on them blindly.[9]

When we talk about rationality, we don't mean the sort most economists discuss. Economists have historically assumed that everyone is automatically "rational"—that, in the words of economist David Friedman, "individuals have objectives and tend to choose the correct way to achieve them." According to Friedman, "Babies are rational. So are cats."[10] This has nothing to do with what we mean by the term "rational." What we mean by rationality is: the volitional choice to use reason rather than emotion to guide your life. To follow reason *all* the time, on *every* issue, *unconditionally*, no matter what. That is not something everyone does—and it is something babies and cats aren't even capable of.

It should now be clear why Rand calls her moral code *rational* selfishness. Rationality is what philosopher Tara Smith calls Rand's "master virtue," the central thread running through every aspect of Rand's ethics.[11]

PRINCIPLE 2: PRODUCTIVENESS

"Production," writes Rand, "is the application of reason to the problem of survival."[12] Tom Hanks breaks off a tree branch and sharpens it into a spear. Thomas Edison turns a pile of glass, metal, and carbonized copper into a light bulb. A factory worker moves a hunk of metal one step closer to becoming a car. That is production.

If rationality is the basic virtue we have to exercise in order to achieve our well-being, production is the main existential activity rationality consists of. It is the virtue of applying reason to the creation of the goods and services that keep us alive.

The principle of productiveness says: Use your mind to create wealth. "Wealth" in this context refers to the creation of any material value—from a meal to a truck, to a medical operation, to a stock analysis, to a symphony. Productiveness doesn't assume any particular level of ability. It says only: Do the best your mind is capable of.[13]

The material benefits of production are obvious. In contrast to other animals, the values we need to flourish don't come ready-made in nature. We use our mind to discover the nature of nature and adapt it to our ends. In their book *The Virtues of Capitalism*, Austin Hill and Scott Rae note that "the word *capital* itself comes from the Latin word *caput*, which means *head*. This refers to the human and intellectual elements of creating capital out of the earth's resources (for example, using sand to make silicon)."[14]

It is the spiritual role of production in human life, however, that requires special emphasis. The deepest source of joy for a producer is not the financial rewards of his work but the process of creation itself. Steve Jobs explained his own attitude toward his career in an address to the Stanford graduating class of 2005:

> I'm convinced that the only thing that kept me going was that I loved what I did. You've got to find what you love. And that is as true for your work as it is for your lovers. Your work is going to fill a large part of your life, and the only way to be truly satisfied is to do what you believe is great work. And the only way to do great work is to love what you do. If you haven't found it yet, keep looking. Don't settle.[15]

A rationally selected career brings purpose to a person's life. It is the central activity that enables him to make his days not a succession of pointless repetitions but a meaningful sum. And since it is a person's main form of creativity, growth, and personal achievement, it is an indispensable source of self-esteem and happiness.

For Rand, production is not a dreary duty but the essence of a moral existence—and so she regards the productive individual as deserving of moral reverence.

In this regard, Rand's view is fundamentally different from the so-called Protestant work ethic, which says hard work is good because it pleases God by teaching men self-denial and self-restraint. Rand's view is that productive work is ennobling because it makes the individual richer—both materially and spiritually.

Productive work plays a central role in the life of a rationally selfish individual. But the conventional image of the selfish person is of a person who cares about nothing but *money*. More money, for him, is intrinsically good—regardless of how he gets it, why he wants it, or how he uses it. Rand rejects that view. Money, she recognizes, is a *tool*—a tool of exchange. The value of a dollar doesn't inhere in the dollar. It comes from the fact that it has been earned through production and can be used to obtain goods and services created by other productive individuals. It is a value only of and for producers. But, as we noted, money is not a producer's *primary* concern. For him it's a means to an end.

Creative work is the essence of a happy and successful life. The producer's chief goal, as Jobs suggested in his commencement address, is the act of creation. While he enjoys the luxury that money can buy, money's true value to him is that it permits him to continually expand his productive capacity. What enables Intel to keep multiplying the power of microprocessors is the financial rewards from its previous successes—every dollar of profit that is plowed back into the company enables it to do more research and development, to build more manufacturing plants, to sell more microprocessors, and then to create new and better chips, *ad infinitum*. Ayn Rand's own attitude toward money is instructive as well. She was extremely poor for most of her early life. The best thing about financial success, she later said, was that it gave her the freedom to write. It took her more than a decade of full-time work to write her greatest novel, *Atlas Shrugged*—something she could not have done without the income from her past works. For producers, whether they are designing microchips or writing novels, their primary goal is to create. Their chief reward is the joy of creating the world's greatest microprocessor, just as Rand's was the joy of having written *Atlas Shrugged*.

All of this implies that money is a value only under certain circumstances. The same reasons that lead a profit seeker to love earned money lead him to spurn *unearned* money, money won in defiance of the need to produce. Whether the money is looted from unsuspecting investors or mooched from overly generous relatives, the money does not represent a productive achievement and does not go to fuel further productive achievements.[16]

In Plato's *Republic,* Socrates declares "the more men value money-making, the less they value virtue."[17] Rand's view is exactly the opposite. The value of virtue is its role in promoting your own welfare—including your economic welfare: The more men value money making, the more they value virtue.

PRINCIPLE 3: TRADE

Business, according to *Wall Street*'s Gordon Gekko, is "a zero sum game. Somebody wins, somebody loses." This represents a widely held view: People's interests inevitably conflict, and if one person gains it's because another person loses.

Well, think about the last car you bought. Who lost, you or the dealer? Contrary to Gekko, nobody lost. *Both* of you benefited. You got a car, which you presumably valued more than what you paid for it. The dealer got a check, which he valued more than the car. No one was made worse off by the deal. It was a classic trade—win/win—and the model of *all* proper human relationships.

> A trader [writes Rand] is a man who earns what he gets and does not give or take the undeserved. He does not treat men as masters or slaves, but as independent equals. He deals with men by means of a free, volun-tary, unforced, uncoerced exchange—an exchange which benefits both parties by their own independent judgment.[18]

Human beings aren't by nature scavengers, and life is not a zero-sum game. We create the values we need through reason and productive action. As a result, human relationships don't require sacrifice. Instead of fighting over a fixed pie, the way other animals do, each of us can create a poten-tially unlimited amount of wealth and then trade it for the things others have produced—an exchange that leaves both sides better off.

Don't be confused by the fact that we sometimes pay more for a prod-uct than we would like or get paid less than we had hoped. The fact that a gain from trade isn't as large as we would have preferred doesn't change the fact that it *is* a gain.

The trader principle governs all of a rationally selfish man's relation-ships. He's always thinking win/win, profit/profit, because he knows that making or accepting losses is not to his interests. This is certainly true of business.

In his best-selling book *The 7 Habits of Highly Effective People,* Stephen Covey suggests why thinking in win/win terms is so important and why trying to gain at others' expense is a sure way to lose:

> Win/Lose is not viable because, although I appear to win in a confronta-tion with you, your feelings, your attitudes toward me and our relation-ship have been affected. If I am a supplier to your company, for example, and I win on my terms in a particular negotiation, I may get what I want now. But will you come to me again? My short-term Win will really be a

long-term Lose if I don't get your repeat business. So an interdependent Win/Lose is really Lose/Lose in the long run.[19]

Although we have had it drilled into our heads since birth that selfishness means exploiting people, it is the trader who time and time again reaps the benefits of dealing with others. This was a lesson Ray Kroc put to good use while developing his McDonald's chain in the early 1960s. In those days, most franchisers saw their franchisees as milk cows and often took cuts of what the franchisees paid to their suppliers. Kroc decided that trying to take advantage of his franchisees was a losing strategy. Instead, he used his buying power to get discounted supplies and passed the savings on to McDonald's operators. As former McDonald's chairman Fred Turner noted, "Our method of collecting revenue was almost totally dependent on the sales volume of the franchised store. And so our economic interests were not in conflict with the franchisee's interest, but compatible with them." Kroc put the point more colorfully. "Our operators know which side their bread is buttered on. And the result is that they are cooperative. When you find a good selfish reason for people to cooperate with you, you are pretty sure of their cooperation."[20]

People sometimes find it hard to accept that trying to exploit others is unselfish. But think about your own life. Would you really be better off if you stole from your coworkers? If you lied to your friends? If you cheated your customers? If you cheated on your spouse?[21]

The rationally selfish person doesn't view other people as playthings to be exploited for his purposes any more than he views himself as a plaything for others to exploit. His attitude is best summed up by a line from Rand's novel *Atlas Shrugged:* "I swear—by my life and my love of it—that I will never live for the sake of another man, nor ask another man to live for mine."[22]

A NEW CONCEPT OF SELFISHNESS

Here, then, is Ayn Rand's new concept of selfishness. Selfishness, for her, refers to the person who places nothing above the pursuit of his own happiness and who actively thinks about and acts to achieve all the values required to promote his long-range self-interest. In order to achieve his well-being, he demonstrates fidelity to the principles of self-interest: rationality, productiveness, and trade chief among them. As a result, he achieves his values, his happiness, and an unbreached self-esteem that comes from showing unbreached fidelity to a code of rational moral principles.

Under this new concept of selfishness, there is no package deal of the moneymaker with the liar, the thief, and the cheat. Bernie Madoff does not qualify as selfish.

If Madoff qualified as selfish, it's pretty obvious what your interests consist of: Just do what you feel like; lie, cheat, steal your way to wealth, power, and fame. If you get away with it for the moment, then you've achieved your interests. Rational selfishness says that defining and achieving your self-interest requires careful, deliberate, scientific thought—about the long term as well as the short—and principled action.

If Madoff qualified as selfish, you have two alternatives in life: You can either act for your own interests at the expense of others or become a dupe who acts for their interests at the expense of your own. Rational selfishness says that the interests of men don't conflict—not so long as they're rational. The essence of a moral existence is pursuing your interests without sacrificing yourself *or other people.*

For Ayn Rand, selfishness is not about giving in to the "lower" part of your nature but about living up to your highest potential. It is not about mere prudence but about the demanding pursuit of joy—a pursuit that involves the grandest values and the noblest virtues.

It should be all too clear that Rand rejects the idea, commonly heard in economics classrooms, that everyone is selfish. Not everyone is interested in his own interests. The mere fact that a person chooses to do something, or wants to do something, does not make it selfish. The question is: *Why* does he want to do it?

We are not deterministic puppets, forced to pursue our own well-being whether we want to or not. Embracing selfishness as a moral ideal is a choice. To be selfish, you have to decide to pursue your long-term best interests, to think about them, to make the effort to abide by them even when you feel tugged in a different direction. That's not something everyone does.

THE EVIL OF SELF-SACRIFICE

If rational selfishness demands a principled pursuit of genuine, life-affirming values, then it categorically condemns self-sacrifice. Yet self-sacrifice is generally considered the essence of virtue. How could anyone say that it's wrong, let alone evil?

Self-sacrifice does not mean giving up something to get something else—it's not synonymous with "cost." A sacrifice means giving up something you care about for something you care about less—or for something you don't care about at all. When you give up a dollar in order to buy a newspaper you value more than a dollar, it is not a sacrifice. When you give up a dollar to some bum out of a sense of duty, it is. When you help a friend pay his rent because he lost his job through no fault of his own and it's a sum you can easily afford, it is not a sacrifice. When paying his rent leaves you unable to pay yours, it is. When an entrepreneur forgoes much-needed sleep to make breakfast for his kids, whom he loves, it is not a sacrifice. When he forgoes working on his business to feed strangers at a soup kitchen because he feels guilty for his wealth, it is.[23]

Self-sacrifice requires *sacrifice*. To sacrifice is to make yourself worse off, to make your life less enjoyable, to see a net reduction in the resources you can use to foster your well-being. The key to virtue, according to this view of morality, is not helping others but harming yourself. Sacrificing for your neighbor, that's okay according to altruism—but sacrificing for a drunk who lost his job, his family, and his friends and now has nothing? That's the stuff moral saints are made of.

This is the reason most people consider Mother Teresa a moral saint but give companies like Pfizer no moral credit. As Francis Sejersted, chairman of the committee that gave Mother Teresa her Noble Peace Prize, put it, "Mother Teresa stands out, in a very positive way, as an example of true self-sacrifice in humanitarian work. She became a symbol to the world."[24] Mother Teresa may or may not have benefited people, but she certainly made herself worse off for their sake: What she symbolized was self-sacrifice.[25] Pfizer, however, clearly has improved and saved the lives of millions—but (gasp) its executives, stockholders, and employees all made themselves well-off in the process.

It's revealing that even partly altruistic companies don't achieve the holy grail of virtue according to the proponents of self-sacrifice—not so long as they profit in the process. Compartamos is a leading for-profit microloan institution, providing small loans to support entrepreneurship by poor South Americans, who might otherwise have to resort to pawn shops and loan sharks. You might think that humanitarians would herald Compartamos for its work. But you'd be wrong. "Microcredit should be seen as an opportunity to help people get out of poverty in a business way, but not as an opportunity to make money out of poor people," said Muhammad Yunus, an economist who won the Nobel Prize for his work on these loans.[26] Yunus is particularly critical of Compartamos. "When you discuss microcredit, don't bring Compartamos into it," he insists. "Microcredit was created to fight the money lender, not to become the money lender."[27] In other words, instead of treating the poor as charity cases, Compartamos treats them as traders, capable of engaging in win-win transactions. For this, it is a moral blackguard.

From the perspective of rational selfishness, sacrifice is bad for the same reason that sickness is bad, that poverty is bad, that starvation is bad, that suicide is bad: It harms your life.[28]

Self-sacrifice is anti-life—so naturally, it is fundamentally in conflict with the virtues self-interest requires. Take them in reverse order.

The trader principle counsels voluntary trade to mutual advantage; to sacrifice is to cultivate losses. A trader seeks out people he can respect; to sacrifice you have to look for people you can pity and serve. A trader doesn't seek or give the unearned; to sacrifice is to give away the things you earn to those who haven't earned them.

The principle of productiveness counsels relentlessly seeking to re-shape the earth in order to raise your standard of living; sacrifice requires that you lower your standard of living. Productiveness says to seek out work you love; to sacrifice you have to direct your labor wherever it is most needed by others. Productiveness is rooted on the premise that wealth is to be celebrated and enjoyed; to sacrifice requires that you not "wear two tunics" but "sell your possessions and give to the poor."[29]

And rationality? Rationality says to place nothing above the judgment of your own mind. The morality of sacrifice says to place nothing above the needs of others—including your own values, standards, and convictions. During the late nineteenth century, for instance, private charity in America was abundant, but it was selective. In most cases, anyone who was able to work had to work in order to receive care, and those who received care were expected to learn new ideas and habits that would enable them, insofar as possible, to get off the dole. But during the twentieth century, more consistent altruists condemned such practices as *selfish*. Why should people in need be denied care simply because they didn't want to work? Why should those offering care have a right to impose *their* views on people just because those people need help? The needy, said the leaders of the new "welfare rights" movement, are entitled to care—and the "more fortunate" have a duty to provide that care, no questions asked.[30] "Those who start by saying: 'It is selfish to pursue your own wishes, you must sacrifice them to the wishes of others,'" writes Rand, "end up by saying: 'It is selfish to uphold your convictions, you must sacrifice them to the convictions of others.'"[31]

Self-sacrifice means subordinating yourself to others—to surrender the things that make you happy in order to serve others. The question no one ever asks is: *Why is that supposed to be good?*

> Why is it moral [writes Rand] to serve the happiness of others, but not your own? If enjoyment is a value, why is it moral when experienced by others, but immoral when experienced by you? If the sensation of eating a cake is a value, why is it an immoral indulgence in your stomach, but a moral goal for you to achieve in the stomach of others? Why is it immoral to produce a value and keep it, but moral to give it away? And if it is not moral for you to keep a value, why is it moral for others to accept it? If you are selfless and virtuous when you give it, are they not selfish and vicious when they take it? Does virtue consist of serving vice? Is the moral purpose of those who are good, self-immolation for the sake of those who are evil?[32]

These questions, Rand argues, have never received a rational, nonmystical answer.

Why, then, is self-sacrifice held in such esteem by most Americans? In significant part because they don't have a clear concept of "sacrifice" or of "selfish." They treat any noble or benevolent gesture as a sacrifice, and they equate selfishness with violating people's rights or never helping anyone for any reason. In other words, the reason we laud self-sacrifice and revile selfishness is not because we've heard some great argument in favor of those views but because sacrifice has been whitewashed and selfishness has been turned into a straw man. Once those concepts are clearly defined, any pretense that altruistic self-sacrifice is noble vanishes.

Perhaps the greatest distortion concerning selfishness is the idea that the selfish person never helps others. But helping others per se is not sacrificial. What rational selfishness says is: Help others when you have a value to gain; don't help others at your own expense—don't do it when it's a net loss. Don't give away 10 percent of your income to charity when you're having trouble making ends meet. Don't allow your no-good sister to stay in your house because you think it's your duty. Don't help your enemy pummel you by turning the other cheek. If you see a stranger drowning and you can save him without significant risk to your own life, do it—but don't then go around the world looking for drowning people to rescue.

If you want a clear picture of what altruistic sacrifice really means in practice—the kind of "help" it demands and the kind of "love" it upholds—allow us to introduce you to David Platt. He's the youngest megachurch pastor in the country, and in his best-selling book *Radical,* he tells the story of a missionary and his wife who went to Indonesia trying to convert the Batak tribe to Christianity. The couple was murdered and cannibalized by the Batak. Sometime later, however, another missionary went to convert the tribe, and—luckily for him—succeeded. According to Platt:

> When I first heard this story, the immediate questions that came to my mind were *Would I be willing for my wife and me to be that first missionary couple? Would I be willing to be killed and cannibalized so that those who came after me would see people come to Christ?*[33]

Platt never says whether he would—but he is clear about one thing: He *should.* And if self-sacrifice is a moral duty, he is right. What could be a greater sacrifice than feeding yourself and your wife to a tribe of cannibals for the sake of the cannibals?

It should go without saying that this is obscene. A man of self-esteem does not regard the lives of others as more important than his own, and he does not hand over his highest personal value to be slaughtered by savages. But that is an egoistic conclusion—a *consistent* altruist can have no truck with self-esteem and must be prepared to renounce any personal value.

Finally, let us note that self-sacrifice has been and has to be the justification (and rationalization) for every dictatorship in history. The dictatorial mentality that seeks power over others does not preach selfishness but self-sacrifice. Rational selfishness says that each individual is an end in himself. Self-sacrifice demands that men turn themselves into fodder for the sake of others—the dictator is there to organize the feast. "It stands to reason," says a character in Rand's novel *The Fountainhead,* "that where there's sacrifice, there's someone collecting sacrificial offerings."[34]

CONCLUSION: THE ONLY WAY TO BE SELFISH

The genuinely selfish individual—the person who pursues his actual long-term interests—is not the brute who sacrifices others and blindly tramples over them. He is the rational, productive individual who deals with others by means of trade.

People often ask, "Isn't the solution to be selfish sometimes and to sacrifice other times?" Economist Deirdre McCloskey, for instance, declares that we mustn't be unbridled egoists. But, she continues, it would be equally disastrous to be consistently self-sacrificial. "It's the Jewish-mother version of goodness: 'Oh, don't bother to replace the bulb. I'll just sit here in the dark.' But the mother, after all, is God's creature, too, and benevolence therefore should include a just benevolence toward herself."[35]

Once you grasp fully that selfishness means pursuing your own interests rationally and without sacrifice, and that self-sacrifice consists of nothing but harming yourself, then there is no longer a temptation to dilute selfishness with a little sacrifice—any more than there is a temptation to dilute a glass of water with a little cyanide.

Rational selfishness, then, is a redundancy—there is no other way to be selfish. From now on, when we speak of selfishness we will do so only in Ayn Rand's sense. We will call Madoff and those like him what they are: evil, self-destructive human beings.

The question now is: What kind of behavior characterizes and pervades a free market? Is it the destructive irrationality of a Madoff or the rational pursuit of a person's genuine interests? To answer that, we need to look at the central activity that takes place on a market: the pursuit of profit by businessmen. That will be the subject of the next two chapters.

SEVEN
THE BUSINESS OF BUSINESS

EARLY IN AYN RAND'S NOVEL *ATLAS SHRUGGED,* SHE DE-
scribes industrialist Hank Rearden walking home on the evening he
has started production of Rearden Metal—a new alloy stronger and lighter
than steel. As Rearden walks, he reflects on the years that had brought him
to this point:

> the nights spent at scorching ovens in the research laboratory of the
> mills . . . the meals, interrupted and abandoned at the sudden flash of a
> new thought, a thought to be pursued at once, to be tried, to be tested, to
> be worked on for months, and to be discarded as another failure . . . the
> one thought held immovably across a span of ten years . . . the thought
> of a metal alloy that would do more than steel had ever done . . . the acts
> of self-racking when he discarded a hope or a sample, not permitting
> himself to know that he was tired, not giving himself time to feel, driv-
> ing himself through the wringing torture of: "not good enough . . . still
> not good enough . . ." and going on with no motor save the conviction
> that it could be done—then the day when it was done and its result was
> called Rearden Metal.[1]

"[T]his," in our colleague Onkar Ghate's words, "—the man alone in his
lab or office, who chooses to exert the effort necessary to think and to
create his values—is *Atlas*'s image of a moral saint."[2] This is the kind of
life that capitalism protects and enshrines. This is the actual nature of the
profit motive.

Consider the case of Andrew Carnegie. Carnegie's long and colorful career began less than auspiciously. Immigrating to America with his family in 1848 at the age of thirteen, he went right to work, earning $1.20 a week in a cotton mill. But he didn't stay there for long. Soon he was working at a telegraph company, where he taught himself Morse code and shocked his coworkers by reading telegraph messages by ear, a feat no one else in Pennsylvania could perform. Still a teenager, he was already earning more than both his parents.

The turning point in Carnegie's career came shortly thereafter. Having recently started as an assistant to Thomas Scott, a division superintendent at Pennsylvania Railroad, Carnegie was in the office alone one day when news came of a wreck on the Eastern Division. Rail traffic started backing up; Carnegie decided to take action. "Mr. Scott was not to be found," he would later write. "Finally, I could not resist the temptation to plunge in, take the responsibility, give 'train orders' and set matters going."[3]

It was no easy decision. Although Carnegie had watched Scott deal with similar problems in the past, lives and property were at stake.

> I knew it was dismissal, disgrace, perhaps criminal punishment for me
> if I erred. On the other hand, I could bring in the wearied freight-train
> men who had lain out all night. I could set everything in motion. I knew
> I could.

And he did, forging Scott's signature and issuing orders until rail traffic was back to normal. "Do you know what that little white-haired Scotch devil of mine did?" Scott later said to a colleague. "I'm blamed if he didn't run every train in the division on my name without the slightest authority." Had he run them right? the colleague asked. "Oh, yes, all right," Scott replied.[4]

Carnegie would demonstrate this initiative and ability throughout his career, ultimately becoming history's greatest steelmaker and the era's second richest man. Toward the end of his life, he would become known for his philanthropy, giving away nearly all his wealth by the time he died. To the extent Carnegie has been the object of moral praise (and it's not often), it is for giving away his fortune. But making it? No one regards that as a moral achievement.

Ayn Rand did.

In reconceiving morality, Rand redefined what it meant to be a moral hero. If a hero is one who embodies a moral ideal, then in Rand's view, the essence of a hero is man the thinker: the Aristotles, the Leonardos, the Galileos. Since the purpose of thought is the achievement of earthly values, her pantheon includes thinking men of action as well: the Washingtons, the Jeffersons, and the Madisons. And, for the same reasons, it includes businessmen: the Carnegies, the Rockefellers, the Jobses—men of colossal daring, ambition, and intelligence, who use their minds to translate scientific knowledge into earthly prosperity.

Unfortunately, aside from a few brief mentions of alleged robber baron exploitation, few people learn about businessmen in history class. Most of us don't have a real sense of what it is that businessmen do. As a result, we not only fail to revere business greatness, we can't even answer the critics who contend that businessmen are mostly useless fat cats we could easily do without. It's easy to demonize something you don't understand.

In this chapter, we'll look at what businessmen do and why anyone who values human life and happiness should esteem their contribution. In chapter 8, we'll examine the virtuous nature of the motive that drives them—and the campaign under way to demonize that motive.

THE BUSINESSMAN: PARASITE OR PRODUCER?

Production, the economist Jean-Baptiste Say observes, consists of three broad stages. It starts with gaining knowledge of reality—scientific knowledge concerning natural laws, the nature and potentialities of raw materials, methods of how to gather and use those materials. "A lock could never have been constructed," Say notes, "without a previous knowledge of the properties of iron, the method of extracting from the mine and refining the ore, as well as of mollifying and fashioning the metal."[5]

The next step, writes Say, involves applying that knowledge in order to serve a human purpose: "for instance, the conclusion, or conviction, that a particular form, communicated to the metal, will furnish the means of closing a door to all the wards, except to the possessor of the key."[6]

Finally, labor is used to carry out the plan set forth in stages one and two, "as, for instance, the forging, filing, and putting together of the different component parts of the lock."

These three operations [Say concludes] are seldom performed by one and the same person. It commonly happens, that one man studies the laws and conduct of nature; that is to say, the philosopher, or man of science, of whose knowledge another [the businessman] avails himself to create useful products, being either agriculturist, manufacturer, or trader; while the third supplies the executive exertion, under the direction of the former two; which third person is the operative workman or labourer.[7]

The scientist, the businessman, and the worker each performs essential components of the process of production. But whereas the scientist is praised for his rationality and the worker is applauded for his productivity, the businessman is scorned as a mindless, unproductive leech. Even Adam Smith seems to have held this view to some extent. "Decades before the birth of Marx," observes one economist, "he proclaimed the view of businessmen and capitalists, and of capitalism as a system, as parasitically feeding off the labor of wage earners."[8] Such a portrait fails to acknowledge the incredible amount of knowledge, thought, tenacity, and sheer endurance a businessman's job requires.

In his book *The Personal MBA,* Josh Kaufman notes that before he started working at Proctor & Gamble as a young man, he "knew next to nothing about what businesses were or how they functioned, other than that they were places people went every day in order to draw a paycheck." It was only after he joined P&G that he started to appreciate "[t]he sheer size and scope of the business—and the complexity required to manage" it. "To this day," he concludes, "I can't help but marvel at the thousands of man-hours, the millions of dollars, and the enormously complex processes necessary to make a simple bottle of dish soap appear on the shelf of the local supermarket."[9] The person who is responsible for initiating and overseeing that complex process is the businessman. He is in charge of making the fundamental decisions that will result either in a thriving business or a short-lived one.

Two facts should already suggest that running a successful business is easier said than done. The first is that enough business books are published each year to fill a library, each with hundreds of pages of advice for increasing sales, besting the competition, inspiring employees, cutting costs, and just about anything else you can imagine. The second is that most new businesses fail in their first five years.

Far from unproductive parasites, businessmen—entrepreneurs, managers, and capitalists alike—are producers *par excellence.* They are among those Rand called "men of the mind," whose decisions determine the fate of companies and the standard of living of countries.

The *entrepreneur* seeks out new profit opportunities, often introducing new products, new services, or new ways of doing business.[10] Entrepreneurs like Bill Gates (Microsoft), Elon Musk (PayPal), and Richard Branson (Virgin) are the risk takers and trailblazers who start new businesses and even new industries. They are the ones who organize and reorganize the division of labor, making it more efficient, more productive, better geared to the requirements of human life.

The word "entrepreneur" comes from the French word *entreprendre,* which means to "undertake" and is thought to have been coined by Jean-Baptiste Say. According to Say, the entrepreneur is the "Master-agent." He sets a business enterprise in motion, often risking his own wealth along with that of other investors. The success or failure rests on his shoulders. Consider the case of leading Internet shoe retailer Zappos and the entrepreneur who made it a success, Tony Hsieh.

Hsieh had invested in the company with the money he had made selling his first company, LinkExchange, and eventually came aboard as Zappos's CEO. Hsieh believed in the Zappos business model, which promised low-cost shoes and ultra-friendly service. But getting a company off the ground is challenging in the best of times, and Hsieh was doing it in the midst of the dot-com crash and the post-9/11 downturn. Like many other start-ups, Zappos found itself in a race against time: It was in the red and its capital was drying up quickly.

To keep the company alive, Hsieh was forced to reach into his own pocket. (His Zappos salary amounted to $1 per paycheck—before taxes.) Eventually, he faced a tough decision: bow out while he still had money in the bank or go for broke. He went for broke: "My plan was to take almost everything that I had left in my name and liquidate it in a fire sale. I would bet the farm and put all the proceeds into Zappos."[11]

More troubles followed, including the loss of nearly a third of Zappos's inventory in a disastrous shipping accident. But in the end, the company survived—barely. It was only through dogged effort and persistence that Hsieh was able to keep Zappos alive and turn it into the success it is today. What this story captures, more than anything, is how much we count on men like Hsieh to see farther than the rest of us, to see how tremendously valuable a company like Zappos could be to consumers long before they do, and to fight through every kind of obstacle to make that vision a reality. That is what it means to be an entrepreneur.

Every business around us started as an idea in the mind of an entrepreneur. Whether that idea matured into a small local business or a vast international corporation, our lives as we know them today would be impossible without his contribution. Without the entrepreneur, the Scientific Revolution would have never become the Industrial Revolution. Without the entrepreneur, we would all still be subsistence farmers.

The *manager* oversees the use of capital and labor in order to ensure that the company's goals are being met and that its resources are being used as efficiently as possible. Managers, from the frontline supervisor to the CEO, coordinate and organize the division of labor within firms. They plan and manage the firm's resources. While workers are focused on individual projects and tasks, the manager's job is to take a broad view of the organization. The top manager—the CEO—takes the widest perspective and the most long-range time frame.

When Lou Gerstner came aboard IBM as its CEO in 1993, the computer giant was on the verge of collapse. Gerstner had to take bold action, and quickly, to keep the company alive. But *what should he do?* How can you save a giant that's hemorrhaging money and whose primary cash cow, mainframe computers, is viewed by many as destined for obsolescence?

One of the first and most critical decisions Gerstner faced was whether to break up the IBM colossus into smaller units. That was what virtually all industry experts at the time thought should happen, including many within IBM. But there was no clear-cut answer. On the one hand, this was IBM's old business model, and the changing computer landscape had helped bring the company to the verge of bankruptcy; breaking up the company would help foster decentralized, market-driven decision making. On the other hand, keeping the company together gave it a unique ability to offer comprehensive solutions other companies couldn't.[12]

Gerstner carefully assessed the market landscape and IBM's competitive advantages. His crucial insight was that the market desperately needed an integrator. Companies were buying different technological solutions from different technological companies to meet different technological needs. As a result, they were put in the position of having "to be the integrator of the technology into a usable solution. . . . [T]he burden was on the customer to make everything work together."[13] Finally, Gerstner decided that this was a role IBM, and only IBM, could fill. He chose to keep the company together, regarding it as "the most important decision I ever made—not just at IBM, but in my entire business career."[14]

The second looming issue was what to do about mainframes. Mainframe computing was IBM's bread and butter, but the market seemed to have shifted in favor of personal computing. According to Gerstner, "it was clear that IBM had an obsessive focus on recapturing the ground lost to Microsoft and Intel in the PC world."[15] This was no idle dream: IBM had already created powerful alternatives to Intel's microprocessors and Microsoft's PC software. And although IBM still led the mainframe market, that market appeared to be crumbling. Even IBM's leadership position within that market was under threat, as its competitors undercut its prices.

Then came Gerstner's decision: IBM would work to revive its mainframe business with an aggressive price reduction strategy and a stronger customer focus. Gerstner noted:

> There was no doubt that a new CEO could take the alternative strategy: Keep S/390 [mainframe] prices high for a number of years, since it wasn't easy for customers to shift to competitive products in the near future. The revenue—hundreds of millions of dollars—would have been a powerful short-term underpinning of a restructuring of the company.[16]

There were scores of other large decisions to be made and thousands of small ones. Gerstner reorganized the board of directors, radically overhauled IBM's compensation and benefits policies, sold off unproductive assets, laid off thousands of employees, and protected the research and development budget to ensure long-term success. Each of those decisions required immense knowledge and rational judgment. In the end, Gerstner succeeded, not only saving IBM but restoring its former status as an industry leader. A lesser mind with lesser judgment would not have been able to pull off this turnaround, one of the most stunning in the history of business. But while Gerstner's story is particularly dramatic, it isn't unique. These are the kinds of critical, thrive-or-die decisions that CEOs have to make every single day.

"[W]hat part of being a CEO could be so difficult—" wonders left-wing radio host Thom Hartmann, "so impossible for mere mortals—that there are only a few hundred individuals in the United States capable of performing it?"[17] Anyone who knows Gerstner's story knows the answer.

The *capitalist* provides the resources, such as financial capital and equipment, that businesses must use in order to produce. He is the shareholder, the banker, or the financier who supplies capital to the economy. His productive role is to take savings—unconsumed wealth from prior acts of production—and direct them toward their best, most productive uses.

This is no easy task. At any time, there are countless people seeking capital investment, from the immigrant who wants to start a drycleaners to the college dropout who wants to pioneer a new technology. But capital is limited. Put capital into the wrong hands, and you could destroy it. (Venture capitalist Kevin O'Leary calls this the crime of "murdering money.") Fail to put it into the right hands, and you lose out on profits. The capitalist is the one who makes these decisions.

In *The Birth of Plenty*, William Bernstein observes that "the lion's share of Western society's prosperity originates in the minds of a few geniuses." But "[t]ranslating their ideas into economic reality requires . . . staggering amounts of capital."[18] Bernstein gives the example of Thomas Edison and his creation of the incandescent light bulb. Mass-producing light bulbs "required building large factories, hiring thousands of trained workers, and purchasing large amounts of raw materials." Not to mention there were no power plants or transmission grids to supply buildings with the electricity necessary to power the bulbs. All of that had to be built as well. Edison turned to the greatest capitalist of his era, J. P. Morgan. But even Morgan did not personally control enough wealth to finance the venture. He had to rely on his unmatched ability to raise capital from outside sources—and in the name of an untested technological venture, something that Morgan as a rule did not do. But, seeing the potential of electric lighting, he made an exception and risked a vast amount of his wealth and the wealth of his investors. Several twists and turns later, the venture finally succeeded.[19] It's no exaggeration to say that while Edison's mind created the light bulb, Morgan's judgment is what lit the world.[20]

Most businesses, big and small, require a capitalist to place capital at risk so they can get started and grow. Without the capitalist agreeing to take on risk and make a loan or an investment, there are no jobs, no products—no businesses. Such is the indispensable importance of capitalists.

The businessman—the entrepreneur, the manager, the capitalist—is not a parasite but a *producer:* He uses his mind to help create the goods and services that enrich our lives.

But what about the people employed by the businessman? Aren't they really the ones responsible for a business's success? Wouldn't they be better off without him around?

A FELLOWSHIP OF TRADERS

In a 1993 installment of the comic strip *Dilbert,* an exasperated Alice complains to her manager that she can't have a family life if she continues to work such long hours. Her manager is unmoved. "This isn't the 'me' generation of the eighties. This is the 'lifeless nineties.' I expect 178 hours of work from you each week." Alice responds that there are only 168 hours in a week. "I expect your family to chip in a few hours."[21]

Many Americans view the business world this way: unfulfilled, overworked employees lorded over by a cruel, overpaid boss. Left-wing radio host Thom Hartmann summed up this view with his usual subtlety: "Corporations and their CEOs are America's new feudal lords. . . . Instead of a landed aristocracy, we increasingly have a corporate aristocracy."[22] This, in one form or another, is what we might call the Dilbert view of business: management as master, employee as exploited serf.

Now, if you work for a company, we'll wager that it's not because someone drags you into work each day at gunpoint, forces you to do the boss's bidding, and sends you home with empty pockets. Most likely, you go of your own volition, do work you enjoy doing, see friends you enjoy seeing, and get paid for your trouble. "A recent survey," notes Deirdre

McCloskey, "finds that even in I'm-All-Right-Jack Britain half of the workers 'look forward to going to work.' In the Tough-Guy United States, two-thirds do, and elsewhere in the developed world still higher percentages."[23] Rasmussen wasn't taking polls back in feudal times, but we would be willing to bet that slaving away for the lord wasn't high on many people's list of eagerly anticipated activities.

A business is not a modern version of feudalism, with serfs laboring to fill the master's pockets. If you don't like your job, the only thing keeping you there is your decision not to leave. The reason many of us choose to work for other people is because we *prefer* to: Businessmen perform a number of crucial functions that most workers either cannot or would rather not perform.

Start with capitalists. When a capitalist funds a new business, he risks his capital on an undertaking that will not pay off for weeks, months, or years—if ever. But the venture's employees collect paychecks all along, courtesy of the capitalist: Their wages come out of his investment. Were it not for the capitalist, workers would have to risk their own savings (if they had sufficient savings), or sell the products of their labor, rather than sell their labor for a wage.[24] Instead of a Nike employee in Ohio being able to go to the local factory and come home with a paycheck, she would have to make her own shoes and sell them herself in order to get paid. In short, capitalists are the ones who enable workers to *be* workers rather than risk-taking entrepreneurs.

What's more, the capitalist is the one who supplies the plant and equipment that make workers dramatically more productive. That same Nike employee, who might be able to turn out a hundred shoes a day in Nike's factory, probably could not make ten pairs a week on her own. Since, on a free market, wages are determined by a worker's productivity, the net effect of the capitalist's contribution is to continually raise workers' standard of living.[25]

What's true of capitalists is true of businessmen more generally. Businessmen raise workers' standard of living through their productive efforts. This is what Ayn Rand calls the pyramid-of-ability principle. The higher the most able producers rise, the more they contribute to the productivity of the less able. Ability, here, means *intellectual* ability. The greatest contributors to production are not those who supply physical labor but those who contribute ideas—new theories, inventions, tools, businesses, and methods—to the productive process.

A factory worker makes a real contribution: He helps turn a pile of parts into a TV or a toaster. But the end product of his work goes no further: It provides particular goods destined for particular consumers. But the man who supplies an idea is able to raise the productivity—and the standard of living—of an unlimited number of other men. It was his contribution that *created* the factory, that *invented* the television, that *designed* the assembly line, and that thereby made it possible for a factory worker of modest ability to produce TVs, earn a wage, and live like a relative king. As Rand explains:

> In proportion to the mental energy he spent, the man who creates a new invention receives but a small percentage of his value in terms of material payment, no matter what fortune he makes, no matter what millions he earns. But the man who works as a janitor in the factory producing that invention, receives an enormous payment in proportion to the mental effort that his job requires of *him*. And the same is true of all men between, on all levels of ambition and ability. The man at the top of the intellectual pyramid contributes the most to all those below him, but gets nothing except his material payment, receiving no intellectual bonus from others to add to the value of his time. The man at the bottom, who left to himself, would starve in his hopeless ineptitude, contributes nothing to those above him, but receives the bonus of all of their brains. Such is the nature of the "competition" between the strong and the weak of the intellect. Such is the pattern of "exploitation" for which you have damned the strong.[26]

Probably the most maligned employer today is Wal-Mart. Far from pursuing win/win relationships, it's said, Wal-Mart offers its employees low pay and paltry benefits. That wasn't the experience of journalist Charles Platt, who in 2009 went undercover as a Wal-Mart employee. Far from finding a company that treated employees only slightly better than toilet paper, his experience led him to praise the retailer. Platt pointed out that the company provided opportunities for unskilled workers to gain work experience and to rise relatively quickly to management positions.

(The company even pays its employees for time spent watching a series of training videos and gives them raises when they complete the course.) What's more, he noted that

> despite its huge size, the corporation turned out to have an eerie resemblance to a Silicon Valley startup. There was the same gung-ho spirit, same lack of dogma, same lax dress code, same informality—and same interest in owning a piece of the company. All of my coworkers accepted the offer to buy Wal-Mart stock by setting aside $2 of every paycheck.[27]

True, he conceded, Wal-Mart pay is nothing to write home about, but it is competitive with comparable big-box chains like Target. From his experience, Platt "came to regard [Wal-Mart] as one of the all-time enlightened American employers, right up there with IBM in the 1960s. Wal-Mart is not the enemy. It's the best friend we could ask for."[28]

The same, in essence, can be said about every productive businessman.

Business is not a feudal manor but a fellowship of traders. It is a cooperative venture where tens, or hundreds, or hundreds of thousands of people pursue common goals. It is perhaps the best illustration of the idea that there is a harmony of interests among rational men.

We need to scrap the Dilbert view of business. While there are no doubt companies that create a stifling environment, and managers and employees who play the respective roles of tyrant and tyrannized, that is a *choice*. It's not inherent in business. It's certainly not inherent in good business. Business by its nature is a relationship of traders—a relationship based on voluntary agreement to mutual advantage. The world of business is a realm in which every employee, from the cashier to the CEO, is able and encouraged to be a rational, productive trader.

A more accurate picture would be what we could call the orchestra model of business. An orchestra is made up of a large number of individual musicians. Together each can play music that no single individual could play alone. But to play together, each must follow a score written by the composer (the entrepreneur) and take direction from a conductor (the manager). Nevertheless, each person plays for his own pleasure and reward and employs his own creativity, within the parameters established by the conductor and the music.

CONCLUSION: THE GREAT LIBERATOR

When you wake up in the morning feeling refreshed because you slept on an inner spring mattress rather than a pile of rags, it is thanks to businessmen. Your ability to pour yourself a hot cup of coffee and to make yourself a fresh bowl of fruit depends on businessmen. The fact that you can drive to work in a car you own—and that you need work only five days a week in order to live comfortably—is thanks to businessmen.

If you get sick, businessmen are hard at work looking for new and better ways to get you well again. If you get bored, businessmen are working overtime to find new ways to thrill and entertain you. If you're seeking new knowledge, businessmen have made it possible for you to learn virtually anything with the press of a button. This book got from our laptops to your library only because of businessmen.

The businessman, Rand concludes,

> is the great liberator who, in the short span of a century and a half, has released men from bondage to their physical needs, has released them from the terrible drudgery of an eighteen-hour workday of manual labor for their barest subsistence, has released them from famines, from pestilences, from the stagnant hopelessness and terror in which most of mankind had lived in all the pre-capitalist centuries—and in which most of it still lives, in non-capitalist countries.[29]

And yet, despite business's record, sociologist Daniel Bell observes that

> romantic or traditionalist, Enlightenment or irrationalist, vitalist or naturalist, humanist or racialist, religious or atheist—in this entire range of passions and beliefs, scarcely one respectable intellectual figure defended the sober, unheroic, prudential, let alone acquisitive, entrepreneurial, or money-making pursuits of the bourgeois world.[30]

Ayn Rand did defend those pursuits. But she did not agree that they were sober and unheroic. On the contrary, she argued that business aims at the noblest end—the individual's self-interest—and requires the noblest means—the principles of rationality, productiveness, and trade.

In this chapter, we've seen part of Rand's defense of business. We've seen that businessmen are men of the *mind* who *produce* material values and *trade* them with other producers. In the next chapter, we'll focus on the issue of business success: what constitutes business success, what motivates it, what moral principles it requires and encourages.

EIGHT

THE NOBILITY OF THE PROFIT MOTIVE

JOHN ALLISON IS PROBABLY THE MOST SUCCESSFUL BANKER of the past few decades. As CEO of Branch Banking & Trust Corporation from 1987 until his retirement in 2008, Allison grew the bank from $4.5 billion to $152 billion in assets and from 300 to 30,000 employees. But Allison is perhaps best known for his principled approach to business—turning down seemingly attractive deals and firing high-performing employees for not living up to the company's values. In one telling incident, Allison recalls:

> Our number-one mortgage producer—this was before the mortgage market busted—number one in production, number one in revenue. . . . We found out he was fudging on his reports, and we fired him. And we fired him immediately, without hesitation or reservation, even though he was our number-one producer. [It didn't matter that] most of our mortgage production is sold in the secondary market, so in a way you can argue there was no "risk" in what he was doing.[1]

But don't accuse Allison of sacrifice. He insists his purpose was always to ensure long-term profits: "There is a widespread misconception about business: that you can either operate by the profit motive—or you can do what's right."[2] That dichotomy is inevitable if you think what's right consists of self-sacrifice. But if doing what's right means taking a principled approach to achieving your self-interest, then, he says, you profit by being principled.

"Profit is a good thing," Allison adds.

> It's simply the difference between the value of what we create and the cost to create it. To be highly profitable, however, you have to *earn* it by being very productive. It's not about taking advantage of your clients. It's not about cheating in the game. It's about running a really good business.[3]

That's not the way most people today think of the profit motive.

"This culture is not, as it sometimes pretends, offended by some bad things that some businessmen do," observed Irving Kristol; "it is offended by what businessmen are or seem to be: exemplars of the naked 'profit motive.'"[4] "[T]here's nothing wrong with utilitarian values like profit, advantage and efficiency, but they lack nobility," writes another commentator.[5] True nobility is reserved for nonprofit pursuits. "Don't go into corporate America," Michelle Obama advised a group of Ohioans. "You know, become teachers. Work for the community. Be social workers. Be a nurse. . . . Make that choice, as we did, to move out of the money-making industry into the helping industry."[6]

Although most people acknowledge that the profit motive has benefits—it sparks entrepreneurship, innovation, and risk taking—we're generally wary of profit seekers. They aren't to be trusted, because while today they might sell you a decent product at a decent price, tomorrow their insatiable greed will lead them to jack up prices, let quality slip, cook their books, or, if Hollywood is to be believed, sell nuclear weapons to anti-American terrorists and then cackle uncontrollably.

What the profit motive actually fosters, however, is creativity, passion, and cooperation to mutual benefit. It is the economic form that the individual's pursuit of self-interest takes. It demands the same virtues and leads to the same results. Not only are profit seekers worthy of respect—at their best, we should regard them as moral exemplars.

WHAT IT SHALL PROFIT A MAN

If we want to understand the profit motive, the first question to answer is: What is profit? Profit, in the broadest sense, means a gain. You profit whenever you make yourself better off. In economic terms, then, profit means *making money*.

In a division-of-labor economy like America, individuals don't produce most (if any) of the goods they themselves consume. Instead, they specialize. Mitch produces cattle prods, sells them for money, and uses the money to buy food, housing, movie tickets, and whatever else he wants.

But the productive process itself has costs. It involves acquiring various factors of production—some mix of land, labor, capital goods, and materials—and combining and rearranging them in the attempt to create something more valuable. Calvin Klein spends a certain amount of money on fashion designers, seamstresses, sewing machines, denim, thread, copper, and other resources and uses them to create designer jeans. If he can sell those jeans for more than the cost of making them, he profits. If he can't, he experiences losses.

Profit, in short, is the money a business has left over after paying its expenses. It is the mark of having produced something that other people in the market value more than the inputs used to produce it. Profit is the standard and reward of productive success in a division-of-labor economy. On a desert island, you make the things that make your life better. In a division-of-labor economy, you make money (by making things) in order to buy the things that make your life better. Profit seeking, in the last analysis, really just means producing in the context of a money economy.

Production—the use of reason to create material values—is the central activity that makes our lives possible. To condemn profit is to condemn production, and to condemn production is to condemn human life. But many *do* condemn profit. As economist Thomas Sowell points out, these people see profits simply as "unnecessary charges added on to the inherent costs of producing goods and services, driving up cost to the customer."[7]

But profits are *created*—not looted, "captured," or added on. There is no difference, in principle, between Tom Hanks's *Cast Away* character turning palm trees into a raft and the chair maker who buys some lumber for $50 and sells a finished chair for $100. Both have engaged in productive effort and have thereby created something more valuable than what they started with.

The rational buyer *wants* the chair maker to profit. To view profit as an unnecessary markup is to reject the trader principle. It implies that producers should toil without gain in order to selflessly dole out benefits to consumers. A trader, however, wants those he deals with to profit too. He knows that if they don't, *he's* the one who will lose in the long run, since no one will continue to produce without rewards.

When Exxon Mobil, for instance, reports billions in profits, too many people think: Look how much has been taken from us. But that has it completely backward. Were it not for the possibility of earning substantial profits, Exxon Mobil wouldn't have risked billions in capital to find, extract, refine, and distribute oil. To the extent that we value our ability to drive our cars, buy cheap food, and have access to goods made out of petroleum products (try finding something that isn't), we should be thankful it's profitable for Exxon Mobil to supply us with these things.

It's funny. Most of us either run a business or work for one. When it comes to our own businesses, we know that profit is a good thing. It's not something we extract from helpless customers—it's something we have to fight for every day by creating as much value as we can for customers who, far from being helpless, are quite prepared to spend their money elsewhere. It's only when we think of other people's businesses that we start viewing profit as a bad thing.

In response, industries often try to justify profit, on those rare occasions when they do try to justify it, by some social standard. Profit "allocates society's resources efficiently," or it "leads producers to serve consumers." From the perspective of rational selfishness, all of this is beside the point. The key issue is that profits earned through voluntary trade, *no matter how large,* require no special justification. They are good because they make the producer who earns them better off. To quote political philosopher Isabel Paterson: "If profit is denounced, it must be assumed that running at a loss is admirable. On the contrary, that is what requires justification. Profit is self-justifying."[8]

PROFITABLE PRINCIPLES

An enterprising manager walks into Larry Ellison's office and lays out his plan for Oracle's future. "It's simple," he says. "Step one, stop giving employees bonuses. Step two, save money by doing away with our Quality Assurance process. Step three, pad our earnings in order to drive up our stock price. What do you think?"

Talk about an indecent proposal. In reality, that kind of plan would get a manager fired. But this reflects the conventional view of how profit-seeking businessmen think: Health insurance companies make money by denying patients covered tests. Doctors make money by giving them unnecessary ones. Speculators make money by recklessly bidding up the price of stupid investments. Short sellers make money by driving down the price of sound ones. Lie, cheat, steal, roll the dice, and cut corners: People think that's the easy path to profits.

In his pitch for Dodd-Frank, President Obama complained:

> In the absence of sound oversight, responsible businesses are forced to compete against unscrupulous and underhanded businesses, who are unencumbered by any restriction on activities that . . . take advantage of middle-class families, or, as we've seen, threaten to bring down the entire financial system.[9]

In Obama's view—a view many Americans share—being "unscrupulous and underhanded" is a competitive advantage. Is it any wonder, then, that laws and regulations shackling businessmen are increasing by the day? If lying, cheating, and stealing really are the road to riches, then economic freedom can't be tolerated.

But think about your own line of work. Think of the time, energy, and money your organization pours into research and development, quality control, motivating employees, and searching for innovative ways to meet its customers' needs. Can *you* succeed via dishonesty and corner cutting? We've spoken to businessmen all over the world and they all say the same thing: "Oh, you couldn't get very far in *my* industry that way. But those other industries. . . ." They're wrong. Business success requires abiding by rational principles for the same reason that success more generally does.[10]

In 1912, America's most successful banker, J. P. Morgan, was hauled in front of Congress to answer questions concerning the alleged concentration of power on Wall Street. In a famous exchange, Congressman Samuel

Untermyer asked Morgan, "Is not commercial credit based primarily upon money or property?"

"No, sir," replied Morgan, "the first thing is character."

"Before money or property?"

"Before money or anything else. Money cannot buy it. . . . Because a man I do not trust could not get money from me on all the bonds in Christendom."[11]

An individual's moral character is central to his success as a producer, and the moral principles a business operates by, as embodied in its corporate culture, are central to its success as well. As Zappos's CEO Tony Hsieh puts it:

> For individuals, character is destiny.
> For organizations, culture is destiny.[12]

What kind of culture does it take to succeed in business? What moral principles pave the way for profit? One place to start is with the values that Allison credits with making possible BB&T's remarkable growth during his tenure:

- *Reality.* "What is, is. . . . Wishing something is doesn't make it so."
- *Reason.* "Reason is our specific means of survival. . . . Reject all beliefs which are inconsistent with reality. . . . Reject all contradictions—contradictions cannot exist."
- *Independent thinking.* "Independent thinking means thinking for yourself. It makes possible responsibility and creativity."
- *Productivity.* "Productivity is a gut-level commitment to get the job done."
- *Honesty.* "Honesty is a foundational value. . . . We must mean what we say and know what we mean."
- *Integrity.* "If you believe something, do it. . . . We will not compromise our principles."
- *Justice.* "Those who contribute the most should receive the most."
- *Pride.* "If you wouldn't tell the people that you care about what you're going to do and why you're going to do it, don't do it."

- *Self-esteem.* "Sometimes people in business get confused. They think money is the end of the game. Nothing wrong with money . . . but money is not an end. . . . Happiness is the end of the game and happiness is based on self-esteem."
- *Teamwork.* "We want people with strong personal goals, that think for themselves, but recognize that, in an organizational context, we're in it together—and that means you have to be a good team player."[13]

You might have noticed that these are startlingly similar to the principles of Ayn Rand's morality. Indeed, they are nothing more than specifications of the three basic principles we've been discussing: rationality (reality, reason, independent thinking, integrity, honesty), productiveness (productivity), and trade (justice, teamwork)—and their rewards: pride and self-esteem. The overlap between Allison's principles and Rand's is no accident. Allison has often cited Rand's profound influence on his thinking.

When you study the traits of successful businessmen, aspects of these same virtues come up again and again. Here's a sampling we found by picking books from our shelves, more or less at random.

- GE's former CEO Jack Welch names as one of his six core principles "Face reality as it is, not as it was or as you wish . . . facing reality is crucial in life, not just in business. You have to see the world in the purest, clearest way possible, or you can't make decisions on a rational basis."[14] (Rationality)
- After studying seven CEOs who turned around troubled companies, Martin Puris attributes their success above all to their effort to "pursue the truth. . . . They display a doggedness, even a kind of compulsion to dig beneath appearances and uncover the true state of affairs in the area of their enterprise."[15] (Rationality)
- In their book *Execution,* former Honeywell CEO Larry Bossidy and author Ram Charan counsel: Insist on realism. "Realism is at the heart of execution but many organizations are full of people who are trying to avoid or shade reality."[16] (Rationality)

- Tony Hsieh explains Zappos value #8, Do More with Less: "We believe in hard work and putting in the extra effort to get things done. . . . We must never lose our sense of urgency in making improvements. We must never settle for 'good enough,' because good is the enemy of great, and our goal is to not only become a great company, but to become the greatest service company in the world."[17] (Productiveness)

- In *Built to Last,* authors James Collins and Jerry Porras state that visionary companies do not settle for "good." "For these companies, the critical question is *'How can we do better tomorrow than we did today?'* . . . Superb execution and performance naturally come to the visionary companies not so much as an end goal, but as the residual result of a never-ending cycle of self-stimulated improvement and investment for the future. . . . Becoming and remaining a visionary company requires oodles of plain old-fashioned discipline, hard work, and a visceral revulsion to any tendency toward smug self-satisfaction."[18] (Productiveness)

- Lou Gerstner lists the qualities he thought running IBM required. He puts "Passion for business" (Productiveness) at the top of the list, along with qualities like "Builds strong team," "Gets the best from others," and "Maniacal customer focus" (Trade).[19]

- In *The Science of Success,* Charles Koch, CEO of the ultra-successful Koch Industries, counsels that the path to success is paved by guiding principles that include knowledge (Rationality), value creation and fulfillment (Productiveness), and customer focus (Trade).[20]

An individual who wants to live a happy and successful life needs to adhere to the principles of rational selfishness, and so does a business enterprise that wants to thrive. In Allison's words:

> Sometimes organizations are successful because of fortunate timing. Sometimes organizations fail due to economic factors beyond their control. However, the most common cause of organization success or failure is the fundamental principles on which the leader of the business acts.

Businesses largely succeed or fail based on basic ideas—i.e., their philosophy—not complex strategies or esoteric activities.[21]

Business success requires rationality, productiveness, and trade.

RATIONALITY AND BUSINESS SUCCESS

A business enterprise committed to rationality fosters a culture committed to discovering facts, facing facts, and acting in alignment with the facts.

One of the most famous cases of a company facing facts, even when those facts did not seem convenient, is Intel's choice in the mid-1980s to abandon its core competency—producing computer memory chips—and focus instead on producing what was then a small part of its business, microprocessors.

Intel started as a memory chip producer. Indeed, it *created* the memory chip market and led the market for much of the next decade. Microprocessors made up only a tiny sliver of its business. But by the 1980s, Japanese memory chip producers had made tremendous gains in chip quality. "In fact," then-president Andy Grove would later write, "the quality levels attributed to Japanese memories were beyond what we thought were possible. Our first reaction was denial. This had to be wrong. As people often do in this kind of situation, we vigorously attacked the ominous data."[22] But when Intel's own research confirmed the claims, the company didn't bury its head in the sand—it got to work competing. Over the next decade, Intel would try to retain and then regain its dominance of the memory chip market. But as the Japanese continued to undercut it on price and match it on quality, the company found its sales plummeting and its inventories piling up.

Finally, Grove asked then-CEO Gordon Moore, "If we got kicked out and the board brought in a new CEO, what do you think he would do?" Moore replied without hesitation, "He would get us out of memories." After a long moment, Grove said, "Why shouldn't you and I walk out the door, come back and do it ourselves?"[23] It was not an easy decision, and there was fierce internal resistance, but shedding the money-losing memory chip business turned out to be a crucial step in Intel ultimately becoming the world's leading microprocessor company. What made it possible was a commitment to facts over feelings.

This ruthless commitment to facts is not a given. Many people allow misplaced loyalty, unjustified optimism, office politics, or a "this is the way we've always done it" attitude to trump concern for facts. Unlike Grove, who went out of his way to discover and act on facts, former Macy's CEO Edward Finkelstein seemed to go out of his way to evade them. As Edwin Locke observed in his 2000 book *The Prime Movers,* Finkelstein's "main agenda seemed to entail denying problems, intimidating subordinates, and spending freely on perks for himself—while waiting for a nonexistent economic upturn to bail the company out of its troubles."[24] The result was bankruptcy. A failure to face reality doesn't change reality—it just increases the odds of, well, failure.

PRODUCTIVENESS AND BUSINESS SUCCESS

A business enterprise committed to productiveness tackles its mission with passion and verve, working relentlessly to become more efficient, more innovative, more productive, more profitable. "[I]n business, I have always been driven to buck the system, to innovate, to take things beyond where they've been," reflected Wal-Mart's Sam Walton.[25] Motivated by a profound love of his work—"[T]here hasn't been a day in my adult life when I haven't spent some time thinking about merchandising," he once said[26]—Walton continually sought to improve Wal-Mart. He described himself as endlessly "fiddling and meddling with the status quo"—an approach he regarded as his biggest contribution to the retailer's success.[27]

Not every company is committed to productiveness as a principle. Some aren't interested in creating any genuine value. When Don was studying Internet marketing, he noticed something fascinating. Many of the people buying Internet marketing books and courses didn't seem to have anything they were trying to market. Marketing, for them, wasn't a means of promoting some value they created—it was a way to sucker people into buying something despite its lack of value. Amusingly, many of these people decided to repackage what they learned about Internet marketing and sell their *own* Internet marketing courses. As a result, much of the Internet marketing world is filled with courses based on courses based on courses leading back to some guy who probably never had any real marketing experience to begin with. We suspect most of these hucksters aren't actually rolling in the cash they claim to be.

Other companies do create real value but eventually start trying to coast on past achievements and find themselves surpassed by the competition. As Robert Sobel observes in his study of business failure, *When Giants Stumble:*

> Frequently the decline and fall of a once-proud product results from the business blunders of managements frozen in time and space, unable to adjust intelligently to change. Safe in their niches, secure in their market share, managements are blindsided by new technologies and customers.[28]

Such was the case with IBM during the late 1980s and early 1990s. Although the company had taken an early lead in the burgeoning personal computer industry, its focus remained on its profitable mainframe business—even as that business declined and the personal computer industry started booming. This passivity in the face of changing market conditions allowed competitors like Compaq to gain a foothold and eventually dominate the PC market. By 1993, IBM—one of the most successful companies in American history—was on the verge of bankruptcy.

TRADE AND BUSINESS SUCCESS

A business enterprise committed to the trader principle seeks to profit by helping others profit. J. J. Hill was convinced that the success of his great transcontinental railroad, the Great Northern Railway, depended on promoting the success of the businesses along his lines. As a result, Hill kept his rates low and even went so far as to give free grain and free *cattle* to farmers who, due to circumstances outside of their control, had temporarily fallen on hard times.[29] The result was that the Northern Pacific was "the best built, the least corrupt, the most popular, and the only transcontinental never to go bankrupt."[30]

Successful companies apply the trader principle at every level—company to customer, shareholder to management, management to employee,

employee to employee, company to vendors, and so on. Fred Mossler, an executive at Zappos, describes how his company deals with its vendors:

> Negotiations at Zappos are a bit different. . . . Instead of pounding the vendors, we collaborate. If we're looking for longer payment terms, we'll present different sales plans based on the days-of-payment terms. We decide together what makes the most sense for the business, the amount of risk we want to sign up for, and how quickly we want the business to grow. . . . We don't believe that negotiations need to be an arm-wrestling match. If both parties are honest about our positions and objectives, we should be able to find an equitable way to get there.

Mossler goes on to report that Zappos even throws an annual Vendor Appreciation Party.[31]

What happens when companies don't abide by the trader principle? Circuit City had notoriously bad customer service. In a case that typified its modus operandi, Matt Southerton purchased a defective laptop from the retailer. But when he tried to return it, Circuit City refused to refund his money—even though it admitted the product was faulty and didn't have a replacement in stock. Unsurprisingly, Circuit City went out of business in 2009.[32]

The consequences of flouting the trader principle are, if anything, more clear when we consider those who resort to outright fraud. Cheating, as we've stressed again and again, doesn't work. The fatal flaw in all dishonest schemes is that they depend on pretending the facts are different from the way they actually are—that your business is more profitable than it really is or that your customer is going to receive a quality product when in fact you're selling snake oil. But pretense doesn't change the facts. They are out there waiting to be discovered, inevitably bringing down the cheater's house of cards. See: Charles Ponzi, Tyco, WorldCom, Madoff, and any episode of *America's Dumbest Criminals*. As for fraudsters who seem to "get away" with their schemes, it's important to remember that happiness comes from practicing certain virtues and achieving certain values; however much loot a criminal is able to grab, it will not make him into a rational, productive trader. (Recall Madoff's confession that he was most miserable precisely when he was "getting away" with his crime.)

To be sure, the principles of rational selfishness cannot by themselves guarantee success in business, any more than moral principles guarantee success in life. The fact is, there are a lot of perfectly moral businessmen who simply aren't very good at what they do. Moral virtue won't turn Joe Shmoe into Steve Jobs. Nevertheless, virtue is the indispensable foundation without which long-range profit is impossible.

And it is *long-range* profit that producers are concerned with. While we are constantly told that the profit motive fosters short-term concern with next quarter's stock price, the fact is that the profit motive drives companies to be long-run oriented.[33] In 1982, when people in Chicago started dying from Tylenol that had been deliberately tainted with cyanide, Johnson & Johnson immediately pulled more than 30 million bottles from stores. Short term, the recall was of course costly, but the decision ultimately saved the Tylenol brand.[34] *This* is what the profit motive encourages and demands.

Are we saying that every successful businessman is moral? No. Are we saying that high profits are proof that a company is ethical? We're not. Our point is simply this: Over the long run and in a free market, businesses that flout the principles of rational selfishness are penalized economically. Evaders miss opportunities. The unproductive lose out to productive competitors. The win/lose model creates once-burned, twice-shy vendors, employees, and customers who will happily take their business to the more moral company.

THE ALTRUISTIC ATTACK ON BUSINESS SUCCESS

In a business context, profit seeking consists of businessmen striving to maximize shareholder value—ultimately, to raise the company's stock price by being as productive as possible. This goal has been attacked by antibusiness altruists, who say that shareholder value maximization is cold, selfish, uninspiring, and harmful to the "public good"—Forbes.com columnist Steve Denning goes so far as to call it "the dumbest idea in the world."[35] Business needs to be "socially conscious" and "socially responsible," critics of shareholder value maximization say. It needs to stop putting profit first and instead make serving the "needs of society" its primary aim.

One company that did just this was Control Data. During the 1960s and 1970s, Control Data was a powerful competitor to IBM. But it also had a corporate philosophy that aimed at using its resources to "meet society's unmet needs."[36] It self-sacrificially built factories in rundown neighborhoods, launched do-gooder agricultural projects in Alaska, and even sent expensive computer equipment to China and the Soviet Union in exchange for unsellable trinkets like Russian-made Christmas cards.

Then there was the program the media would eventually dub "cars for cons." Observing that released convicts had trouble finding work in part because they lacked transportation, Control Data started leasing cars to convicted felons on favorable terms. According to a company vice president, "We're not concerned about a quick profit here."[37] There was no danger of that. It turned out that many of the convicts decided to steal the cars rather than make good on the loans. Imagine that.

This focus on sacrificially serving "society's needs" eventually helped destroy the company. One author notes:

> A lot of people believe that because the leaders of Control Data said the brand was all about meeting society's unmet needs, the company began to neglect the base business, the mother lode, the goose that laid the golden eggs. Resources that should have helped Control Data keep up with the ferociously competitive technology market were frittered away.[38]

Not a big surprise. Everyone talks about how tough it is to succeed in today's competitive environment—how much harder is it when you deliberately spend time, energy, and resources on programs that are unproductive? Corporate "social responsibility" is, in the end, nothing more than corporate altruism—and like mixing "a little" self-interest with "a little" self-sacrifice, it is as sensible as "balancing" a nourishing meal with "a little" poison.

Nevertheless, many businessmen continue to buy into the "social responsibility" philosophy. Why? Exhibit A:

> As the CEO of Hasbro, nothing is more important to me than the safety and well-being of the children who enjoy our products. In fact, because

of its importance, I lead the committee of Hasbro executives that over-sees our company's corporate social responsibility efforts.[39]

Who could doubt that the safety and well-being of children who en-joy its products is of vital interest to a toy company? If that's the kind of thing that "social responsibility" demands, then every successful business is "socially responsible." But, of course, that's not *all* "social responsibility" demands. Back to Hasbro:

> Our belief in CSR [corporate social responsibility] shows up in a wide variety of areas including the quality and safety of our products, en-vironmental, safety and health initiatives, ethical manufacturing pro-grams, philanthropy initiatives, community relations, human resources, governance and our code of conduct. . . . [I]n the area of community relations, in 2010, Hasbro donated more than $22 million in grants and products to programs that helped more than 3.6 million children around the world.[40]

In other words, corporate "social responsibility" is a hodgepodge or, more precisely, a package deal—which is exactly why many businessmen support it. It labels as "socially responsible" both legitimate concerns of profit-seeking businesses (e.g., safety, customer and employee satisfac-tion) and concerns that aren't relevant to a business (e.g., the fact that some people in their communities have unmet "needs," to be addressed with "philanthropy initiatives").

The way businesses seek profits in a free market is through producing valuable products and services, which requires having motivated employ-ees, safe and satisfied customers, and a whole lot else. Their ability to do so is affected by things like the economic well-being of their surrounding community and the amount of political freedom they have. To be focused on profits requires paying attention to those kinds of issues. But it doesn't require giving away shareholders' money to charity and sending salesmen out to soup kitchens.[41]

To get them to swallow the idea that it's their duty to serve and sac-rifice, the altruistic push for corporate "social responsibility" has taught businessmen that their choice is either some monomaniacal focus on the "bottom line"—one that involves ignoring many of the factors that *determine* a company's bottom line—or a mawkish pursuit of a "service" agenda. But that's a false alternative: it leaves out men like Steve Jobs—that is, producers.

Businessmen should erase the term corporate "social responsibility" from their vocabularies. A business should be focused on *production and profit*—with everything that requires and implies. Any company that achieves productive success should self-confidently reject calls to "give back." It created wealth—it has nothing to atone for.

CONCLUSION: THE "PUBLIC GOOD" BE DAMNED

If profits are material gains earned through production, then the profit motive is the selfish desire to earn material gain by producing wealth. The goal of someone driven by the profit motive isn't to *get* money, by hook or by crook; it's to *make* money, by trading his best effort for the best effort of others. The path to profits, then, is paved in principle. True profit seekers have no motive to resort to chicanery or crime.

In *Atlas Shrugged*, Hank Rearden is put on trial for violating the government's edicts restricting his ability to make and sell a new metal alloy he has invented, Rearden Metal. His courtroom speech captures the essence of the profit motive:

> "I work for nothing but my own profit—which I make by selling a product they need to men who are willing and able to buy it. I do not produce it for their benefit at the expense of mine, and they do not buy it for my benefit at the expense of theirs; I do not sacrifice my interests to them nor do they sacrifice theirs to me; we deal as equals by mutual consent to mutual advantage—and I am proud of every penny that I have earned in this manner. . . . I made my money by my own effort, in free exchange and through the voluntary consent of every man I dealt with—voluntary consent of those who employed me when I started, the voluntary consent of those who work for me now, the voluntary consent of those who buy my product. . . . I refuse to apologize for my ability—I refuse to apologize for my success—I refuse to apologize for my money. . . . I will not say that the good of others was the purpose of my work—my own

good was my purpose, and I despise the man who surrenders his. . . . If it is now the belief of my fellow men, who call themselves the public, that their good requires victims, then I say: The public good be damned, I will have no part of it!"[42]

The profit motive represents the best in us—and, as we'll see in due course, the profit system represents the best for us.

NINE
SELFISHNESS UNLEASHED

ALTHOUGH HENRY FORD HAD NO FORMAL EDUCATION IN engineering, few were as adept with machines. Ford started building cars in the early 1890s while working at Thomas Edison's company. He assembled his first one by hand in his shed; it turned out to be too wide to fit through the door, and he was forced to chop down the shed walls to get it out. It was a harbinger of things to come: Throughout his career, Ford would have to break down walls again and again.

After three years of testing, Ford decided to launch his career as a carmaker. His first company, however, went bankrupt. So did his second. Finally, in 1903, he launched the Ford Motor Company. The basic idea behind the company was both elegantly simple and completely revolutionary: Use mass production to achieve economies of scale and thereby sharply reduce the cost of automobiles. "I will build a car for the great multitude," Ford said. "It will be so low in price that no man making a good salary will be unable to own one."[1] It would certainly not be easy. As business historian Richard Tedlow describes it:

> Henry Ford understood . . . that anyone who wanted to build such a car would have to fight like hell to do so. He would have to fight his financial backers, who would constantly push him toward building heavier, more expensive models. He would have to fight his competitors. . . . He would have to fight engineering barriers which stood in the way of manufacturing enough inexpensive yet rugged and dependable vehicles to make an acceptable profit while keeping the retail prices low. In fact, he would

have to fight everything and everybody with one exception. The exception was the consumer.[2]

After a few missteps, Ford developed the Model T and made it available in 1908 to Americans at the astonishingly low price of $850 (most cars of the day cost two to three times that amount). Sales grew quickly. As Ford continued to innovate and refine the production process, he was able to bring down the cost even more. In 1913, he unveiled his greatest innovation, the moving assembly line, which by 1916 had slashed the time required to assemble the chassis from twelve hours to less than two. Now Ford was able to sell each Model T for only $345—and he sold nearly 750,000.[3] He had succeeded in making America mobile.

As Ford's career neared its end, another career was just beginning. Rexford Tugwell was an American economist enamored with central planning and an admirer (to some degree) of planning efforts in Communist Russia and Fascist Italy. A member of FDR's Brain Trust, Tugwell became part of the president's administration, starting as assistant secretary of agriculture in 1933. There he became instrumental in designing two of the most prominent—and infamous—early New Deal programs, the National Industrial Recovery Act (NIRA) and the Agricultural Adjustment Act.

Tugwell was openly hostile toward capitalism, declaring in one speech, "The jig is up. The cat is out of the bag. There is no invisible hand. There never was."[4] He went so far as to say—it was not meant as a criticism— that government planning "amounts, practically, to the abolition of 'business.'"[5] He hoped for an end to competition, preferring the establishment of massive industry cartels. These cartels, in turn, would be run not by greedy businessmen chasing profits but by selfless central planners—like Tugwell himself, no doubt—acting in "the public interest." (For a time, Tugwell got his wish: The NIRA, for instance, cartelized huge portions of American industry, restricting the production and raising the prices of all sorts of goods, from automobiles to household appliances.)

According to economist Lawrence White, "In the planned future, [Tugwell] declared, speculative profit-seekers like Henry Ford will not be allowed to decide independently where to risk investment funds. They will have to get the approval of an investment planning board." White then quotes Tugwell: "New industries will not just happen as the automobile industry did; they will have to be foreseen, to be argued for, to seem probably desirable features of the whole economy before they can be entered upon."[6]

Ford's spectacular success came at the tail end of America's freest days; Tugwell's rise marked the beginning of the end for economic freedom in America. There is a certain tragic eloquence in that fact: Capitalism *is* the system that liberates the Fords from the Tugwells. It is the system that liberates the human mind from physical force and allows men to pursue their own goals, their own vision, their own profit, their own happiness.

We've said in earlier chapters that the economic system that has existed for the last century in America is not a free market but a mixed economy. In this chapter, we'll discover what a real free market is. We'll see that it is designed to protect a certain way of life—the life of an individual who pursues his own interests via thinking, producing, and trading. The profit system *is* the system that protects, rewards, and enshrines the profit motive. What that means in practice, however, is not the dog-eat-dog chaos envisioned by capitalism's critics but a constant upward climb fueled by the reasoning mind; not a Madoff economy or a Tugwell economy, but a Ford economy.

Capitalism, in short, is the system of selfishness—of *rational* selfishness.

A SOCIETY OF PRODUCERS

The businessman as we understand him is a relatively recent phenomenon. While there has been commerce throughout the ages, men who relentlessly pursue profits by transforming abstract theory into wealth can flourish only under certain political-economic conditions—conditions that did not exist for most of mankind's history. Professional profit seekers like Ford were made possible by the birth of capitalism.

The essence of business, as we've seen, is translating scientific knowledge into material wealth. But from the fall of Rome until about the sixteenth century, science was virtually extinguished by Christianity. St. Augustine had condemned the pursuit of scientific knowledge as "the lust of the eyes."[7] It was one "sin" Christians did manage to suppress.[8]

Science finally began to reemerge during the Renaissance, thanks to a few heroes willing to risk their lives to bring men out of the Dark Ages. (Some of those heroes, like the astronomer Giordano Bruno, were declared heretics and burned at the stake for their trouble.) It was Newton who finally ended the church's position as an earthly authority: His discoveries showed conclusively that *reason,* not revelation, was the means to knowledge. The publication of his *Principia* in 1687 ushered in the Enlightenment or, as it has accurately been called, the Age of Reason.

The Enlightenment's explosion of scientific knowledge spawned a trickle of technological innovations: Ben Franklin's lightning rod, Eli Whitney's cotton gin, John Fitch's steamboat. But if thought was essentially free, production remained chained. Guilds restricted competition in countless trades. Crippling tariffs undermined free trade. Taxes drained the pockets of anyone hoping to work and become rich. Mercantilist economic policies shackled producers in the name of filling the government's coffers with silver and gold.[9]

There were other, cultural factors that kept the profit motive under wraps. As late as the mid-eighteenth century, Americans generally looked down on "greedy tradesmen and moneymakers." These sentiments were so strong that colonial mobs would regularly form to

> support traditional customs and moral relationships against changes brought on by new impersonal market conditions, maintaining by force, for example, customary prices and traditional ways of distributing goods against the perceived forestalling and gouging practiced by unscrupulous shopkeepers and middlemen.[10]

But in 1776, two powerful intellectual statements helped sweep aside these attitudes and lay the groundwork for capitalism: the Founding Fathers' declaration of inalienable individual rights and Adam Smith's eloquent defense of economic freedom, *The Wealth of Nations*.[11] Their combined effect was so powerful that by the mid-1800s, Tocqueville could write that in America, "nothing is more great or more brilliant than commerce: it attracts the attention of the public and fills the imagination of the multitude; all energetic passions are directed towards it."[12]

The mercantilist policies of the eighteenth century were giving way to new free market policies. Tariffs were reduced, government monopolies were abolished, and taxes were cut to historic lows. The new economy was no longer geared toward enriching the government (or merchants with political pull) but to freeing individuals so they could enrich themselves.

Not only were the mercantilist policies of the past being stripped away, but new institutions that supported commerce were being developed. The corporate form was established, increasing access to capital. Intellectual property rights were refined, protecting the rights of creators and encouraging them to create. Liberty of contract became legally sacrosanct, fostering trade of all sorts. The result was the first free economies in human history—and an unprecedented explosion of invention, innovation, and advance.[13]

The path to capitalism was not an accidental one. It followed an irresistible logic. America, which would become the world's freest economy, had been founded on the principle that each individual has an inalienable right to his life, liberty, and the pursuit of his own happiness. To be an American was to be an entrepreneur in the deepest sense: "to be the master of your own fate and the captain of your own soul."[14] It was to take responsibility for exercising your own thought, your own creative effort, and to carve out for yourself a life of happiness and worldly success. As a result, the economic system of America became more and more geared to the life of a rational and industrious trader—an Edison, a Carnegie, an Allison, a Ford. Such men exemplified what would become known as the American or capitalist way of life, and it was the desire to protect that way of life that led men to create capitalism.

Men flocked to America not for the easy life but for freedom. Capitalist America did not guarantee you success, but it offered you an unobstructed road: In this country, you could make your own way. Today the supporters of Big Government are fond of telling us that "a hungry man is not free." Those who immigrated to America during the nineteenth and early twentieth centuries knew otherwise. They arrived poor—even famished—but ambitious. Carnegie, recall, arrived in America a penniless Scottish immigrant. But, as Tedlow notes, he arrived "a free man in a free land. Nothing could stop him. One new frontier after another—that was

America to young Andrew Carnegie."[15] In another biographer's words, "For Andrew, 'America was promises,' promises of growth [and] opportunity."[16] Liberated from the bonds of their home countries, men like Carnegie were free to rise as high as their ambition and ability would take them.

Not every American shared this attitude toward life, of course. No nation is filled only with the rational and industrious, who seek nothing more than the right to live an independent existence. There were thieves, crooks, moochers, and bums—but the system was not designed for them. It was designed for the best among men and the best in each man—not only the productive genius but anyone willing to think and produce.

PROTECTING THE PROFIT MOTIVE

What is capitalism? How exactly did it free men to think, produce, and trade? Well, just consider the central pillars of capitalism: the right of individual liberty, the right of private property, and the right of voluntary association.

Individual liberty says that because morally you *should* think, you have an inalienable *right* to think and to act on your own judgment.

Individual liberty means that if you develop a scientific theory that holds that the earth revolves around the sun, no pope can silence you. If you want to follow your dream of becoming an electrician, no bureaucrat can demand that you first get a government license. If you and your doctor judge that an experimental new drug is the best shot you have at saving your life, you don't have to consult some FDA official. If you want to revolutionize transportation, you don't have to explain yourself to Rex Tugwell.

Economic progress depends on innovation—on discovering more and more knowledge about the natural world and on finding new ways to use that knowledge to improve human life. This process, in turn, requires that "authorities did not have the power to divert inquiring minds from areas of inquiry and did not punish by law . . . people who undertook innovations that would disturb the traditional workplace."[17] Innovators challenge convention and upset the status quo. It is only the existence of individual liberty that allows them to do it.

Early in his career, nineteenth-century entrepreneur Cornelius Vanderbilt went into competition with the Hudson River Steamboat Association. A master of efficiency and innovation, he cut the standard passenger fare from $3 to *nothing,* making all his income on meals and drinks. The association was so alarmed that it offered to pay Vanderbilt $100,000 plus $5,000 a year not to compete. (Vanderbilt accepted, but it didn't matter: He had shown what was possible, and the association soon found itself facing other competitors.) There's no question that without the individual liberty to compete, Vanderbilt would have been barred from revolutionizing steam traffic on the Hudson. Indeed, Vanderbilt had started his career by challenging and defeating Robert Fulton's govern- ment-protected monopoly on the New York steamboat traffic—a monop- oly designed to keep innovators like Vanderbilt at bay.[18]

The right to private property says that because morally you *should* pro- duce, you have an inalienable *right* to keep, use, and dispose of the product of your work. The right to property says that the material values you cre- ate are *yours.* It doesn't guarantee that you'll successfully acquire property. It guarantees only that whatever property you do acquire won't be seized or disturbed by others. Government's job is not to take your property, to restrict its use, or to redistribute it to other people—but to protect it.

We tend to equate property with land. But actually property is anything you own—from a car, a shirt, or a paper clip to a paycheck, a business, or a patent on an invention. To own something is to have the exclusive right to determine how it is used. If you own a car, you can drive it, or add rims and a new stereo system, or paint it green, or put it in a showroom, or sell it, or lend it to a friend, or donate it to charity, or scrap it for parts.

The right to property means that if you want to build an extension on to your home, you don't have to obtain permission from some zon- ing board. If you want to allow patrons to smoke in your restaurant, no busybody can stop you (and you, in turn, cannot force nonsmokers in the door). If you want to spend your paycheck on expanding your business or on a weekend getaway in Lake Tahoe, no politician can make you spend your money on your neighbor's retirement or his appendectomy.

Ownership means that you can use your resources as you judge best, regardless of what others think: No one can step in and say "society" would prefer you to use your property in a different way. You use it by right, not by permission.

The right to individual liberty requires the right to property (and vice versa). What enables an innovator to try his idea, even if the rest of the world thinks he will fail, is his freedom to use his property as he sees fit. If all property belonged to the state, as it does under socialism, individual liberty would be impossible: To gain the resources for a venture, you would have to convince Rexford Tugwell or his equivalent that your venture is in "the public interest." His judgment, not yours, would be supreme. When the government owns and controls everything, observed Trotsky, opposition "means death by slow starvation. The old principle, who does not work shall not eat, has been replaced by a new one: who does not obey shall not eat."[19] In a free market, you can use your private property, and the property of any other individual you can persuade to help you, to pursue your vision.

The principle of *voluntary association* says that because morally men *should* deal with each other as traders, each has a *right* to trade voluntarily with others, free from physical coercion.

The principle of voluntary association means that no matter how noble someone thinks his goals are—whether it's building wind farms or sending other people's children to college or providing people with health care—he has no right to force them on you. And it means that no matter how misguided someone thinks *your* goals are, so long as you are not coercing others, he has no power to stop you from pursuing them.

In economic terms, the principle of voluntary association means that individuals deal with one another only via voluntary trade to mutual benefit. As economist Ludwig von Mises describes it:

> The worker does not depend on the good graces of an employer. If his employer discharges him, he finds another employer. The consumer is not at the mercy of the shopkeeper. He is free to patronize another shop if he likes. Nobody must kiss other people's hands or fear their disfavor. Interpersonal relations are businesslike. The exchange of goods and services is mutual; it is not a favor to sell or to buy, it is a transaction dictated by selfishness on either side.[20]

Looking back at some of the examples of profit seeking in previous chapters, we see that the principle of voluntary association is what helps make them possible. When Edison created the light bulb and offered it for sale, the principle of voluntary association meant that kerosene makers like Standard Oil could not stop him—nor could they stop consumers from flocking to him. When Gerstner laid off thousands of employees in his effort to turn IBM around, he was counting on the principle of voluntary association—his employees had no *right* to their jobs. When Wal-Mart employees agree to work for nine dollars an hour, that is voluntary association—they are free to look for higher pay elsewhere. When Oracle shareholders agree to pay Larry Ellison tens of millions of dollars a year for his consistently strong performance, that is voluntary association—they are free to offer him less or find a new CEO. And if a given shareholder doesn't like Ellison's pay, he can choose *not* to be a shareholder by selling his stock. In all of these cases, voluntary association makes it possible for people to engage in win/win relationships (regardless of how outsiders evaluate those relationships) or to go their separate ways.

INDIVIDUAL RIGHTS

All three of these rights—individual liberty, private property, and voluntary association—form a unity. You can't have voluntary association without individual liberty and private property. And when individual liberty and private property are fully protected, the inexorable result is voluntary association. The basic unifying principle behind the three pillars of capitalism is this: The individual is sovereign. He has a moral right to exist for his own sake, to keep and use the values he creates, and to deal with others only on terms that are voluntarily agreed upon and mutually beneficial. He does not owe allegiance to any man or any group; his only obligations are those he chooses to assume.

Capitalism is the system focused squarely on the individual. On the individualist approach, society is not something above the individual to which he owes a duty—it is merely a group of individuals, each with his own dreams, goals, and purposes. If you have a right to take a given action, then no one else—no matter how high his office or how large his gang—can morally stop you. You don't have to seek anyone's permission or gain anyone's approval in order to act by right. Rights say: Morality requires a certain course of action on the part of an individual, and if anyone interferes with your freedom to take such action, he is *wrong*. In

Rand's definition, "A 'right' is a moral principle defining and sanctioning a man's freedom of action in a social context."[21] In a crucial elaboration, she adds:

> *Rights* are conditions of existence required by man's nature for his proper survival. If man is to live on earth, it is *right* for him to use his mind, it is *right* to act on his own free judgment, it is *right* to work for his values and to keep the product of his work. If life on earth is his purpose, he has a *right* to live as a rational being: nature forbids him the irrational. Any group, any gang, any nation that attempts to negate man's rights, is *wrong*, which means: is evil, which means: is anti-life.[22]

A society of rights is one in which you are as free as you would be alone on an island. You are fully free to think, to act on your judgment, to create and use material values. The premise underlying rights is that in order to retain that freedom in society, you have to treat other men not as resources to be exploited but as other independent, sovereign beings. Other men are not like fish or rivers or trees, which you can fashion to your purposes. They are like you: ends in themselves who need to fashion nature to their own purposes. You deal with nature by rearranging it to your own ends. You deal with other men by voluntarily cooperating to achieve your separate ends.

We've wandered a long way from the Founders' vision. The intellectual turning point was the complete obliteration of the concept "rights" during the twentieth century, when individual rights were "supplemented" with collective "rights" and when rights went from protecting a man's freedom of action to guaranteeing him certain outcomes (so-called welfare rights).

It should be obvious that there can be no such thing as group rights or collective rights. A group—whether a business, a union, a race, a sex, a class, or a nation—is merely a number of individuals. Those individuals don't gain special rights by forming a group, any more than they lose rights by forming a group. A legitimate association, such as a corporation or a (voluntary) labor union, has only the rights its members choose to delegate to it—and they can delegate to it only those rights they have as individuals.[23]

Nor can there be such a thing as a "right" to health care, a "right" to an education, a "right" to a mortgage. Rights, as the Founders understood, are rights to take certain kinds of action: rational, productive, self-interested actions. They are not a guarantee of success. These modern "rights" are different: They are rights to certain kinds of outcomes. But since nature doesn't and can't guarantee those outcomes, the bill has to be paid by *other men.*

Take the "right" to health care. What does that mean? It means that if you get sick, some doctor or nurse has to take care of you. Can they charge you for their services? Morally, no—their services are yours by "right." What does that make them? It makes them your serfs. (The fact that, in most cases, medical practitioners are paid by the government doesn't change the essential issue. It merely transfers the burden for your care from doctors and nurses to taxpayers.) The same goes for the "right" to an education and the "right" to a mortgage. The "right" to an education means that some people are going to be forced to pay for other people's education (and it has led government to nationalize the entire field of education via public schools). A "right" to a mortgage means that Americans are to be forced to cosign on Fannie Mae's and Freddie Mac's debt in order to make mortgages more affordable. These "rights" inevitably conflict: Your right to your paycheck conflicts with my "right" to have you pay for my health care.

Genuine rights don't conflict—they enable us to live together *without* intractable conflicts. They don't saddle other people with obligations save one: to respect the equal rights of others. The fact that Bob down the street has a right to life doesn't mean you have to provide him with a living. It means that you can't *stop* him from making a living by clubbing him over the head, or picking his pocket, or demanding that he get a government license in order to sell real estate or cut hair.

FORCE

There is only one way someone can violate your rights: physical coercion. The initiation of physical force is the only way others can stop you from pursuing your rational self-interest. It is the only way someone can stop you from acting on your judgment, from using the values you have earned to further your life and happiness, or from dealing with people only on mutually agreeable terms.

A thief uses force to deprive you of your property. While you still have a moral *right* to your cash or your car, it is no longer available to serve your life. You can't buy the cell phone you were saving for. You can't get to work as you were planning to. Instead of spending the afternoon playing fetch with your dog, you're stuck filling out police reports.

A kidnapper uses force to deprive you of your freedom of movement. He keeps you away from your home, your work, your friends, your family. He chooses what you eat and when you sleep.

A rapist uses force to deprive you of your right to decide what you do with your own body.

A murderer uses force to deprive you of your very life.

Force can also be indirect, as with fraud. A con artist who convinces you to write him a check for a plot of land that doesn't exist continues to hold your money not by right (the deal you consented to is not the deal that actually took place) but only by means of your inability to physically reclaim it from him.

The unique evil of force is that it is the only way another person can negate your *mind*. Following reason, as we've seen, is the basic requirement of success and happiness. Others can do a lot of bad things to you— lie to you, hurt your feelings, refuse to deal with you at all—but so long as they do not use force against you, they cannot stop you from thinking and acting on your rational judgment. Physical force, in contrast, does just that. When a person initiates force, he says, in effect: Don't conform to reality, conform to my will. Don't think, obey. As Leonard Peikoff put it in his book *Objectivism: The Philosophy of Ayn Rand*, force "places the individual in an impossible metaphysical situation. If he does not act on the conclusions of his mind, he is doomed by reality. If he does, he is doomed by the forcer."[24]

This is true whether the man holding the gun is Al Capone or Uncle Sam. Suppose you want to buy a new car. You decide to research various cars and their features, and along the way you discover evidence that, given your height, car airbags are more likely to harm you than help you.[25] You judge that airbags are bad, and so you go to the car dealership and request a car without airbags. But, you are told, the government mandates that *all* cars have airbags—if anyone tries to make a car without airbags, the government will forcibly stop him. The government's coercion has negated your judgment. The thinking you did about whether an airbag will keep you safe is rendered irrelevant to your life. It doesn't matter what you think—you simply have to obey Washington's orders and suffer whatever consequences may follow.

The same holds true for every other instance of government force. When antitrust lawyers tell AT&T and T-Mobile that they cannot merge, it is the telecom companies' judgment concerning how best to produce that the government obliterates. When regulators tell bankers that they have to lend to people in "underserved" communities via the Community Reinvestment Act, it is the bankers' judgment concerning who is creditworthy that the government wipes out. When bureaucrats try to "control" health care costs by dictating which medical tests are "necessary," it's the judgment of you and your doctor that's abolished. When a member of your local zoning board tells you that you can't plant vegetables in your front lawn, it is your judgment concerning how to use your property that's squashed. When the IRS reaches into your pocket in order to dole out entitlement benefits to other Americans, it is your judgment concerning how to spend your wealth that's rendered impotent. Force, regardless of who initiates it, is an attack on your mind.

In a civilized society, when men disagree, they appeal to others via persuasion. If you don't like the fact that your neighbors are overweight, you can try to convince them to eat better and exercise—you don't ban trans fats or tax sugary treats. If you think solar panels are the wave of the future, you invest in them and try to convince others to buy them—you don't force taxpayers to subsidize them. Force is the antithesis of persuasion. Persuasion involves offering a man reasons to accept that something is true or good and then leaving the matter to his judgment. Force negates his judgment.

Because it stops a man from exercising his judgment, from pursuing his own interests, from adhering to the virtues success requires, the initiation of physical force is the means—the *only* means—by which others can violate his rights. If the purpose of rights is to create a society where people deal with each other by reason, then a society of rights is one that removes coercion from human affairs.

It's crucial, here, that the use of force be *physical*. There is no such thing as forcing someone via emotional or intellectual means. If your loser brother-in-law guilts you into paying his bills, he didn't *make* you pay his bills. If Amazon runs a really great commercial for the Kindle Fire, Jeff Bezos didn't *make* you buy one—he persuaded you. If peer pressure leads you to jump off a bridge, you still had the power to heed your mother's advice.

Only the initiation of physical force stops you from following your rational judgment, and so only the initiation of physical force closes off the capitalist mode of existence. Nothing but physical coercion can give the Tugwells the power to stop the Fords.

What about retaliatory force? What about punishing those who resort to force? That's not simply okay—it's vital. If individual rights are to be protected, retaliatory force must be used against thieves, fraudsters, rapists, kidnappers, murderers, and the like.

GOVERNMENT

If your purpose is to create a society that safeguards the pursuit of self-interest, then the only proper role of the government is to protect individuals from the initiation of force. The "sum of good government," said Jefferson, is

> a wise and frugal Government, which shall restrain men from injuring one another, shall leave them otherwise free to regulate their own pursuits of industry and improvement, and shall not take from the mouth of labor the bread it has earned.[26]

This is why we need government. What makes a government a government is its monopoly over the legal use of force in a given geographical area. What makes a government a *good* government is that it uses force only in retaliation against aggressors. It is our agent of self-defense.[27]

By barring force and fraud from human affairs, the government secures our rights. That is its only moral purpose. To implement this purpose, a capitalist government employs three basic arms: the military, the police, and the courts. The military's role is to protect the freedom and lives of its country's citizens from foreign threats. The role of the police is to protect a country's citizens from domestic criminals. The court system's chief role is to serve as an impartial arbiter administering objective laws, which enables individuals to resolve their disputes without having to resort to force themselves. That, in essence, is it—that is what a truly limited government looks like.

A limited, rights-protecting government does not guarantee that everyone will be happy and successful. The enemies of limited government think because some are poor and miserable in a free society, this justifies curtailing freedom. But while freedom from force is not a sufficient condition for success, it is a *necessary* condition. A happy and successful life, as we've seen, depends on exercising the virtues of rational selfishness, and that can be done only by each individual through his own free will. No government can guarantee that individuals will use their freedom well. It can only guarantee that they *are* free.

Is a capitalist government democratic? Well, it's certainly true that political representatives are chosen by vote. Capitalism, in that sense, is democratic. But if democracy means a system governed by majority rule and that anything goes so long as 51 percent of the voters agree, then capitalism is resoundingly antidemocratic. It's instructive, in this regard, that the Founding Fathers were outspoken opponents of unlimited democracy, which they regarded as rule by the mob. "[T]he people," warned John Adams, "when they have been unchecked, have been as unjust, tyrannical, brutal, barbarous and cruel as any king or senate possessed of uncontrollable power."[28] The principle of individual rights restrains the mob. It says that even if 99 percent of people want to violate the individual's rights—say, by sending Socrates to his death for preaching ideas the community disapproves of—they are *wrong*.

LAISSEZ-FAIRE

Capitalism is the system that institutionalizes freedom in order to protect a specific way of life: a life of reason, productiveness, and trade. Capitalism's raison d'être is to make possible the individual's selfish pursuit of life and happiness, including the selfish pursuit of profit. It does this by establishing a strictly limited government that removes coercion from human affairs. In terms of man's economic existence, the government's policy is: hands off.

> The fundamental principle of capitalism [writes Rand] is *the separation of* State and Economics—that is: the liberation of men's economic activities, of production and trade, from any form of intervention, coercion, compulsion, regulation, or control by the government.[29]

Government and economics are kept separate in order to protect the free mind—men's conclusions about production and trade must not be subject to the rule of force.

What career should I pursue? How much pay should I accept? Should I start my own business? What kind of business? How much should I charge for my products? What process should I use to manufacture them? Who should I hire and how much should I offer them? What should I do with the profits? Pour them back into the company or spend them on a lavish lifestyle? Should I invest some of my income? With whom? On what terms? What goods should I buy? From whom? For how much? Should I sell my company? Merge it with a competitor? Under capitalism, all of these questions, and countless others, are yours and yours alone to make. No one has a right to step in and force you to substitute his whims for your judgment.

When we say "separation," we mean it: The separation of state and economics must be *total*. Anything less is not capitalism. Capitalism means no social welfare schemes, no corporate welfare schemes, no regulations, no controls, no economic central planning. A capitalist society has no Social Security, no welfare, no Medicare, no Medicaid, no government-run "public" schools. It has no FDA, FCC, SEC, EPA, or any of the hundred other regulatory agencies. It has no Federal Reserve, no czars, no economic maestros. Whatever form they take, regulations and wealth redistribution schemes like these inject force into our economic affairs, violating our rights and stifling our ability to pursue happiness.

Whatever the enemies and alleged defenders of free markets might say, capitalism *means* a laissez-faire, hands-off, fully free market, where the government performs a single, vital function: It protects individual rights. Writes Rand in an important summary:

In a capitalist society, all human relationships are *voluntary*. Men are free to cooperate or not, to deal with one another or not, as their own individual judgments, convictions, and interests dictate. They can deal with one another only in terms of and by means of reason, i.e., by means of discussion, persuasion, and *contractual* agreement by voluntary choice to mutual benefit. The right to agree with others is not a problem in any society; it is *the right to disagree* that is crucial. It is the institution of private property that protects and implements the right to disagree— and thus keeps the road open to man's most valuable attribute (valuable personally, socially, and *objectively*): the creative mind.[30]

That's nothing close to what we have today—and nothing less can fully protect the profit motive.

CONCLUSION: MARKETS ARE MORAL

In a 2011 interview with publisher Steve Forbes, the chairman and CEO of Honeywell, David Cote, attacked the popular image of businessmen as villains. "We're the good guys," Cote said again and again. "In total, if we take a look at the standard of living we have today, our position in the world, our military strength . . . it's all driven by U.S. business." Cote even went on to dismiss the notion that businessmen have to "give something back." "I never took anything," he exclaimed.[31]

Few businessmen are so willing to defend their vocation. The businessman, H. L. Mencken once observed, "is the only man . . . who is forever apologizing for his occupation."[32] But then Forbes asked Cote, "When your kids ask you, how do you say markets are moral? How do you make that case?"

For a moment, Cote was at a loss. Finally he said, "Well, I don't know that markets are always moral. I think that markets are markets." He stammered awkwardly for a while before concluding, "I can't say that's moral or immoral, it's just kind of the way it works."[33]

If we want to stop the growth of the state, this is the view that has to change. Americans need to understand what the free market is, how it works—and why it is profoundly good. Not just okay. Not just the worst economic system except for all the rest. We need to grasp that the free market is an *ideal*—a profoundly, perfectly, flawlessly moral economic system—and that anyone who opposes it to whatever extent is *wrong*.

Capitalism is the system of selfishness—of *rational* selfishness. It doesn't guarantee that each individual will be rational, be productive, and abide by the rule of trade. What it does do is leave men *free* to be rationally selfish, *reward* them for being rationally selfish, and prevent those who default on that goal from imposing the consequences of their irrationality on others. *This,* Ayn Rand argued, is what it means for capitalism to be a moral system.

Capitalism is more than an economic system; it is a social system that protects freedom: intellectual, political, and economic. This book's focus, however, is on this last. We're now ready to turn our attention to the economics of capitalism.

TEN
THE DYNAMISM OF THE MARKET

A S THE HEAVILY REGULATED FINANCIAL MARKETS WERE melting down in 2008, economist Joseph Stiglitz announced that

the reason the invisible hand often seems invisible is that it is not there. The pursuit of self-interest by Enron and WorldCom did not lead to societal well-being; and the pursuit of self-interest by those in the financial industry has brought our economy to the brink of the abyss.[1]

No image is more closely associated with the free market than Adam Smith's invisible hand. There is debate among scholars as to what exactly Smith meant by the metaphor, but today most people read it as describing how markets transform individual acts of self-interest into "socially desirable" outcomes. The greedy butcher wants to line his own pockets, but the invisible hand ensures that he can do so only by providing society with safe, tasty, affordable cuts of meat. This account smuggles in two assumptions: that self-interest is immoral and that our aim should be the achievement of some collective "social good." As we've seen, these assumptions are deadly to capitalism. If people view the profit motive as immoral and unjust, no amount of hand-waving, invisible or otherwise, will convince them to embrace the profit system. They, like Stiglitz, will see disasters that are in fact caused by government intervention as emanating from ruthless profit seekers.

The invisible-hand metaphor does capture something important, however. Critics claim that the free market is a chaotic free-for-all. The truth is that it is an orderly *system* of production and trade, but the forces that make it orderly are not self-evident. They emerge not from top-down central planning but from the free, voluntary choices of individuals seeking their separate interests. Smith's great contribution was to take the first important steps in identifying these forces—to make the invisible hand visible.

In this chapter, we will look at some of these forces—the division of labor, the price system, and competition—and their result: innovation. We'll see that the profit system *is* a system—and that government intervention distorts and blocks the forces that make the system work.

THE DIVISION OF LABOR

A market is made up of people who voluntarily cooperate. The folks at Apple help you listen to music. Your trainer helps you exercise. Your grocer helps you put food on your table. We (hopefully) help you understand capitalism. You help your company produce whatever it is your company produces. Now notice something interesting. With rare exception, human cooperation doesn't involve a group of people working on the same exact task, like rowers rowing a boat. Most human cooperation involves dividing up tasks and exchanging the results—or *specialization* and *trade*. Adam Smith called this the division of labor.

Under economic freedom, Smith explained, most individuals don't produce the goods that they consume; they specialize. They produce one or a few things that others want, which they then trade for the goods they consume. They, in effect, strike an agreement: I'll focus on making some things, you focus on making other things, and then we'll exchange our respective goods for all the things we want.

Why bother? Because, when we specialize, we become vastly more productive than when we produce everything ourselves. Smith famously gives the example of a pin factory. He noted that a self-sufficient pin maker "could scarce, perhaps, with his utmost industry, make one pin in a day, and certainly could not make twenty." If you gathered ten such makers in a room, you would at the end of the day be lucky to have two hundred pins. But if they divided their labor? Smith describes the process:

One man draws out the wire, another straightens it, a third cuts it, a fourth points it, a fifth grinds it at the top for receiving the head; to make the head requires two or three distinct operations; to put it on, is a peculiar business, to whiten the pins is another; it is even a trade by itself to put them into the paper.

The result, said Smith, is that ten men could produce up to forty-eight *thousand* pins a day.[2]

The division of labor makes everyone incredibly more productive: A given person in a given quantity of time can create exponentially more wealth. How? Time saved by not having to switch tasks, for one. The ability to take advantage of labor-saving machinery, for another. But the most important way the division of labor makes us more productive is by enabling us to *leverage human intelligence*.

The fundamental source of wealth is the rational human mind. It is by exercising our capacity for thought that we gain the knowledge required to develop and improve nature in order to satisfy our needs. The more knowledge we can bring to bear on production, the wealthier we become, and the higher our standard of living.

In a non–division-of-labor society, most people live as self-sufficient farmers. As a result, they each have roughly the same knowledge. You may know more about your particular plot of land and your neighbor may know more about his, but your methods for planting and harvesting are basically the same. Since both of you have to perform every step in the agricultural process, neither of you has the time or specialized knowledge to, say, invent a better plow. And even if one of you happened to design a better plow, how would anyone else ever find out about it?

In a division-of-labor society, however, knowledge isn't duplicated—it's multiplied. Specialization allows us to acquire a huge body of knowledge possessed by few others—and trade allows us to benefit from everyone else's knowledge. In a division-of-labor society, you *can* spend all your time thinking about how to improve plows, and the profit motive will drive you to spread the results of that knowledge far and wide by making cheaper, better plows. You're able to trade the results of your knowledge of plows for the results of other people's knowledge of things like medicine, construction, and textiles. As a result, everyone is better off.

One consequence of this multiplication of knowledge is that a division-of-labor society can produce goods that *could not exist* without the division of labor. The amount of knowledge that goes into building a car, even a simple car like the Model T, is astronomically greater than the knowledge any given individual possesses. It requires knowledge of engineering, mining, metallurgy, electricity, chemistry—knowledge that itself could be acquired only in a society where individuals specialize. Indeed, no technology, aside from a few rudimentary tools like arrowheads, could exist without the specialized knowledge made possible by the division of labor. As economist Russell Roberts has observed, "Self-sufficiency is the road to poverty."[3]

But the division of labor cannot exist under just any economic system. It is inextricably connected to the institutions of capitalism: individual liberty, private property, and voluntary association. Only when men are free to think, to own property, and to trade freely can the division of labor flourish.

Knowledge can't be multiplied unless independent individuals are free to acquire knowledge, to exercise their independent judgment, and then to take independent action. If everyone had to receive permission from a central planner before acting, the productive benefit of specialized knowledge would vanish. Independent action, in turn, requires private property. It is private property that enables an entrepreneur like eBay's Pierre Omidyar to pioneer an untested idea no bureaucracy or central planner would approve. And no less important, it is private property that gives entrepreneurs the selfish incentive to take big risks in the pursuit of big gains.

To the extent that property is owned or controlled by the state, the division of labor breaks down. Economic coordination is hampered and ultimately destroyed by central planning, so chronic shortages develop, encouraging increasing self-sufficiency in production. The following is from a report on production in the Soviet Union (written by two Russian economists):

For a Soviet factory—or a Soviet research institute—the best response to unreliable business partners is self-sufficiency. When the planners decided to build the giant Fiat factory, they decided to make it almost entirely self-sufficient. Except for electrical equipment, window glass and tires, every part used in Zhiguli—every nut, bolt, seat cover, and piston ring—is made in the factory itself. Gersh Budker's Institute of Nuclear Physics in Novosibirsk couldn't buy the instruments it needed, so the scientists there began to make their own. This kind of self-reliance is expensive and inefficient. Yet no amount of planning can provide the trust and reliability that could substitute for it.[4]

As for voluntary association, it is the institution that protects free exchange. Specializing wouldn't do you much good if you weren't free to trade the product of your labor. Even Jeff Bezos couldn't make much use of a million Kindles.

Initially the process of trade took the form of direct exchange, or barter: Sam the Shoemaker would make shoes, which he would trade with Freddie the Fisher for fish. But the benefits of direct exchange were limited. What if Freddie didn't need shoes at that particular moment?

The next great advance in the process of trade was indirect exchange. Although Freddie didn't need shoes, he did want bacon. While Sam himself didn't eat pork, he realized he could trade shoes for bacon and then bacon for fish. Nevertheless, this process was cumbersome and still relied on having a lot of personal knowledge about the people you wanted to trade with.

What followed was a quantum leap forward in the process of trade: the birth of money. Today we think of money as pieces of paper issued by the government, but originally money was a material good—usually gold. Gold was the most marketable good in the economy: Individuals would trade whatever they produced for gold, confident that when they found a good *they* wanted to acquire, the seller would be willing to accept gold in return. Now the division of labor could flourish like never before. Sam no longer had to worry about whether Freddie wanted shoes; he no longer had to worry about what Freddie wanted at all. So long as *someone* wanted shoes, he could trade shoes for gold and use gold to get his fish. Money is what allowed the division of labor to extend beyond the confines of a small town to cities, nations, and ultimately the entire world.

Some commentators have argued that because the division of labor involves producing things that others want rather than the goods you yourself are going to consume, it is a form of altruism.[5] But to anyone who doesn't have a vested interest in trying to disguise or downplay capitalism's selfish nature, that claim is simply not credible. Although you produce goods to trade with others, your ultimate goal is to benefit yourself (just as the buyer's goal is to benefit himself). You pick the career that will bring you the most joy and demand payment for your work. The division of labor would be altruistic only if it required making shoes or sandwiches to *give* away to others.

The division of labor is the way in which free, rational, productive beings selfishly cooperate to create wealth; by dividing their labor and trading its products, they magnify the power of thought to almost unimaginable levels.

PRICES

Hedrick Smith was a reporter for the *New York Times* when, during détente, he had the opportunity to spend time in the Soviet Union, getting to know the Soviet people and becoming familiar with the trials and tribulations of life under communism. This was the Brezhnev era—Russia at its "best."

> I had heard about consumer shortages before going to Moscow but at first it seemed to me that the stores were pretty well stocked. Only as we began to shop in earnest as a family did the Russian consumer's predicament really come through to me. First, we needed textbooks for our children (who went to Russian schools) and found that the sixth-grade textbooks had run out. A bit later, we tried to find ballet shoes for our 11-year-old daughter, Laurie, only to discover that in this land of ballerinas, ballet shoes size 7 were unavailable in Moscow. . . . Leningrad can be overstocked with cross-country skis and yet go several months without soap for washing dishes. In the Armenian capital of Yerevan, I found an ample supply of accordions but local people complained they had gone for weeks without ordinary kitchen spoons or tea samovars. I knew a Moscow family that spent a frantic month hunting for a child's potty while radios were a glut on the market.[6]

Needless to say, that's not what life is like under economic freedom. When you walk into your local grocer, the shelves are always stocked with things that consumers actually want to buy. When you stop to refuel your car, you don't usually worry that the station will have run out of gas. When you move to a new town, you aren't shocked to discover that there are people willing to work as plumbers, janitors, and trash collectors. There seems to be an order to a free economy. But where did it come from? There is no cadre of economic rulers telling us what to make, and we don't all get together in a room and collectively vote on what to produce. We're each making our own independent judgments in pursuit of our own separate interests—and the result is the opposite of chaotic.

A capitalist, division-of-labor economy is an *integrated* system of production. It involves millions and even billions of people working in concert to satisfy all their diverse wants. What integrates it? *Prices.*

"Prices," notes Center for Industrial Progress Senior Fellow Eric Dennis, "are the language of the economy."[7] They coordinate an economy by conveying knowledge that allows individuals to decide what to produce and how best to produce it.

Market prices reflect two underlying facts: the amount of a given good available (supply) and how much people value that good relative to other goods (demand). Thus, the law of supply and demand: When the demand for a good decreases and supply remains unchanged, its price falls. When the demand for a good increases and supply remains unchanged, its price rises. When the supply of a good decreases and demand for it remains unchanged, its price rises. When the supply of a good increases and demand for it remains unchanged, its price falls.

That's pretty abstract, so consider one price: the price of gas. At the current market price of, say, $4 a gallon, the market for gasoline clears: Everyone who wants to buy a gallon of gas for $4 a gallon can find a willing seller, and everyone who wants to sell a gallon of gas for $4 can find a willing buyer. If a gas station tried to charge $6 a gallon, it would find its inventory piling up. If a buyer was willing to pay only $2, he would find that his vehicle would not get him very far.

What happens if supply or demand changes? What if, for instance, people decide to do more traveling, increasing the demand for gas? There will be shortages of gas and long lines at the pump, right? Wrong.

Instead, some people will bid up the price of gasoline to, say, $4.50 a gallon. At the new price, everyone who values a gallon of gas more than $4.50 can buy it. Some of the people who would have bought a gallon of gas at the old price of $4 might now opt to carpool, or bike to work, or consolidate multiple trips to the grocery store. Meanwhile, profit-seeking entrepreneurs will continue to monitor the market and decide whether it is profitable to increase their production of gasoline given the higher price.

In an economy where prices are determined by the market, no one has to force consumers to use less gasoline or force producers to make more gasoline. Those decisions are made voluntarily. People seeking their own interests adjust their behavior to the facts of supply and demand conveyed to them through prices.

This is the invisible hand at work. All this happens even though most people know nothing about Americans' changing travel preferences. What they do know is: Gasoline is more expensive. And that, it turns out, is all they need to know.

We've only scratched the surface of this enormously complex process. The price for any particular good doesn't reflect the supply and demand for just that good but also for all its inputs and substitutes as well as *their* inputs and substitutes, and so on. Ultimately, the price for any one good reflects the supply and demand for every other good in the economy. That is what it means to say a division-of-labor economy is an *integrated* system of production.[8]

Importantly, prices don't merely convey information; they also come ready-made with an incentive to act on that information. In the case of consumers, that's pretty straightforward. If the price of gas rises, you have to decide whether to purchase less gas or to spend less money on all the other things you want to buy. But why do producers respond to price changes? Why does the fact that consumers are willing to bid up the price of gasoline lead businessmen to consider producing more gasoline? The main thing to understand is that what businessmen are interested in is not a single price but the *difference* between the price of their inputs and the price they can get for their output. It is the difference between these two sets of prices that represents their economic profit (or loss). If the price of their product goes up but the prices of its inputs don't go up (or don't go up as much), a *profit opportunity* is created.

We said in chapter 8 that profits are the businessman's goal. Now we can see the broader economic role of profits and the way in which the profit motive is indispensable for a functioning economy.

The basic difficulty a division-of-labor economy faces is how billions of people making billions of goods using billions of inputs can know that they're being productive. How can they be sure that their output is more valuable than their inputs? And, just as important, how can they tell whether resources are being put to their *most* productive uses? The answer is supplied by economic profit and loss.

For someone marooned on an island, his efforts are profitable when he thinks the resulting state of affairs (say, a fire) is preferable to the work and resources that went into creating it (e.g., chopping down a tree and rubbing sticks together for fifteen minutes). But in a division-of-labor economy, it's not so obvious. A restaurant owner may work really hard to cook good food. He may even succeed. But if people don't choose to eat there because they like the restaurant across the street even more, then from the standpoint of other market participants, he isn't being productive. As a result, he will not reap economic profits.

Economic profit is a signal that an individual or a company is, from the standpoint of other market participants, creating wealth and creating it efficiently. When McDonald's reaps huge profits, that is, in effect, a message from consumers: "We value the use you're making of economic resources way more than any alternative use: Keep it up!" Profits are a green light to production: They signal to a businessman that he is creating wealth and give him the means to expand his productive activities. Losses, in contrast, are a red light to production: They signal to a businessman that he is not creating wealth, and they move his business closer to bankruptcy.

It is this—the pursuit of economic profit—that keeps all the different industries in an economy in balance. High profits in a given industry—say, the tech industry during the PC boom—draw people and resources into the industry, increasing production. The same pattern works in reverse. When the automobile came along, there were lots of people working in the horse-and-buggy industry. As consumers started buying cars, horse-and-buggy profits shrank. Young people who might have gone into the horse-and-buggy industry a decade earlier now sought higher-paying work elsewhere. Investors who might have poured capital into the industry now invested in other industries. Whip makers and other businessmen who served the horse-and-buggy industry found their income drying up and had to find a different line of work. The profit motive drove individuals to regear their productive activities from a horse-and-buggy economy to a car economy, just as today it is helping us transform into an information economy.

Economist Henry Hazlitt summarizes the point: "One function of profits, in brief, is to guide and channel the factors of production so as to apportion the relative output of thousands of different commodities in accordance with demand."[9] (The other economic function of profits, according to Hazlitt, is to "put constant and unremitting pressure on the head of every competitive business to introduce further economies and efficiencies," which we touched on in chapter 8 and will talk more about in this chapter when we turn to competition.[10]) The profit motive—*selfishness*—is not simply a by-product of economic freedom. It is what makes economic freedom work.

People often treat prices as if they could be set arbitrarily by producers. When gas prices go up, for instance, we accuse oil companies of greedily "gouging" us. But why, then, do gas prices ever fall? And why, when they do fall, don't we thank oil companies for their generosity? The truth is that businesses don't arbitrarily raise prices in order to exploit consumers, any more than they arbitrarily drop prices in order to altruistically benefit consumers at the expense of their own profits. On a free market, prices are the product of voluntary trade and reflect facts of supply and demand. Prices are at once a product of individuals pursuing their own self-interest and a means by which individuals coordinate their economic goals in concert with others.

COMPETITION

Do you remember the first cell phones? The Motorola DynaTAC 8000X (the one used by Michael Douglas in the film *Wall Street*) cost as much as a used car, was the size of a brick, and had the reception of a paper cup. But then came improvement, with Motorola's lineup becoming smaller and cheaper. Later, Nokia came out with the 1011, the first 2G digital cell phone to hit the market. But it was surpassed by the Motorola StarTAC—a clamshell phone that could fit easily into your pocket. Soon Nokia was back with the 5110, which, thanks to its size, weight, and simplicity, became the most popular phone of its day. The back-and-forth continued, as phones got smaller, battery life increased, displays got larger and clearer, and features were piled on top of features. New phone makers joined the rivalry, including Ericsson, Siemens, LG, and, later, Apple, which would revolutionize the industry with its iPhone. Today, many of us have phones in our pockets that are more powerful than the average computer circa 2000.[11]

Welcome to the fruits of capitalist competition.

When people are free—free to buy from whomever they want, free to seek work from whomever they want, free to set prices however they choose—the result is competitive rivalry. Businesses compete for customers. Workers compete for jobs. Employers compete for workers. Buyers compete for the goods and services they want to consume. This rivalry, as paradoxical as it may sound, works to harmonize the interests of everyone involved in trade.

One way to see this is to take a look at places where economic competition has been absent—say, the Soviet Union. In a world where people aren't free to shop elsewhere, there's no incentive for businesses to concern themselves with offering value to consumers. When McDonald's first opened in Russia after the collapse of communism, it found that cashiers wouldn't greet customers with a friendly smile. "Why should we?" the bosses were told. "We have the burgers. They don't have the burgers." In a capitalist economy, you may have the burgers—but others are free to offer better burgers, or cheaper burgers, or a cleaner, friendlier environment to eat burgers in. No, you don't have to try to best them. You'll just go out of business and have to find another line of work.

The best way to grasp the power of competition is to look at the kind of actions it encourages and the kind of results it produces. Here are a few aspects:

- *Innovation.* As we'll see in the next section, competition is what pushes profit seekers to put a premium on constant improvement and innovation.
- *Lower prices.* All else being equal, the company with the lowest price wins. So-called robber barons like Vanderbilt, Carnegie, and Rockefeller all came to dominate their respective industries by vastly lowering prices, the same way that Wal-Mart today has come to dominate its industry by offering super-low prices.
- *Improved quality.* Companies will strive to make sure that all else *isn't* equal. By increasing the quality of its wares, it can attract customers. One of the reasons Japanese auto companies were able to gain a foothold in the American market was because they gained a reputation for quality, in contrast to the perception that American-made cars were substandard.
- *Increased efficiency.* One way to reap higher profits while actually cutting prices is to cut costs—to produce more with less by rooting out waste, introducing labor-saving technology, and so on. One of our favorite stories about Rockefeller tells of him walking through one of his plants and seeing a man seal tin cans of kerosene using forty drops of solder. Rockefeller suggested the man try thirty-eight drops. It turned out that with thirty-eight drops the cans occasionally leaked, but with thirty-nine drops, none did. Even late in his retirement, Rockefeller would proudly note that this one small change ultimately saved Standard Oil hundreds of thousands of dollars.[12]
- *Improved customer service.* Buyers value a pleasant buying experience. Zappos has become the leading online shoe retailer largely by making sure that customers are satisfied not only with its products but with its service. There's a reason why profit seekers tend to greet you with a smile.
- *Wages based on performance.* If a company can't attract good employees, it won't be able to attract customers. Competition for good employees leads to employers offering pay in line with an employee's productive contribution. That's why Henry Ford started paying his lowest-paid employees $5 a day in 1914, more

than $110 in today's dollars.[13] He had to: Turnover at the company was *370* percent in 1913.[14]

- *Improved working conditions.* Employee compensation involves more than just higher wages—it also involves making the workplace more pleasant (e.g., air conditioning, break rooms, even free food and massages in some companies).
- *Advertising.* If an iPhone is invented and no one hears about it, does it make a sale? Advertising informs us of all the wonderful things available to buy and helps us decide whether to buy them.
- *Better methods.* Profit seekers are constantly learning from other profit seekers, which means that good ideas proliferate while bad (or outdated) ideas die quick deaths. When Motorola showed that its Six Sigma management strategy could lead to increased profitability, the strategy soon became an industry standard.

When people are free to pursue their own goals and interests, we benefit. Sure, sometimes we don't like the short-term outcomes of living in a free economy. Maybe we don't get the job we want, or maybe our business goes out of business. But any short-range inconvenience is far outweighed by the benefits of living in a world where no government czar can tell us where to work or what business we can start—a world with better products, lower prices, and rising pay. Politically, far from there being inherent conflicts of interest among people, we all have the same fundamental interest: freedom.[15]

At the same time that capitalism is condemned for its "cutthroat" competition, it is alleged to stifle competition by fostering monopolies. But there is no reason to equate a Microsoft with the United States Postal Service. If one keeps in mind what the actual definition of a monopoly is—a business *legally immune* from competition—then it is only government that can create monopolies by coercively barring competition. The Postal Service is a monopoly: Private businesses are legally barred from entering its market. If UPS tries to deliver first-class mail, it will be forcibly stopped by the government. This is why the Postal Service can continue to operate inefficiently (at least as long as the government will continue to pump tax dollars into it). Microsoft is not (and never was) a monopoly: Any private company can enter its markets and compete with it. The fact that, for a time, Microsoft held a huge market share in operating systems meant only that other companies couldn't match what it was offering customers. When Google and Apple and others figured out ways to compete, they grew spectacularly.[16] Large, successful, profitable companies like Microsoft, Google, and Apple are examples of competition in action, not of its absence.[17]

A free market, in other words, can have dominant competitors, but it cannot have monopolies. And dominance can be achieved and maintained only by incredible productivity. There's no better example of that than history's most famous "monopoly," John D. Rockefeller's Standard Oil. Standard Oil achieved its dominant place in the market not by raising prices but by lowering the price of petroleum products while simultaneously improving their quality. And once it achieved that dominance, it couldn't have raised prices significantly even if it wanted to—not without inviting competition. Indeed, by the time the antitrust case against Standard Oil went to court in 1909, the company had well over one hundred competitors in the United States alone.[18] This included one competitor no one had expected or could have foreseen: Thomas Edison and his electric light bulb. Whereas most of the demand for oil in those days came from people buying kerosene to light their homes, electricity provided a cleaner, safer, cheaper alternative.

Free markets *are* competitive. Government intervention can't create competition, it can only destroy it.

INNOVATION

Capitalism remade the world, radically transforming the way human beings lived. "[U]ntil the capitalist era," observes commentator Michael Novak, "the world had been understood as relatively static."[19] Men sowed and they reaped. Monks passed down an unchanging body of dogma to their understudies. Craftsmen passed down an unchanging method of production to their apprentices. Invention was rare, and innovation as a way of life was unheard of. At the end of your life, the world looked pretty much the same as it did at the beginning.

Capitalism changed that. Rejecting aristocratic status seeking and religious self-denial, most men sought their own earthly happiness. They valued ambition, they prized knowledge, they esteemed (earned) wealth, and they admired (earned) success. The result, economically, was a world of continuous progress, what historian Joyce Appleby calls "the relentless revolution."[20] A man born in the early nineteenth century could scarcely have recognized the world of the twentieth—a world where railroads crisscrossed the continent, where radio waves carried men's voices across the span of miles, where buildings could scrape the sky, and where sundown no longer sentenced families to darkness. Economist Joseph Schumpeter, writing in the mid-twentieth century, elaborates:

> [T]he history of the productive apparatus of a typical farm, from the beginnings of the rationalization of crop rotation, plowing and fattening to the mechanized thing of today—linking up with elevators and railroads—is a history of revolutions. So is the history of the charcoal furnace to our own type of furnace, or the history of the apparatus of power production from the overshot water wheel to the modern power plant, or the history of transportation from the mail-coach to the airplane. The opening up of new markets, foreign or domestic, and the organizational development from the craft shop and factory to such concerns as U.S. Steel illustrate the same process of industrial mutation . . . that incessantly revolutionizes the economic structure *from within,* incessantly destroying the old one, incessantly creating a new one.[21]

Schumpeter called this process "Creative Destruction."[22] But that phrase is misleading. The automobile industry didn't destroy the horse-and-buggy industry—it surpassed and replaced it. There is no destruction in capitalism. What the relentless revolution actually illustrates is the power of reason under political freedom. When men are free to think, the result, economically, is constant progress, constant *innovation.*

According to the *New Oxford American Dictionary,* to innovate is "to make changes to something established, esp. by introducing new methods, ideas, or products." If we looked merely at the division of labor, prices, and competition, our picture of a free market would not capture its dynamism. It would fail to reflect the innovative spirit of capitalism:

> A free market [writes Rand] is a *continuous process* that cannot be held
> still, an upward process that demands the best (the most rational) of
> every man and rewards him accordingly. While the majority have barely
> assimilated the value of the automobile, the creative minority introduces
> the airplane. The majority learn by demonstration, the minority is free
> to demonstrate.[23]

Every element of a market is suffused with innovation. When men are
free to think and produce, their ambition leads them to continually divide
and subdivide their labor in new and better ways; they relentlessly seek
to reduce the cost of their inputs and increase the value of their output;
they compete with one another by introducing new goods, better goods,
cheaper goods, more convenient goods, always striving to improve, to advance, to do better and be better.

It is this process of reason-guided innovation under economic freedom that explains—to borrow the title of Nathan Rosenberg and L. E.
Birdzell's work—how the West grew rich. Innovation bred unprecedented
economic growth.

> Growth is, of course, a form of change, and growth is impossible when
> change is not permitted. And *successful* change requires a large measure
> of freedom to experiment. . . . The great majority of societies, past and
> present, have not allowed it. Nor have they escaped from poverty.[24]

Innovation thrives under capitalism, and it's only capitalism that sanctions innovation.

Although virtually everyone today pays lip service to the value of innovation, innovation is under attack. When President Obama blamed
ATMs, as opposed to his Big Government policies, for creating unemployment, he was attacking innovation.[25] When protesters urge government
to block Wal-Mart from opening stores in their neighborhood for fear
that its low prices and wide selection will put mom-and-pop stores out of
business, they are attacking innovation. When we hear complaints about
outsourcing—that is, free trade—for "taking away jobs from Americans,"
the target is innovation.[26]

Lurking beneath these attacks is a view that Ayn Rand's then-colleague
Nathaniel Branden, writing in Rand's collection *The Virtue of Selfishness*,

called "the Divine Right of Stagnation." It's the belief that a person should be able to go to the same job at the same factory and perform the same motions for forty years, without having to bother to learn or to grow. And it's the belief that the innovators who do learn and grow should be rebuked for disturbing other people's routine.

A free market doesn't pander to this sort of view. It is geared toward the rationally selfish individual, the person who recognizes and prepares for the fact that there is no such thing as a guaranteed job for life and that constant growth is not an inconvenience imposed by troublesome innovators but a principle of human survival. As Branden observes:

> Capitalism, by its nature, entails a constant process of motion, growth and progress. It creates the optimum social conditions for man to respond to the challenges of nature in such a way as best to further his life. It operates to the benefit of all those who choose to be active in the productive process, whatever their level of ability. But it is not geared to the demands of stagnation.

And, he adds, "*Neither is reality.*"[27]

GOVERNMENT INTERVENTION

Government controls and regulations inject force into capitalism's system of voluntary cooperation. Like a wrench in the gears, the result is to handicap the price system and competition, and thereby the entire division of labor.

PRICES

We've seen that market prices aren't arbitrary—they are determined by the facts of supply and demand. But government edicts concerning what prices "should" be *are* arbitrary. Economists call these price controls, and they devastate economic coordination. When the government sets prices above the market price, supply exceeds demand and there is a glut of products no one wants to buy. When it sets prices below the market price, demand exceeds supply and shortages ensue.[28]

For example, to combat rising gas prices during the 1970s, Washington put price controls on oil. The results weren't pretty. Shortages developed in some areas, and many drivers were forced to wait in line for hours to fill up their tanks. (Meanwhile, thanks to the economic discoordination created by the price controls, others areas were awash with more gasoline than they knew what to do with.) Anyone who has spent more than twenty minutes waiting in line for anything can guess what happened next.

> "These people are like animals foraging for food," says Don Jacobson, who runs an Amoco station in Miami. "If you can't sell them gas, they'll threaten to beat you up, wreck your station, run over you with a car." Laments Bob Graves, a Lexington, Mass., Texaco dealer: "They've broken my pump handles and smashed the glass on the pumps, and tried to start fights when we close. We're all so busy at the pumps that somebody walked in and stole my adding machine and the leukemia-fund can."[29]

To try to deal with the problems caused by its price controls, the government resorted to further controls—this time, gas rationing. It announced an odd-even system whereby your government permission to buy gasoline on a given day depended on the last digit of your license plate. To the surprise of central planners everywhere, when the price controls were ultimately repealed, not only did the gas lines disappear, the price of gas fell as well.

Or what about the minimum wage, which says that the price paid for labor can't fall beneath a certain floor ($7.25 an hour as of this writing)? What it actually does is prevent any worker whose labor is worth less than the minimum wage from finding employment and building his skills. If an hour of your time brings only $6 into a business, then no government decree will convince an employer to pay you $7.25. You'll simply find yourself out of work. (The employer, meanwhile, may find himself out of business, unable to afford the help he needs.) And, indeed, unemployment—especially among young people and minorities—has been shown to grow whenever the minimum wage is increased.[30]

And then there is the Federal Reserve controlling interest rates. Interest rates are a price (the price that coordinates the borrowing and lending of money). We saw what happened when the Fed lowered interest rates during the early 2000s: It spawned a housing bubble and ultimately a financial crisis.

COMPETITION

In today's mixed economy, competitive rivalry is impeded in all sorts of ways, but three stand out as particularly damaging: government monopolies, bailouts, and antitrust.

In a number of fields, the government prevents competition outright. Sometimes it runs an enterprise itself (e.g., Amtrak). Other times it allows a nominally private business to operate without competition (e.g., utilities). Either way, buyers have no alternative. And when buyers are forced to submit, sellers won't go out of their way to provide. The Postal Service, anyone?

It's not simply that government monopolies attract mediocrities who don't care about customers. It's that even if a state-sanctioned monopoly *wants* to provide good service, the lack of competition provides an almost insurmountable barrier. We noted earlier, for instance, that learning is central to competition. When Apple showed that there was a market for tablets, many other companies noticed and created their own tablets. That doesn't happen when government bars competition. There is no Apple Airport to show LAX or LaGuardia how to make air travel more pleasant, safe, and efficient.

As for bailouts, few Americans were happy to see the banks and car companies rescued during the 2008 financial crisis. But this was nothing new: By that point, the U.S. government had been bailing out companies that were "too big to fail" for thirty years.[31] If a large company goes under, we're told, it will cause a chain reaction that can cripple the entire economy. But, setting aside certain special cases, businesses fail all the time, and the result is that the price system—if it's free to function—allows the economy to adapt relatively quickly and painlessly.[32] When Enron failed, it was one of the largest companies in the world, and yet the effects of its failure were barely noticeable economy-wide. Far from a problem, business failure is an important and integral part of competition. A business that is unprofitable is misusing, even *destroying*, wealth. In a free market, it can't continue to lose money forever. But in a bailout-happy nation, it can.

The direct costs of bailouts can be immense. But the indirect costs are perhaps greater. One such cost is what economists call moral hazard. In a free market, each of us must carefully assess risk and reward. We're free to make risky bets, but because we face both a potential upside *and* a potential downside, we have a powerful incentive to make rational decisions. But when we can enjoy the upside of taking on risk and are protected from the downside by government bailouts, the result is that we are encouraged to take on far more risk than we would (or even *could*) on a free market. Think back to chapter 4 and the shenanigans of government-sponsored companies like Fannie Mae and Freddie Mac. If market participants hadn't been conditioned by Washington to expect these companies to be bailed out whenever things got rocky, Fannie Mae and Freddie Mac could not have operated so recklessly during the 2000s.

Another unseen cost of bailouts is the competitors that *would* have succeeded were it not for the state's actions. In 2011, columnist E. J. Dionne penned a piece titled "G.M. Is Back, Thanks to Uncle Sam." Well, it's true that the bailout saved GM (for now). But the assumption is that this is a good thing. It ignores questions such as: What would have happened had GM been allowed to fail? What kind of message would this have sent to the other auto manufacturers? Would competitors have benefited from being able to buy GM's assets at fire-sale prices? What about all the things taxpayers would have done with their money had they not been forced to hand it over to failing carmakers?

Bailouts are fundamentally unjust: They reward unproductive companies at the expense of productive ones, they destroy wealth, they foster bad behavior, and they generally wreck the market system.

And so does our final anticompetitive measure: antitrust. Antitrust is a body of laws that "regulate" competition. Although its details are complex, vague, and contradictory, the basic idea is that the government will intervene in the market to "promote" competition and keep it "fair." It will, for instance, break up companies that are "too big," or punish companies that charge prices that are "too high," or stop companies from charging prices that are "predatorily low," and so on.

Of course, none of this protects actual competition. True competition, as we've seen, means *freedom* of competition—the freedom of a businessman to use his property the way he thinks will maximize his profits. Antitrust allows the government to violate property rights on a massive scale by banning and punishing perfectly voluntary acts.[33]

The *reductio ad absurdum* of antitrust is the war on Google. Although antitrust has always been sold as a way to protect the consumer—to keep prices low, quality high, and so on—Google has come under attack for the "crime" of offering tremendously valuable products for free.[34] Will the suit "promote" competition? Or will it make Google think twice before deciding to enter (and likely revolutionize) a new field?

If the free market is an integrated system of production and trade, government intervention is an attempt to break up the system. The attempt can come from without, by central planners, or from within—by favor-seeking businessmen.

Not every businessman is a profit seeker. Some are the kind of money chasers we described in previous chapters. They go into business not because they seek to create wealth but because they view it as a fast track to unearned loot. These businessmen often seek to grow rich not through production but through political pull. Ayn Rand called these men "Money-Appropriators," as against "Money-Makers."[35]

In a free market, the government has no power to dispense special favors, privileges, subsidies, or franchises. It has nothing to offer businessmen except what it offers all citizens: protection from physical force.

But when the government has the power to control and regulate the economy, the government is a potential source of unearned rewards (and undeserved punishments). How would you like billions of dollars to build a high-speed railroad or an electric car? How would you like to be the only company able to offer cable TV in your neighborhood? Are you finding it hard to compete with foreign steel producers? How about a protective tariff? Are you finding it hard to compete with a domestic rival? How about an antitrust suit? When the government stops protecting individual rights and starts coercively intervening in markets, Money-Appropriators scramble to extract what benefits they can.

Economists call this process of seeking government favors "rent seeking." More commonly it is known as crony capitalism. But that name is totally misleading. Cronyism isn't a form of capitalism. As philosopher Andrew Bernstein suggests, "since it is made possible only by significant government control of the marketplace, it is fitting to call it by its proper name: 'half-assed socialism.'"[36]

When we speak of ending Big Government, what we want to end is all government intervention in the economy. In its place we want to establish a fully capitalist, rights-respecting system. Writes Rand:

> A full, perfect system of capitalism has never yet existed in history. Various degrees of government intervention and control remained in all the mixed, semi-free economies of the nineteenth century, undercutting, hampering, distorting, and ultimately destroying the operations of a free market. But during the nineteenth century, mankind came close to economic freedom, for the first and only time in history. Observe the results. Observe also that the degree of a country's freedom from government control was the degree of its progress. America was the freest and achieved the most.[37]

Critics have done their best to distort, ignore, and erase capitalism's record. Ask them what have been capitalism's results and their answer will be: exploitation, according to Karl Marx. Depressions, according to John Maynard Keynes. Inequality, according to Barack Obama. The chorus of anticapitalist voices is always singing the same song: In one way or another, capitalism leads to tragedy and disaster. The facts paint a much different picture.[38]

There were, to be sure, genuine problems and injustices during the nineteenth century; these were a result of precapitalism's legacy of poverty and the unfree elements that remained in the economy. But whatever the flaws and contradictions, in the period between the Civil War and World War I, the United States became an economic juggernaut and the symbol of freedom and prosperity. Those decades saw real gross domestic product per capita more than double at the same time that population—much of it from a flood of immigration—exploded.[39] They saw a rise in life expectancy from about forty years to more than fifty-five.[40] The cost of living plummeted while the amount of leisure time soared.[41] Those years saw the birth of the skyscraper, the camera, the telegraph, the oil industry, the electric light, the automobile, the airplane, modern medicine, and the middle class.

Today, the remnants of capitalist freedom continue to propel us forward. It is entrepreneurs pursuing profits who have made it possible for us to buy fresh fruit and fresh seafood any time of year, to ship gifts to distant friends overnight, to wake up to freshly brewed coffee, to surf the web while flying through the air, to live comfortably for eighty years or more.

That is capitalism's actual legacy. People don't flee from Hong Kong into China. People don't risk their lives to travel from South Korea to North Korea. They don't hop on poorly constructed rafts in order to make their way from Florida to Cuba. The Berlin Wall wasn't built to keep West Berliners from flocking to East Berlin. People flock to free (or, as has been the case, *relatively* free) economies because they provide them with the opportunity to flourish, materially and spiritually—to live the life of a producer rather than a serf.

CONCLUSION: THE PROFIT SYSTEM

A capitalist economy is a free economy. When men are left free to pursue their self-interest, they divide up their labor, rendering it more productive; they use prices to coordinate their productive activities, they compete with one another for profits—and they innovate their way to prosperity.

History has not provided us with a picture of a completely free market, but it has provided us with snapshots. We see the effects of freedom when we compare the precapitalist world's poverty and stagnation to today's riches. We see the effects when we compare semifree West Germany to East Germany's dictatorship. We see the effects when we compare Mao's China to today's China, or today's China to today's Hong Kong, or the tech industry to the housing industry. The lesson is clear: The freer a country or an industry, the more productive and prosperous it is.

The conventional picture of the free market is wrong. It is not a reckless, senseless, Wild West race to the bottom but a dynamic race to the top. It is the system where "good" is not good enough, where only the relentless pursuit of "more" and "better" will do.

In the next two chapters, we will see how the attempt to limit capitalism in the name of "greed" and "need" harms the rational and industrious individual. We'll see how the alternative to "hands off" is the government's hands around the necks and in the pockets of producers.

We'll see, in other words, why nothing less than laissez-faire will do—not if we want a fully moral and fully practical economic system.

ELEVEN
THE REGULATORY STATE
AND ITS VICTIMS

JULIE MURPHY IS NOT THE KIND OF PERSON YOU WOULD typically regard as a threat to public health and safety. But when the seven-year-old opened a lemonade stand to serve patrons at a local art festival, county health inspectors shut her down. She had not, it seemed, shelled out $120 to obtain the temporary food-safety permit required in order to sell refreshments.[1]

Regulations aren't synonymous with laws. Proper laws protect individuals from force and fraud by punishing the initiators of force. When the government puts Bernie Madoff in prison for defrauding customers, or when a court fines a business for causing property damage to its next-door neighbor, that is the rule of law. Regulations, however, are themselves the initiation of force to control or proscribe the voluntary decisions of market participants.

What happened in Julie's case was not the rule of law but regulation: In order to sell a water and Kool-Aid mix, she had to gain the government's permission, and because she failed to, individuals who wanted to purchase lemonade from her—even knowing it was not government approved—were forcibly prevented from doing so.

Without regulations, we're told, businessmen would more or less destroy the universe:

- Without health and safety regulations, businessmen will serve us poisonous food and sell us dangerous products.

- Without financial regulations, businessmen will take crazy risks, lose (or steal) tons of money, and bring the economy to its knees.
- Without labor regulations, businessmen will pay workers less than a "living wage," subject them to rotten working conditions, and make them work brutally long hours.

All of these fears, in one way or another, come down to this: The unrestrained profit motive creates a dog-eat-dog world, and the only way to protect us from the profit motive is to override people's voluntary choices with coercive regulations. Or: Businessmen are motivated by self-interest, and therefore they need to be shackled. This is the Argument from Greed.

We've already discussed why this view of selfishness and of a capitalist economy is wrong. In this chapter, we'll apply that understanding to two areas where we're often taught that regulation is essential: consumer and worker protection. What we'll see is that these kinds of regulations do not safeguard consumers or workers—but they do throttle producers and limit everyone's freedom.

PROTECTING THE CONSUMER

"Consumer regulation" is a wide-ranging category that includes everything from price controls to anti-monopoly legislation.[2] For our purposes, it suffices to focus on consumer regulations that aim to promote safety and quality and to ensure that consumers can make "informed decisions." When the Food and Drug Administration tells doctors what drugs they can prescribe, that is consumer regulation. When the Federal Trade Commission tells toy makers what information has to be on their package labels, that is consumer regulation. When hairstylists are told they must get certified in order to cut hair, that is consumer regulation.

Let's get the obvious out of the way: No one wants poisonous food, an incompetent doctor, or a car that explodes from time to time. But why wouldn't a free market enable you to buy all the safety and quality you want?

Imagine a world with no government regulation of food. Anyone and his brother can bake cupcakes or grow carrots to sell in any store willing to carry them. How will you respond? Will you:

a. Carelessly buy anything that sounds enticing and hope it won't kill you?
b. Stop buying food and become a self-sufficient farmer?
c. Exercise a little common sense and buy food from reputable sellers?

In a world without food regulation, *caveat emptor* would rule the grocery store. Far from giving food providers license to skimp on safety, this would give them a powerful incentive to build reputations for impeccable quality.

That's what went on in America before the FDA. Upton Sinclair's socialist propaganda aside, historian Gabriel Kolko notes that food makers "learned very early . . . that it was not to their profit to poison their customers, especially in a competitive market in which the consumer could go elsewhere."[3] This is not the conclusion of some free market apologist— it is the frank admission of an anticapitalist historian.

The same is true for safety and quality more generally. The idea that profit seekers would as a rule skimp on high standards makes little sense in light of the competitive value of *reputation*. Maybe you remember the classic *Saturday Night Live* skit where Dan Akroyd, playing the shady-looking head of a toy company, is taken to task for his company's dangerous product line, a pantheon that includes the Pretty Peggy Ear-Piercing Set, General Tron Secret Police Confession Kit, and Bag O' Glass, which, as its name suggests, was nothing more than a bag of jagged glass bits. (Defending the product, Akroyd declares, "Look, we put a label on every bag that says, 'Kid! Be careful—broken glass!'")[4] Akroyd is described in the skit as "a ruthless profiteer," but in reality, profit is the last thing such a businessman would reap.

In a free market, consumers know there isn't a government watchdog vetting businesses, so many are willing to pay more to buy from a company that has proved itself reliable over a long stretch of time. If you're driving through Nowheresville, Kansas, you're probably willing to shell out an extra fifty cents for a McDonald's burger rather than eat at Marie's Discount Beef Joint because you know that McDonald's has proven itself over many decades to be clean, tasty, and trustworthy. (This is one of the values of middlemen. We may not be able to keep track of which company consistently produces untainted beef paddies, but McDonald's *can* keep track of that, and we in turn know that McDonald's has a reputation for selling safe food.) This fact, combined with the relentless pressure of competition, leads businesses to go out of their way to safeguard their reputations; remember how Johnson & Johnson was quick to recall Tylenol in an attempt to save its brand.

Now, you might think, "That's not good enough for me. I want businessmen who negligently dispense dangerous wares to be stopped." They would be. Remember: A free market has strict laws against force and fraud.

You might also think, "That's *still* not good enough for me. I want to know that some impartial party is looking in the refrigerators and under the counters to make sure I'm safe." Well, that's exactly the kind of thing a free market would provide—privately and voluntarily. A free market leads to widespread use of private certification agencies. Such agencies exist even today. Sports autograph collectors, for instance, can turn to companies like Professional Sports Authenticator to make sure the ball they're buying was autographed by the 1927 New York Yankees and not by Ralph from Kentucky. In a free market, private voluntary certification services would be in high demand, and those companies would stake their reputation on the quality of their inspections. Restaurants, doctors, pilots, plumbers, and mechanics would have an incentive to meet the standards of independent inspectors in order to compete for customers. And don't forget: Customers can do a lot to encourage businesses to maintain high standards. The freer the market, the more indispensable are great reviews on services like Angie's List and Yelp.

In the days before omnipresent regulation, writes one historian,

> merchants stood ready to provide customers with as much information as they desired. . . . In contrast to the modern view of consumers as incompetent to judge the quality or safety or a product, *caveat emptor* treated customers with respect, assuming that a person could spot shoddy workmanship. Along with *caveat emptor* went clear laws permitting suits for damage incurred by flawed goods.[5]

Safety and quality are not benefits bestowed upon us by a beneficent government in the face of protests by profit-seeking businessmen. Safety and quality are values created by profit seekers looking to outcompete rivals.

It's profit seekers who discover and create longer-lasting preservatives; better storage methods for perishables; cleaner ways to slaughter animals and transport meat; safer ways to build cars, planes, and buildings; more effective drugs, pesticides, and medical procedures. One of the great injustices of the regulatory state is that we give the credit for these advances not to the profit seekers who forge them but to the bureaucrats who come along and dictate what counts as "safety" or "quality."[6]

Just as people fail to see how markets improve safety, quality, and the like, so they often fail to appreciate the real harms caused by the regulatory state.

For starters, the regulatory state discourages private certification agencies (by offering similar services for "free") and in general dilutes the value of reputation. Since buyers have been told that they need not beware, they are often unwary—reputation gets replaced with reliance on the judgment of regulators. So long as an outfit has a government stamp of approval, a fly-by-night operation has basically the same status as a company with a proven track record. (And as anyone who watched the proliferation of dubious mortgage companies during the housing boom can attest, a bustling regulatory state by no means prevents fly-by-night businesses.) A spotless reputation is no longer as much of a competitive advantage, which means that there is less of an incentive to gain and maintain a spotless reputation in the first place.

That's what happened to banks in the wake of deposit insurance. In order to attract customers, it no longer mattered whether a bank had a reputation for sound banking practices. All that mattered was whether it had an FDIC-insured sticker and how high an interest rate it paid. FDR himself—the man who signed deposit insurance into law—had warned that it "would lead to laxity in bank management and carelessness on the part of both banker and depositor."[7] (Hardly a surprise, then, that today's banks are so susceptible to crises.[8])

The regulatory state's problems don't end there.

In life, you regularly have to assess the value of safety and quality in the context of the pursuit of all your other values. You could, for instance, very simply reduce your chance of dying in a car crash to zero—simply stop driving. The reason you don't is because you judge that the risk of a car crash is worth it: Driving helps make possible a whole host of values in your life, such as getting to work easily or visiting distant friends. But you *do* value safety. What happiness and success require is thinking about such things as: Is it worth it to me to spend an extra five hundred dollars for antilock brakes and an electronic stability control system? Is it worth it to me to spend an extra thousand dollars for airbags? Government regulation short-circuits that thought process. Instead of leaving you free to decide how much you value extra safety features, government forces you to pay for these sorts of things *regardless* of how much you actually value them. (And if you can't afford the extra costs, well, then you just have to go without a car.)

The same goes for the disclosure of information. When ObamaCare forced restaurant chains with twenty or more stores to list how many calories are in each menu item, many people thought: Who could possibly object to giving consumers more information? But information isn't costless. Whether it involves scientific experiments to discover how many calories are in a slice of cheese or printing new menus, providing customers with information imposes genuine costs on businesses. One small businessman noted that, under ObamaCare's caloric mandate, his company would have to pay tens of thousands of dollars to replace all of its store menus, brochures, and drive-through signs—every time it changes a single ingredient. The FDA itself puts the total cost at $315.1 million in initial costs and $44.2 million in ongoing compliance costs.[9] On a free market, by contrast, companies would compete to find the best cost/information mix for their particular customers.

Part of pursuing our own happiness means constantly making these kinds of assessments, based on our own judgment and values. Regulations prevent producers and consumers from figuring out how best to pursue their individual values by saddling everyone with one-size-fits-all solutions. They treat us as a homogeneous group and elevate regulators to the status of elites who "know" what our preferences should be.

In a 2011 *Forbes* column, small business owner Warren Meyer tells of trying to set up a new modular office near the docks of his campgrounds in Ventura County, California.

Somewhere along the way an enterprising employee of mine made coffee in our new (not yet legal) office for the early morning fishermen, but we soon found that to continue to provide coffee would require the installation of a triple cleanup sink, which in turn would add marginally to the load on the current septic system, which in turn would trigger a county requirement for us to build a new $2.5 million sewage treatment facility. Uh, never mind on that coffee.[10]

In a free market, the fishermen would be free to decide whether to buy coffee brewed in the absence of a triple cleanup sink. In today's regulatory state, it's in the hands of a bureaucrat. You may think that the risk of a single sink is negligible (even nonexistent). You may think that few things in life are more important than a hot cup of joe in the morning, but in a regulatory state, what you think doesn't matter. Your judgment is irrelevant.

To take another example, if the FDA approved only drugs that were "perfectly safe," then about the only approved "drug" would be water—except that too much water can be deadly too. What the FDA does in reality is decide how much risk you're allowed to accept. The arthritis drug Vioxx, for instance, was pulled from the market after it was found that among patients taking high doses for a year and a half, 1.5 percent suffered a heart attack or stroke (versus .75 percent of those taking a placebo).[11] Why should an arthritis patient be stopped from deciding that Vioxx is effective enough at treating his symptoms to be worth that extra risk? The only answer regulators can give is: because we say so.

Sometimes the stated justification for interfering with our ability to act on our judgment is that some people won't choose to be rational. But whenever government intervenes in our affairs in order to protect people from their supposed irrationality, it ends up doing so at the expense of the *rational* person. In 2009, Washington passed the Card Accountability Responsibility and Disclosure Act, claiming the act would protect consumers against credit card companies by limiting penalty fees and interest-rate adjustments. Of course, consumers had always been protected from those penalties and adjustments so long as they regularly paid their credit card bill. But after the government barred credit card companies from charging higher fees to consumers who weren't so diligent, prudent credit card users found that their interest rates went up, other fees increased, and their credit limits were reduced to make up the shortfall.[12] Regulations don't help the consumer—they merely sacrifice the rational consumer to the irrational (or irresponsible) one.

The most severe cost of the regulatory state may also be the most elusive. While we can easily see the apparent benefits of regulation, what we cannot see is how the market would have evolved absent regulation.

Regulations, in theory if not always in practice, are attempts to deal with real problems through government dictate. How, for instance, can we safely and efficiently run gas lines into homes? Instead of leaving builders free to search for the best methods, regulations specify in loving detail who is allowed to run gas lines, what materials they can use, what kind of procedures must be adhered to, what approvals are necessary, and so on. (If you have a few months to spare, try thumbing through the International Fuel Gas Code and marvel at just how detailed these regulations can get.)

What we see in this case are guidelines to keep our homes from blowing up. What don't we see? We don't see what kind of creative solutions builders might have come up with had they been free to use their own judgment. Maybe, for instance, there is a vastly cheaper material that could be used that is just as safe as those specified in the code. Or maybe there is a more reliable method for testing the safety of gas lines. But in the regulatory state, profit seekers aren't free to seek out new methods or try out new materials (not without government permission, anyway). They have to stick to the code no matter what. This closes off entire avenues to experimentation, competition, and innovation by wealth creators.

Imagine if the same approach had been taken with computers back in the 1970s. What if the government came up with a Computer Code that mandated how computers were to be wired and powered and how memory was to be designed? Or what if it dictated how cell phones were designed in the early 1980s? There's little doubt we'd have missed out on decades of innovation that today we take for granted. The reason that the bulk of America's economy isn't as innovative as high tech is that it *has* been subject to the regulatory state's shackles.

More broadly, what we don't see when we look at today's regulatory state are all the entrepreneurs who decided not to start businesses because of the costs of regulation. We don't see the innovators who did not innovate because they were unwilling to seek (or unable to get) the permission of bureaucrats. We don't see the drugs that weren't produced, the factories that weren't constructed, the power plants that weren't built. It is hard to project how much better life would be if it weren't for the pernicious influence of regulations.

The fact is, the ability to produce higher-quality and safer products depends not on regulatory dictate but on the amount of knowledge, technology, and wealth in an economy. As an economy advances and grows richer, people can *afford* to buy safer and higher-quality goods—they can afford to buy the new Ford Focus loaded with the latest safety features rather than a forty-year-old VW Bug. It's probably no coincidence that rich countries have vastly lower traffic-related fatalities per capita than poorer countries.[13] By retarding economic progress and making us poorer than we would otherwise be, regulations actually make us less safe.

No system can eliminate the risks of living. But only under capitalism are you free to rationally assess and manage life's risks.

PROTECTING THE WORKER

Worker protection regulations govern things like unionization, wage rates, working hours, and working conditions. The basic idea is that employees are at the mercy of profit-seeking employers and that were it not for government (and unions backed by political power), they would still be working twelve hours a day in hazardous factories for subsistence wages.

We've seen in earlier chapters how distorted this picture is, how it is rooted in a false conception of the relationship between businessmen and workers, and how it ignores the fact that businessmen have to *compete* for labor by offering higher pay and better benefits (including a safer, more pleasant work environment). But the myth of the exploited worker is ubiquitous, so it's worth reviewing the actual facts concerning the rise in wages and working conditions since the beginning of the Industrial Revolution.

The starting point for any analysis of the conditions of workers during the early days of capitalism has to be the recognition that they voluntarily chose to work in those conditions and for those wages. No factory owner could force them to work—he could only offer rewards, which workers were free to accept or reject. By and large, people accepted, because they rightly judged the factories by what other opportunities were available to them. At a time before capitalism had created the vast abundance we take for granted today, the factories were often the best option available and, indeed, offered men and women the chance at a *better* life.

For most factory workers, the only real alternative was going back to the farms from which they had fled. Capitalism's critics have glamorized the pastoral life, but this ignores the brutal reality of the farm. Biologist Matt Ridley relates the not untypical story of William Turnbell,

> born in 1870, [who] told my grandmother that he started work at thirteen, for sixpence a day, working six days a week, from 6 a.m. to 6 p.m., usually outdoors whatever the weather, with just Good Friday, Christmas and half of New Year's day as his only holidays. On market days he started herding sheep or cattle to town, carrying a lantern, at 1 or 2 a.m.[14]

As economist Deirdre McCloskey notes, "There's a reason that most people, when given the choice, prefer to work under roofs and inside heated and air-conditioned offices and in busy cities."[15]

The factories, although relatively primitive, were a savior to many. It was not simply that the factories rescued them from the farm. The harsh fact was that, were it not for capitalist industrialization, many of those who made a living in the factories would not have been able to make a living at all. An agricultural society simply could not have sustained the growing population that capitalism fostered.[16]

It was capitalism, not government, that slowly improved life for workers. With new equipment and technology making workers more productive than ever, businessmen could afford to offer higher wages, better hours, and better working conditions. In fact, because businessmen had to compete for productive employees, they couldn't afford *not* to. (Recall Ford and the five-dollar-a-day starting wage.)

Even Karl Marx had to come to terms with the rising standard of living among workers. In the period between *The Communist Manifesto* (1848) and the publication of the first volume of *Capital* (1867), the real wage of factory workers had risen 17 percent while the average number of hours worked declined.[17] As one economist observes:

Marx's earlier writings argued that [workers'] absolute standard of living [under capitalism] falls. But in *Capital,* written in the face of indisputable evidence that workers were better off than they had been, he retreats, claiming only that workers have a smaller share of the wealth than before.[18]

It's worth repeating: The rise in workers' standard of living started *before* any government interventionist policies designed to come to their aid.

Capitalism didn't impoverish workers; poverty is mankind's natural state. Instead, by unleashing the wealth producers, capitalism transformed the way people thought about poverty. It was, for the first time in history, a problem to be solved, because, for the first time in history, it was a problem that *could* be solved.

So there was never a good reason for government to grant special, coercive powers to unions. But during the 1930s, it did. In a free market, of course, employees are free to unionize or not—and business owners are free to deal with unions or not; unions, like every other organization on a free market, are totally voluntary. But in 1932, President Hoover signed the Norris-La Guardia Act. The act (1) prevented businesses from asking, as a condition of employment, that workers not join unions; (2) exempted unions (but not business) from antitrust prosecution; and (3) eliminated the ability of employers to get federal court injunctions in cases of labor union coercion. In 1935, unions were given even more political power via the Wagner Act: Among other provisions, the act forced companies to recognize and bargain with labor unions and simultaneously allowed a majority vote to force *all* employees into the union, even if some preferred not to join. "The effects of the Act were immediate and dramatic," notes one economist.

Massive labor organizing occurred over the next two years, and in a period of extreme job scarcity and enormous unemployment, such that opportunities to change jobs to avoid unpleasant circumstances were essentially nonexistent, literally millions of workers who did *not wish to be unionized* were forced into unions. . . . In 1937 . . . the unions initiated a massive series of strikes to force wage rates up. *As a predictable result of these pervasive forced wage increases, the economy, which had been recovering since 1934, was shocked into deep depression in 1938.*[19]

Whether the downturn in the economy was actually caused by the Wagner Act, there is no question that it made a bad situation worse.

Today, the power of unions has much abated (although the power of government employee unions has exploded). Nevertheless, those sectors of the economy where unions continue to have power, such as the U.S. automotive industry, are suffering for it. Government-protected unions are notoriously hostile to productive workers. Protected from competition by government, with pay and promotions usually determined by seniority rather than ability, the incentive of each worker is to produce as little as possible—while anyone who dares show exceptional ability is chastised by his fellow workers "for making the rest of us look bad."

PUNISHING THE PRODUCER

So far we've been talking mainly about the groups allegedly helped by regulation. Now we turn to the greatest victims of the regulatory state: producers.

When Jill Bigelow and her husband decided to open Provecho, a Mexican restaurant in downtown Los Angeles, they knew regulation came with the territory. Every business-related construction project in L.A. has to go through a dozen different city departments, and restaurants have to go through even more, with fees running into the thousands of dollars—assuming everything goes smoothly. For Jill Bigelow, things did not go smoothly.

First she was ping-ponged back and forth between a plumbing inspector and the Department of Public Works to get a decorative water wall approved, with neither side being quite sure what approvals Bigelow actually needed. Then the department held up the approval process, insisting that Provecho was sitting on top of a landfill—even though the restaurant was in a high-rise office in downtown L.A. Then the city demanded that Bigelow replace most of her perfectly serviceable kitchen appliances—from refrigerators to coffee grinders—because they hadn't been certified by the Los Angeles Mechanical Testing Laboratory. Then came the coup de grâce.

In order to construct Provecho's restroom, Bigelow had to submit plans and sample materials to the city. The city approved the plans, and Bigelow built the restroom accordingly. After the construction was completed, a public health inspector decided that the dark brown tile did not have enough "reflective value" to enable him to assess whether it was sufficiently clean. Bigelow had two choices: tear out the tile and rebuild, or bar her employees from using the restroom. She was able to work out a deal with the building manager whereby she remodeled an existing restroom elsewhere in the building and designated it for her employees' use. As for her customers, the city was fine with *them* using the ambiguously clean restroom.

"In all," concludes Institute for Justice senior attorney Michael Bindas, "these and other problems delayed the opening of Provecho by five months and resulted in a cost overrun in the six figures."[20]

In a September 2010 interview, Whole Foods CEO John Mackey was asked about his company's merger with the Wild Oats grocery chain. "[I]t's been great," said Mackey. "Our Wild Oats same-store sales were up like sixteen percent in the second quarter." But when asked whether he would do the merger again, Mackey answered with an emphatic "No."

> We'll never do another merger that requires FTC approval. It was the worst experience of Whole Foods' corporate life. All my e-mails were examined by the FTC. The thirty million dollars in legal fees. . . . For what? To prove we weren't a monopoly? Everyone knows we're not.[21]

Under the government's 2010 "catch-share" fishing regulations, fishermen were hit with severe restrictions on the number of fish they could catch. By mid-2011, one New Hampshire fishing cooperative was already reporting $750,000 in lost business. The regulations destroyed countless jobs and even reportedly led some fishermen to commit suicide.[22] According to Hampton, New Hampshire, town manager Fred Welch, "If they don't do something to modify the fishing regulations, we won't have a fishing industry on the Seacoast."[23]

Regulatory horror stories like these are about as common as a cold. After a century of government controls piled on top of controls, anyone with the temerity to try to make a profit faces two challenges: the challenge of creating wealth and the challenge of obeying government authorities. Or: the challenge of mastering nature and the challenge of assuaging bureaucratic masters. In the name of fighting selfishness, the state treats profit seekers like convicted criminals and vests "public servants" with incredible amounts of arbitrary power.

Regulation, in short, is nothing more than government force directed at the minds of America's producers. It paralyzes their thinking, undermines their productivity, and restricts their ability to engage in voluntary, value-for-value trade.

Consider the effects of one of the worst, most arbitrary, most nonobjective, and uncontroversial regulations around today: antitrust.

Can a businessman organize and reorganize the division of labor as he sees fit—say, by merging with a competitor? No. Not if the Federal Trade Commission, or the Justice Department, or some jealous competitor objects.

Can a businessman set his prices so as to maximize his profits? No. If he sets his prices "too high," he could be guilty of "intent to monopolize." If he sets them "too low," he could be guilty of "predatory pricing" or "restraint of trade." And if he tries to play it safe and match his competitors' prices? Why, he could be guilty of "collusion."[24]

Can a businessman compete by becoming more innovative, efficient, and productive than his rivals? God help him if he does: That's proof the market is not "perfectly competitive." Indeed, the cardinal sin that provokes the antitrust authorities is: *incredible business success.* If you want a list of history's most successful companies, you would do well to look up companies accused of antitrust violations. In the tech industry, for example, which companies have come under the antitrust microscope? Microsoft, Intel, Google, Apple—the best of the best of the best. Under the threat of antitrust, innovation can occur only to the extent that enforcement is lax and inconsistent, and at a much slower pace than it would in a free market.

Antitrust, of course, is just one particularly perverse body of regulations. But the essence is the same. Shrink the range of options open to businessmen, force them to wade through a morass of often contradictory commandments, make them submit to endless costs and intrusive investigations—and expect them to go on producing, innovating, providing jobs, creating wealth. And if they should persevere and succeed? The same motives that lead us to shackle businessmen with regulations in the first place lead us to spit in their faces, denounce their greed, sneer at their profits, and damn them as selfish should they so much as protest the growing burden of the regulatory state.

Isn't this what we saw during the financial crisis? As we noted in chapter 4, regulators warped the price system through their manipulation of interest rates, they stick-and-carroted bankers into lowering their lending standards, they helped Fannie and Freddie buy up half the mortgage market, they made it profitable for Wall Street to leverage to the hilt—and then when it all came crashing down, we made businessmen Public Enemy Number One, vilified them, and slammed them with regulatory nightmares such as Dodd-Frank.

CONCLUSION: ANSWERING THE ARGUMENT FROM GREED

The Argument from Greed says that the profit motive leads businessmen to cut corners, take crazy risks, and lie, cheat, and steal their way to another buck—and that the only way to protect ourselves is to rein in the profit motive through ever more government regulation. Over the course of the preceding chapters, we have laid out our answer to that argument, which we can now summarize: *It isn't selfish to sacrifice others to yourself.*

A free market does unleash selfishness—not the range-of-the-moment irrationalism of a Bernie Madoff but of the rational, productive pursuit of life and happiness in a society of trade. The profit motive drives businessmen not to cut corners and slit throats but to invest, build, expand, create, produce. Free markets are about self-interest—not in the conventional sense, but in Ayn Rand's sense.

As we have seen, far from unleashing men's vices, the free market encourages the best among men and the best in men. It fosters their thought, their creativity, their ability, their ambition. The free market does not guarantee that everyone will be rational (nothing can guarantee rationality, since it's a free-will choice). Some businessmen will make stupid or immoral decisions. Others will resort to crime. But the free market provides the greatest protection possible from the irrational by leaving people free to avoid, denounce, and boycott those who make poor products and poor decisions and by bringing down the full weight of the government on anyone who violates others' rights.

What the Argument from Greed amounts to is this: In order to protect ourselves from the arbitrary power of businessmen, we have to give arbitrary power to politicians. But what we've seen is that the power of businessmen is not arbitrary. It is not the power to force others to bend to their will. It is economic power, *earned* through voluntary trade. The regulatory state—government force interjected into men's peaceful economic affairs—is not a necessity of human life. It does not protect the consumer or the worker. But arbitrary power placed in the hands of government bureaucrats does harm the rational and productive.

TWELVE
THE IMMORAL ENTITLEMENT STATE

I N AYN RAND'S NOVEL *ATLAS SHRUGGED,* ONE OF THE CHARAC-
ters describes how he once worked at a factory that tried to implement, faithfully and consistently, the Marxist principle of "From each according to his ability, to each according to his need."

> Do you know how it worked, that plan, and what it did to people? Try pouring water into a tank where there's a pipe at the bottom draining it out faster than you pour it, and each bucket you bring breaks that pipe an inch wider, and the harder you work the more is demanded of you, and you stand slinging buckets forty hours a week, then forty-eight, then fifty-six—for your neighbor's supper—for his wife's operation—for his child's measles—for his mother's wheel chair—for his uncle's shirt— for his nephew's schooling—for the baby next door—for the baby to be born—for anyone anywhere around you—it's theirs to receive, from di- apers to dentures—and yours to work, from sunup to sundown, month after month, year after year, with nothing to show for it but your sweat, with nothing in sight for you but their pleasure, for the whole of your life, without rest, without hope, without end. . . . From each according to his ability, to each according to his need.[1]

The worker goes on to describe how each person's need was determined by a company-wide vote. He recounts how, in the face of declining produc- tivity, the factory voted on who the best workers were—and made them work overtime (without pay) to keep the factory afloat. He explains how each worker did what he could to hide his ability, which would bring him nothing but longer hours, and to flout his ineptness and his need, which would bring him rewards.

> What was it they'd always told us about the vicious competition of the profit system, where men had to compete for who'd do a better job than his fellows? Vicious, wasn't it? Well, they should have seen what it was like when we all had to compete with one another for who'd do the worst job possible. There's no surer way to destroy a man than to force him into a spot where he has to aim at not doing his best, where he has to struggle to do a bad job, day after day. That will finish him quicker than drink or idleness or pulling stick-ups for a living. But there was nothing else for us to do except to fake unfitness. The one accusation we feared was to be suspected of ability. Ability was like a mortgage on you that you could never pay off. And what was there to work for? You knew that your basic pittance would be given to you anyway, whether you worked or not—your "housing and feeding allowance," it was called—and above that pittance, you had no chance to get anything, no matter how hard you tried.

In 2010, a Harris poll found that 42 percent of Americans believe that the slogan "From each according to his ability, to each according to his need" came not from Karl Marx but from the Founding Fathers.[2]

On one hand, it's pretty shocking that so many of our countrymen confuse history's preeminent defenders of freedom with its preeminent opponent. But on the other hand, who can blame them for being confused? After all, doesn't that slogan name the moral ideal behind so much of what our government currently does? Isn't it *need* that entitles people to Social Security? To Medicare and Medicaid? To unemployment "insurance"? To an education? To food stamps, farm subsidies, and home loans? Isn't the only difference between socialism and the entitlement state one of degree? Isn't the entitlement state simply the *inconsistent* implementation of Marx's dictum?

Well, yes—and that's the point. The entitlement state is fundamentally at odds with the system of government set up by the Founding Fathers. Theirs was a system based on the principle that each of us has the right to live for our own sake, to use our wealth as we see fit, to pursue our own

happiness. The entitlement state is based on the principle that need entitles people to your money and that their life is your responsibility.

The entitlement state, in short, is the product of the view that we have
a moral duty to sacrifice for the needs of others.

BEFORE THE ENTITLEMENT STATE

America has not always had an entitlement state. For the first 150 years or
so of this country's existence, there was no Social Security, no Medicaid or
Medicare; there were few public schools, and only minimal government
antipoverty measures. How did it work out? The rational and productive
thrived.

We've already seen how, in a relatively brief span, capitalism enabled
men to escape millennia of stagnation. For the first time in history, the lot
of the average man began to rise, as the burgeoning division of labor made
his work more productive and innovation gave birth to new goods, better
goods, and cheaper goods.

According to one textbook, "For most workers . . . the antebellum period was one of rising wages and higher standards of material well-being."[3]
The trend accelerated following the Civil War: Between 1860 and 1890,
real wages doubled.[4] This, even though the population was exploding. As
a result, people could afford to work *less*. In 1870, for instance, the average
worker worked 3,069 hours a year. But as his productivity increased, by
1913, he could enjoy a much-improved standard of living working only
2,632 hours.[5] Or consider this: In 1900, it took 56 minutes to earn enough
money to buy a half gallon of milk and over 107 *hours* to earn enough to
buy 100 kilowatt-hours of electricity; by 1930, it took only 31 minutes
and 11 hours respectively.[6] Life was hard (as it had always been), but for
anyone willing and able to work, life was getting better.

America was the land of opportunity, the place where the Carnegies
and Rockefellers could rise from rags to riches and where men of modest ability could live better than their fathers. But with new opportunities
came new challenges. Capitalism provided radical freedom—and so it demanded radical self-responsibility. In capitalist America, *you* were responsible for gaining the knowledge and skills necessary to make yourself into
a productive individual. You were responsible for finding a productive

career. If you lost your job, it was your responsibility to find yourself another one. If your job became obsolete, it was your responsibility to develop new skills. In a free economy, it was your responsibility to save your money to provide for life's unexpected twists and turns. It was your responsibility to provide for your own health care, your own retirement, your own children's education. You could turn to others for help, but you couldn't claim their help by right.

The great majority of people were able to meet these new challenges, and, thanks to the freedom that went along with it, they prospered to a degree unmatched in human history. (What else could explain why so many immigrants flocked to pre-entitlement America?) It was a minority of a minority who depended on assistance and aid. It's hard to pin down exact numbers, but in 1824, the Yates Report put the number of paupers in New York state at 22,111 (less than 2%)—6,896 of whom who were considered permanently in need of outside support.[7] (The entire population of the state in 1820 was 1.37 million.[8]) And sociologist Charles Richmond Henderson estimates that as of 1890, the ratio of paupers to population was 1,166 : 1,000,000 (0.1%).[9]

Whatever the exact figure, the evidence suggests that by the time the Industrial Revolution was in full swing, less than 1 percent of the adult population were paupers. And this small sliver was on the receiving end of an astonishing amount of private aid. By the mid-nineteenth century, groups aiming to help widows, orphans, and other "worthy poor" were launched in every major city in America. There were some government welfare programs, but they were minuscule compared to private efforts.

> In fact [writes historian Walter Trattner], so rapidly did private agencies multiply that before long America's larger cities had what to many people was an embarrassing number of them. Charity directories took as many as 100 pages to list and describe the numerous voluntary agencies that sought to alleviate misery, and combat every imaginable emergency.[10]

This of course does not count the massive amount of individual assistance that people took advantage of during this time. Most people who needed help, in fact, didn't rely on charity—they turned instead to their friends, families, and neighbors. But not, in most cases, right away. Typically people who hit tough times would first dip into their savings or the savings of immediate family members. They might take out loans and get their hands on whatever commercial credit was available. If that wasn't enough, other family members would be asked to find paying work. It was only after that point that people would generally seek out loans and gifts from their community.[11] Formal charity was almost always a last resort.

One of the most fascinating phenomena to arise during this time was mutual aid societies—organizations that provided *voluntary* protection against the risks that entitlements were created to address. These societies were not charities. They were private associations of individuals that offered an array of affordable member benefits, including life, permanent disability, sickness and accident, old-age, and funeral insurance.[12] These were not fringe institutions: Between 20 and 35 million Americans belonged to a mutual aid society in 1930, more than any other kind of organization besides churches.[13] Whom did these societies cater to? According to one contemporary source:

> [T]he middle-class workman, the salaried clerk, the farmer, the artisan, the country merchant, and the laborer [seeking to] insure their helpless broods against abject poverty. Rich men insure in the big companies to create an estate; poor men insure in fraternal orders to create bread and meat. It is an insurance against want, the poorhouse, charity, and degradation.[14]

Ask yourself: If the rational and productive could thrive without an entitlement state a century ago, how much easier would it be today, when Americans are incredibly richer? When more than three-quarters of *poor* Americans own at least one car, and more than 90 percent of them have a stove, refrigerator, and color TV,[15] who are the true beneficiaries of the entitlement state?

BORN OF IDEOLOGY

The entitlement state came into existence not because Americans were starving in the streets but because a growing number of Americans were ideologically committed to expanding the size and power of the state: They regarded the entitlement state as a *moral* imperative.

Influenced by the philosophy coming out of Germany, which was rabidly altruistic and collectivist, the American Progressives of the late nineteenth century attacked the Founding Fathers' ideals of individual rights and limited government. President Woodrow Wilson dismissed talk of inalienable individual rights as "a lot of non-sense."[16] Progressive Jane Addams declared that "we must demand that the individual shall be willing to lose the sense of personal achievement, and shall be content to realize his activity only in connection to the activity of the many."[17] They wanted to expand the power of government so it could redistribute wealth in the name of taking care of its citizens "from cradle to grave."

Above all, this goal required the government to become the primary source of poor relief. The Progressives said that, although there was abundant private charity, there were still people "slipping through the cracks." As much as was being done, writes Marvin Olasky in his fascinating history of American charity, *The Tragedy of American Compassion,*

> The question, nevertheless, continued to ring out: Why not do more? For many people dire poverty was only a short-term curse—but why did they have to suffer at all? Yes, charity and challenge aided individuals to escape from poverty, and yes, economic growth led to upward mobility, but was it fair that many citizens advanced slowly, and some not at all?[18]

Just as altruism tells an individual that however much he is sacrificing, his duty is to sacrifice more, the Progressives concluded that however much Americans were giving, morality required them to give more. Government would step in and do what private individuals could not or would not do.

Figures such as Benjamin Franklin had long criticized government welfare schemes for encouraging pauperism and for reducing the amount of private aid. The Progressives simply shrugged and declared that, in Olasky's words, "none of these reservations made any difference when newspapers were filled with gripping accounts of particularly worthy families living in poverty that could be helped by the proposed programs."[19] If need was an entitlement, as altruism said it was, then government's duty was to *act*—to supply that entitlement.

Besides, the Progressives argued, private charities were not sufficiently altruistic. At the time, most charities went to great lengths to distinguish between the deserving poor and the undeserving poor—those unable to support themselves and those who were simply unwilling. No one had a *right* to be supported at other people's expense, and it was thought that blindly handing out goodies would, in the long run, do more harm than good. Subsidize the unwilling, you get more unwilling. Charities thought it incumbent to encourage good habits in the needy so that they could, insofar as possible, become self-supporting.

The Progressives maintained that it was wrong for charities to distinguish between the unwilling and the unable. Who were they to decide which needs were genuine? It was selfish to blame the poor for being poor, the shiftless for being out of work, the drunkard for being out of control. True charity should be unconditional: "Give and ask no questions" went one maxim.[20] Demanding that a man work "was cruel, because a person who has faced a 'crushing load of misfortunes' should not be faulted if he does not choose to work."[21]

But did a lazy, shiftless bum really deserve other people's wealth? Absolutely, said the Progressives. As Edward Bellamy put it in his popular 1888 novel *Looking Backward: 2000–1887,* "By what title does the individual claim his particular share? . . . His title . . . is his humanity. The basis of his claim is the fact that he is a man."[22] Wealth is your birthright—never mind that if you don't produce it, someone else has to.

The conclusion from all this was simple: Government entitlement programs should "become the outer form of the altruistic spirit—the unselfish, loving, just nature of the new man."[23]

But when it came to building an entitlement state, the Progressives were largely unsuccessful. Their open attacks on the Founding Fathers, on capitalism, on individual rights—these were too much for most Americans. The entitlement state came into existence, and probably had to come into existence, dressed in sheep's clothing.

Franklin Roosevelt was, if anything, an exceedingly clever politician. Instead of presenting himself as an opponent of the Founding Fathers' ideals, he claimed to be their protector. Instead of claiming to throw out individual rights with his Big Government schemes, he claimed merely to be expanding them. He wasn't ending capitalism, it was said, but saving it.[24]

At a programmatic level, Roosevelt presented the New Deal not as a permanent shift in the American way of life but as a series of mostly temporary emergency measures. But selling Americans on Social Security, which was always intended to be permanent, was a tougher challenge.[25] To begin with, the original bill was packaged with more popular programs, such as child health services. It was also not touted as a bold new undertaking but simply as an expansion of existing (albeit relatively tiny) government aid programs for widows and orphans. Perhaps most ingeniously, Social Security's supporters portrayed the act not as a welfare measure but as an insurance program. (This was manifestly untrue. With genuine insurance, you voluntarily pay a fee that gives you a contractual right to a defined schedule of benefits. With Social Security, you have no contractual rights: Government can alter or rescind your benefits at will. That's to say nothing of the fact that your tax dollars are not invested in a retirement account but are used to pay current beneficiaries, Ponzi scheme style.) Decades later, Medicare would follow the same model.[26]

With the passage of the Social Security Act, America officially changed direction. The entitlement state was born, and with the New Deal as precedent, it would continue to grow. Once need was declared an entitlement, people very quickly started bandying about their need. As William Voegeli asks in his study of the entitlement state:

> Once the enterprise of positing that people have a right to a decent life
> is launched, on what basis can we tell people who repeatedly demand
> additions to the honor roll that some things are indeed conducive to a
> decent life but, at the same time, are not rights?[27]

No such basis, Voegeli correctly concludes, exists. The result was that old programs expanded, and new programs—Medicare, Medicaid, food stamps, and ObamaCare, among others—sprang up. Once altruism replaced the individual's right to pursue happiness as the ruling principle of American politics, the growth of government was unstoppable.

Today, we're seeing the climax of this trend: We're on the precipice of an entitlement crisis that threatens to cripple your standard of living. Who will pay the price? The same people who have been paying the price since the New Deal established the entitlement state: the rational and productive. "From each according to his ability, to each according to his need."

THE ENTITLEMENT STATE'S WAR ON THE
RATIONAL AND PRODUCTIVE

The entitlement state is enormously expensive: Americans pay $1 trillion a year just to help the poor.[28] It's important to be clear on what effect this has on the lives of actual individuals, who are forced to spend a significant portion of their working hours toiling for other people's health care, other people's retirement, other people's food, other people's homes.[29]

In a division-of-labor economy, making the most of your life requires *money*. Whether you want to start a business, buy a house, take a trip, raise a child, eat a meal, watch a movie, or hike through a nature preserve, pursuing values takes cash. The more money you have, the wider your range of action and the greater your potential values. Whatever else is true of wealth redistribution schemes, one thing is for certain: They strip you of money you could use to make your life happier and more enjoyable.

Put it another way: When you are forced to shell out thousands of dollars a year to support others, your life gets worse. You may have to live in a high-crime neighborhood rather than a low-crime neighborhood. You may have to drive around in an old junker rather than a newer, safer car. You may have to put off starting your own business, or having kids, or changing careers.

If we reject the collectivist premise, then it's pretty obvious: Nothing can justify that sort of redistribution. On the individualist premise, a man's life is not interchangeable with the lives of others. If a rationally selfish individual is told that by surrendering his paycheck he will help "the economy," his attitude should be: "To hell with you; it won't help *my* economy!"

The entitlement state is fueled by altruism, but it is sustained in part by a pseudo–self-interested cover-up: You are buying security, you'll be told. No matter what happens to you, the entitlement state will make sure your basic needs will be taken care of. There is an alleged consolation prize for your service and sacrifice: You have a duty to bear responsibility for the needs of others, but don't worry—some other sucker will take responsibility for yours.

In reality, what the entitlement state buys you is not security but insecurity: The government gets to dispose of your wealth as it sees fit, and you get to cross your fingers and hope there will be something left for you. Really, how secure can you be when the government is sitting on $100 trillion of unfunded liabilities? How secure do you feel knowing that it has no legal obligation to pay you a single solitary dime in Social Security and that its "trust fund" is as trustworthy as a used car salesman with a gambling problem? Real security comes from freedom, economic progress, and the choices you make to forge yourself into a responsible, self-supporting being.

We've seen how, in the days before the entitlement state, the rational and productive dealt with life's inherent risks without going on the dole. They didn't reach into their neighbors' pockets. We shouldn't either. The rational and productive have no use for "security" purchased at the expense of freedom. Who, then, does?

Consider Social Security. In a free market, the rational and productive individual would think about his own long-range plans and interests. He might rationally decide that he loves working and never wants to retire, or that he'd rather invest his current income in growing his business today and start saving once he has established himself. When he does invest, he will think carefully about where to park his savings, consulting experts, and judiciously diversifying. For him, Social Security is all downside. All its alleged benefits he could attain much better on his own. Who then wants Social Security? The irrational and the unproductive. The person who can't be bothered to think four weeks into the future, let alone forty years. The person who won't save a dime or who, having cobbled together a few dimes, forgoes diversification and invests them all in Enron. Social Security, and the entitlement state more broadly, institutes a basic injustice: The rational and productive are sacrificed for the sake of the irrational and unproductive, just as altruism demands. "From each according to his ability, to each according to his need."

The worst victims of this injustice are the *ambitious poor*. By sapping immense amounts of capital from productive individuals, the entitlement state cuts down on the number of businesses that get launched, the number of jobs that get created, the amount of economic progress that takes place, the amount of economic opportunity that is available. Although the wealthy can get by in an entitlement state, at least for a while, those wishing to climb out of poverty often cannot.

The problem is not only economic. English psychiatrist Theodore Dalrymple describes the plight of intelligent children born in the British slums:

> [T]he culture of the slums is monolithic and deeply intolerant. Any child who tries to resist the blandishments of that culture can count on no support or defense from teachers or any other adult, who now equate both freedom and democracy with the tyranny of the majority. Many of my intelligent patients from the slums recount how, in school, they expressed a desire to learn, only to suffer mockery, excommunication, and in some instances outright violence from their peers. One intelligent child of fifteen, who had taken an overdose as a suicidal gesture, said she was subjected to constant teasing and abuse by her peers. "They say I'm stupid," she told me, "because I'm clever."[30]

This anti-ability atmosphere, which is ubiquitous in America's underclass communities, is not a consequence of poverty per se. Before the growth of America's entitlement state, there were plenty of poor communities. But such communities tended to prize intelligence, effort, and ambition and to look down on dependency.[31] The entitlement state, however, teaches people that being taken care of by others is their right and that all of their problems are caused by factors outside of their control. So it's no mystery why people on the government dole tend to resent anyone who takes responsibility for his own life and lifts himself up by his own initiative. Such a person is a reproach: His very existence communicates to his neighbors, "It's your own fault you're a failure."[32]

But the full story is even uglier. This entitlement mentality was not an accidental side effect of a well-intentioned entitlement state; it was deliberately cultivated by the entitlement state's proponents.

FROM ENTITLEMENT MORALITY TO ENTITLEMENT MENTALITY

We would hate to live in the world supporters of the entitlement state think we live in. In that world, most of us are powerless, helpless, hopeless, and pathetic. We are on the verge of destitution, and it is only by banding together and expropriating the wealth of the powerful and lucky few that we are able to limp through life.

But that world is a myth. It doesn't exist, not in a free economy. When entitlement statists insist that all of us could potentially be welfare recipients, it's simply not true. (Set aside conditions of mass unemployment: Significant and sustained unemployment is a result of the regulatory-entitlement state, not the free market.[33])

To the extent an economy is free, your ability to support your own life depends fundamentally on your character: Have you made yourself into a rational and industrious trader? The person who exercises the virtues of rational selfishness can support his life—whether he is of modest intelligence and ability or a productive genius. If it were otherwise, mankind would never have survived in the first place.

The truly unable do exist—but they are the rare, rare exception, and a tremendous amount of help is available to them in a capitalist world. A free, prosperous economy is inevitably a benevolent one. A capitalist society is a society that can be created only by individuals who value human life. Although collectivists sing hymns to "humanity," their hostility to the individual makes them, in practice, totally indifferent to human suffering. (See, on this point, the atrocities perpetrated by Communist regimes—and the widespread support for communism among Western intellectuals even after its crimes became known.) A free economy, by contrast, is one in which individuals grow and prosper together, where one person's gain is another's gain, and where economic progress more and more turns poverty and hardship into the exception. In such a society, it would be bizarre if there were widespread indifference toward those who suffered through no fault of their own. Under capitalism, if you're worried about the fate of those in need, the answer is simple: You are free to help them.[34]

The basic moral issue, however, is that no one has a *right* to other people's wealth. Need—even the genuine need of someone suffering through no fault of his own—is not a license to steal. In Ayn Rand's words, "misfortune is not a claim to slave labor; there is no such thing as the *right* to consume, control, and destroy those without whom one would be unable to survive."[35] Does that sound harsh? Consider your own case: Would *you* regard your hardships as a claim on your neighbor's paycheck? Would you march into his house waving your need around like a gun and helping yourself to his food or his medicine cabinet? Would you think very much of a neighbor who did that to you?

The entitlement state is based on a very different assessment: It is based on the idea that the world owes you a living, that your need is a claim, and that if you did show up on someone's doorstep, gun in hand, demanding a handout, then in principle you would be in the right, while the person who wanted to keep his money would be *wrong.* In the words of Saint Ambrose, "You are not making a gift of your possessions to the poor person. You are handing over to him what is his."[36] Or, as Beulah Sanders, then vice president of the National Welfare Rights Organization, put it in her 1970 testimony in front of the Senate: "You can't force me to work! You'd better give me something better than I'm getting on welfare."[37]

The entitlement state breeds this sort of entitlement mentality. If altruism is right and need is an entitlement, then people *should* regard themselves as entitled to others' wealth—they *should* treat their needs as claims on other people's lives. If altruism is right, then so long as I've done nothing, accomplished nothing, achieved nothing, my life is your responsibility. "From each according to his ability, to each according to his need."

In championing this notion of collective responsibility, the entitlement state is fundamentally opposed to individual responsibility. What's astonishing—and tragic—is how hard entitlement statists had to work to beat that sense of individual responsibility out of Americans.

"I'd rather be dead and buried than be on the dole" went the common refrain during the Great Depression.[38] Even when government aid was available, few people at the time took it. It was considered shameful—a last, desperate resort. Roosevelt himself understood that "in this business of relief we are dealing with properly self-respecting Americans to whom a mere dole outrages every instinct of individual independence," which is one reason he focused on creating make-work projects.[39]

The entitlement statists regarded this attitude—individual pride and individual responsibility—not as a virtue to be respected but as a problem to be overcome. One contemporary bemoaned that "established mores are undoubtedly too deeply embedded in the American spirit for the present to permit adequate relief to employable persons without requiring work in return." But, he added, "traditional attitudes toward 'getting something for nothing' are already undergoing change."[40]

So they were. The real shift came in the 1960s when, to borrow Olasky's eloquent phrase, the entitlement statists declared war on shame. Before the 1960s, "the public dole was humiliation, but thereafter young men were told that shining shoes was demeaning, and that accepting government subsidy meant a person 'could at least keep his dignity.'"[41] It worked. To take just one measure: AFDC (Aid to Families of Dependent Children) rolls jumped from 4.3 million in 1965 to 10.8 million in 1974—despite the fact that America as a whole had become wealthier during that time.[42]

The disintegration of individual responsibility has not been confined to the poor, however. Many middle-class Americans regard themselves as entitled to a work-free retirement and an unlimited supply of medical care to be financed by future taxpayers. Many wealthy Americans regard themselves as entitled to subsidies, bailouts, and handouts, regardless of how many dumb decisions they've made. And like the underclass, a growing number of Americans don't celebrate others' success—they view it with cynicism, derision, and envy.[43]

Here's the bottom line. If the vast majority of people can and should be responsible for their own lives, if even those unable to support themselves have almost always been able to find support in a world without an entitlement state, and if the entitlement state was created in order to impose altruism, then the entitlement state is geared not to the unable but to the *unwilling*. The sacrifice of the rational and productive to the irrational and unproductive is not some unintended consequence of a noble plan—it is the whole point.

CONCLUSION: ANSWERING THE ARGUMENT FROM NEED

Behind the many justifications and rationalizations offered for the entitlement state is a single basic premise: A person's need entitles him to other people's wealth. This is the Argument from Need. We can now summarize the answer we've laid out over the course of this book: *It is wrong to sacrifice yourself to others.*

Why are Americans willing to take on millions and billions and trillions in debt in order to give people unearned handouts? Because they guiltily believe that other people's need is a claim. The only way to counter that belief is by *knowing* that morally you have a right to exist for your own sake and that the morality of need—altruism—is wrong.

People require a sense that what they're doing is right—that the kind of life they're living is good. But the only morality most of us know is altruism, and it says that the good is to sacrifice values. Few Americans try to follow altruism consistently. Instead, we spend our time tending to our lives and trying to pursue our own happiness. We go to work, to the gym, to the beauty parlor, to the baseball game—all for the sake of what we think will bring us joy. But our altruistic notions of morality tell us: This is not what we should be doing in life. We feel guilty, and so we try to assuage the guilt. We give money to beggars to prove we care about "the poor." And we vote for politicians who promise to dole out benefits to "the needy." "Worrying," in columnist Mark Steyn's words, "is the way the responsible citizen of an advanced society demonstrates his virtue: he feels good about feeling bad."[44]

To see altruism at work in the nation's political arguments, look for what William Voegeli calls the "to be sure" line in statements by the political right. Whenever a self-described free marketer advocates some sort of limitation on Big Government, he trips over himself to make sure no one mistakes him for a cold, selfish bastard who believes in eliminating the entitlement state. *We need to end Big Government . . . but, to be sure, we need reasonable regulations and wealth redistribution programs.* Voegeli quotes Ronald Reagan's 1980 acceptance speech, in which Reagan declares that "it is time for our government to go on a diet"[45]—but, to be sure, not a starvation diet:

> It is essential that we maintain both the forward momentum of economic growth and the strength of the safety net beneath those in society who need help. We also believe it is essential that the integrity of all aspects of Social Security are preserved.[46]

Voegeli goes on to observe:

> Effectively, conservatives concede that the . . . premises that undergird
> the critique of the welfare state are going to be honored at a high level
> of abstraction, but not followed very far in practice. "We mean it, but we
> don't *mean it* mean it." As government expands, liberty contracts, and
> as government contracts, liberty expands—but, don't worry, voters, the
> sorts of contractions of government that would expand liberty by weak-
> ening the safety net or stop government from providing opportunity are
> not part of our plans.[47]

The Argument from Need is irrefutable—so long as the morality of
need is considered unquestionable. The only way to resolve this conflict
is to reject altruism and to self-confidently defend your moral right to
pursue "more": more wealth, more pleasure, more happiness for *yourself.*

We don't need the entitlement state to survive and thrive—we need
freedom. The entitlement state is not a safety net but a spiderweb that en-
snares and strangles rational, productive, creative, ambitious individuals
in order to dole out unearned rewards to the irrational and unproductive.
It is fundamentally at odds with the capitalist way of life, a way of life captured with powerful eloquence in the mid-twentieth century by politician
Dean Alfange:

> I do not choose to be a common man. It is my right to be uncommon—
> if I can. I seek opportunity—not security. I do not wish to be a kept citi-
> zen, humbled and dulled by having the state look after me. I want to take
> the calculated risk; to dream and to build, to fail and to succeed. I refuse
> to barter incentive for a dole. . . . I will not trade freedom for beneficence
> nor my dignity for a handout. I will never cower before any master nor
> bend to any threat. It is my heritage to stand erect, proud and unafraid;
> to think and act for myself, enjoy the benefit of my creations, and to face
> the world boldly and say, this I have done. This is what it means to be an
> American.[48]

THIRTEEN
YOU ARE NOT YOUR BROTHER'S HEALTH CARE PROVIDER

AS SHE CELEBRATED THE PASSAGE OF OBAMACARE, THEN–
House Speaker Nancy Pelosi announced, "Today, we have the opportunity to complete the great unfinished business of our society and pass health insurance reform for all Americans that is a right."[1]

The view that health care is a right, and not something that has to be earned and paid for, isn't new. It's merely the Argument from Need applied to health care: The fact that people *need* health care gives them a *right* to health care.

But health care is not a right. Rights, as we've seen, are freedoms of action—there can be no *right* to something that someone else has to produce. And genuine rights protect us from coercion—the only means of implementing a "right" to health care is by coercing doctors, nurses, and taxpayers.

Yet health care, we're told, is something that each of us desperately needs, and unlike other needs (food, for instance), the market does a lousy job of providing it. Indeed, we hear every day that America is suffering from a health care *crisis,* where costs are rising, quality is declining, and the only solution is to cede more power to the government.

Few issues are as important—and as misunderstood—as health care. In this chapter, we'll examine some of the causes of our health care problems. What we'll see is that this crisis, like the financial crisis, is not a consequence of a free market (which does not exist in health care) but of more than half a century of government intervention, done in the name of a "right" to health care.

Along the way, we'll show how the ideas we've discussed in this book—the good, the bad, and the ugly—work out in practice. And we'll see how Ayn Rand's defense of the profit motive and the profit system lays the groundwork for a real and lasting solution to America's health care crisis.

THE CAUSE: HOW GOVERNMENT MADE HEALTH CARE INEFFICIENT AND EXPENSIVE

Americans are understandably worried about the rising cost and deteriorating quality of health care. And they've been told that the explanation of this health care crisis is our free market in medicine. As Lyndon B. Johnson's deputy assistant secretary for health put it in 2004, "Today's dysfunctional health care system is a palpable example of the lessons that come from our national obsession with markets at all costs."[2]

But markets don't lead to mounting bureaucracy and skyrocketing prices—they lead to ever-improving customer satisfaction and steadily declining prices. It's no accident that we don't have a computer crisis, or a hair salon crisis, or a veterinary crisis. Nor is it an accident that we *did* have a housing and financial crisis. Along with housing and finance, medicine is one of the most regulated industries in the United States, and those regulations take center stage in precipitating the health care crisis.

As with the financial crisis, health care regulations are mind-numbingly complex, and we don't pretend to give a full account of all the factors—not even all the important factors—that are responsible for today's ills. Our focus is restricted to some of the most obvious instances of government malfeasance driving up costs and driving down quality.[3]

If you want to identify the cause of spiraling prices and declining quality, Econ 101 tells you to look for government interference with the law of supply and demand. And if ye seek, ye shall find. In the name of providing Americans with a "right" to health care, government has artificially driven up demand by promoting the perverse idea that health care should be free, and it has restricted supply by regulating those tasked with doling out this "free" care. Here are a few select examples.

GOVERNMENT-PROVIDED HEALTH COVERAGE

Even before ObamaCare, more than half of U.S. health care spending was government spending.[4] (Some free market.) The primary drivers? Medicaid, which provides health subsidies to the poor, and Medicare, which subsidizes the elderly.

Medicare and Medicaid were products of LBJ's Great Society. "You can help build a society," said Johnson, "where the demands of morality, and the needs of the spirit, can be realized in the life of the Nation."[5] What altruistic morality demanded was reaching into the pockets of some Americans in order to give unearned health care to other Americans. We acquiesced.

Shortly after Medicare was passed, Americans were told it would cost $12 billion in 1990. Actual cost? $98 billion. Americans were also told that the cost of Medicaid would be less than $1 billion in 1992. Actual cost? $17 billion.[6] Costs have only continued to balloon. Writing in 2011, analyst Mary Meeker observes:

> As more Americans receive [government] benefits and as healthcare costs continue to outstrip GDP growth, total spending for the two entitlement programs [Medicare and Medicaid] is accelerating. Over the last decade alone, Medicaid spending has doubled in real terms, with total program costs running at $273 billion in F2010. Over the last 43 years, real Medicare spending per beneficiary has risen 25 times, driving program costs well (10x) above original projections.... Amid the rancor about government's role in healthcare spending, one fact is undeniable: government spending on healthcare now consumes 8.2% of GDP, compared with just 1.3% fifty years ago.[7]

As we've noted elsewhere, this course is not sustainable. Meeker again: "By 2025, entitlements plus net interest payments"—Medicare is the chief cost—"will absorb all—yes, all—of [the federal government's] revenue, per CBO [Congressional Budget Office]."[8]

By lowering the direct cost of health care to tens of millions of Americans, this massive wave of government spending leads to an incredible rise in the demand for medical services and, along with it, an incredible rise in health care costs.

Take one of the biggest sources of Medicare costs—care in the last year or two of life. On a free market, where you are responsible for your own health care, you could have all the end-of-life care you were willing to pay for. Some people, no doubt, would save and spend much of their money on prolonging their lives for a few extra months. Others would not, so they could enjoy a higher standard of living during their healthy years. Medicare says that no such decision is necessary—spend freely today and have your neighbors pick up your health tab tomorrow.[9]

And the tab is enormous. It costs about $10,000 a day to treat a patient in the intensive care unit, where about 20 percent of Americans will spend their last days, weeks, or even months.[10] It's hardly surprising, then, that 25 percent of Medicare costs are incurred by patients during the last year of their lives—and almost half of that amount is incurred in the last thirty days.[11]

By the way, it's estimated that many of these expenses have virtually no impact on patient welfare.[12] That should come as no surprise. When people are spending their own money, they tend to carefully assess whether they're getting sufficient bang for their buck. When they're spending other people's money? Not so much. This is not a problem confined to end-of-life care. The less that people are responsible for their own health care costs, the less incentive there is to demand efficient care.

The government's massive intrusion into medicine has directly affected not only the cost of medicine, but also the quality—and not for the better.

Medicare was initially intended to be nothing but government-provided health insurance. According to Robert Ball, one of the founding fathers of the program, "our posture at the beginning was one of paying full costs and not intervening very much in how hospitals, at least the better ones, conducted their business." But that was never tenable. With the government paying the bills, it was not going to allow the system to function without "oversight." As Ball later admitted: "We did have to interfere."[13]

That interference included, among other things, the diagnosis-related group (DRG) system—that is, price controls. Prior to the 1980s, the government had been paying hospitals on a cost-plus basis (i.e., the government guaranteed them a price that covered all their costs plus an additional markup to allow for profit), which predictably led hospitals to incur as many costs as possible. Under the DRG system, hospitals received a flat fee for each patient, regardless of what that patient cost to treat. Once again, the results were predictable: Hospitals now had an incentive to give each patient as *little* care as possible. To add insult to incomprehension, the DRG system was labeled a "market-based solution" to health care costs.[14]

We've all seen medical dramas that feature ongoing conflicts between doctors, who want to give their patients the best care possible, and hospitals, which seem committed to giving each as little care as possible in order to hold down costs. Such conflicts are all too real, and it is government controls like the ones we've described that are responsible. A market, of course, does lead to cutting costs—for a given level of quality (e.g., finding cheaper ways to make a magnetic resonance imaging machine). But what the DRG system illustrates is that a controlled market, to the extent it cuts costs, does so by *cutting* quality. Things will only get worse with ObamaCare, which gives the government even more power to decide how doctors treat patients.

The meaning and ultimate result of such a policy is eloquently captured in *Atlas Shrugged*, in which a brain surgeon explains why he refuses to practice under government-controlled medicine.

> "Do you know what it takes to perform a brain operation? Do you know the kind of skill it demands, and the years of passionate, merciless, excruciating devotion that go to acquire that skill? *That* was what I could not place at the disposal of men whose sole qualification to rule me was their capacity to spout the fraudulent generalities that got them elected to the privilege of enforcing their wishes at the point of a gun. I would not let them dictate the purpose for which my years of study had been spent, or the conditions of my work, or my choice of patients, or the amount of my reward. I observed that in all the discussions that preceded the enslavement of medicine, men discussed everything—except the desires of the doctors. Men considered only the 'welfare' of the patients, with no thought for those who were to provide it. That a doctor should have any right, desire or choice in the matter, was regarded as irrelevant selfishness; his is not to choose, they said, but 'to serve.' That a man who's willing to work under compulsion is too dangerous a brute

to entrust with a job in the stockyards—never occurred to those who proposed to help the sick by making life impossible for the healthy. I have often wondered at the smugness at which people assert their right to enslave me, to control my work, to force my will, to violate my conscience, to stifle my mind—yet what is it they expect to depend on, when they lie on an operating table under my hands? . . . Let them discover the kind of doctors that their system will now produce. Let them discover, in the operating rooms and hospital wards, that it is not safe to place their lives in the hands of a man they have throttled."[15]

Medicare, Medicaid, and all the rest don't simply drive up health care costs—they cost us the best, brightest, most rational minds: minds that will not take orders from bureaucrats.

PERVERSE TAX INCENTIVES

We don't buy food, diapers, or car insurance through our employers, so why in the world do most of us buy health insurance this way? It's not because it's more efficient for every car dealership and paper towel manufacturer to learn the ins and outs of administering a health insurance plan. It's because we can buy health insurance through our employer with pretax dollars. No such luck if you want to buy your own health insurance package.

Under this setup, our employers pay all or most of the cost of our premiums, hiding from us—the consumer—a significant portion of the cost. The effects are predictable: We demand more medical insurance and use more medical services than we otherwise would. Notice the bizarre phenomenon of paying for routine checkups with insurance, when insurance is by its nature designed to protect against unexpected, costly tribulations. The costs of administering our "pay-for-everything-with-insurance" system are immense. There's a reason we don't use car insurance to pay for oil changes.

In total, patients today pay on average only $0.14 of each dollar of medical care.[16] Think about that. If people had to pay only $0.14 for each dollar spent on food, how do you think they would behave? Would they shop for bargains? Or would they gorge themselves on steak, lobster, and caviar? Would they carefully economize? Or would they pack their fridges and pantries, knowing full well much of it would spoil before it's eaten? When medical costs are so hidden, note Cato Institute scholars Michael Cannon and Michael Tanner,

> [patients] have less need to weigh the benefits of health care against the costs. They end up utilizing care that provides little value. Since patients are not very particular about costs and benefits, neither are providers. They have less incentive to focus on innovative ways of meeting patients' needs or to furnish information about prices and quality. Costs cannot help but rise in such a market.[17]

LICENSING

Government licensing of medical practitioners actually stretches back to colonial times, although licensing was largely eliminated or ignored from 1830 until about 1850.[18] Did that lead Americans to blindly lap up snake oil from charlatans? Hardly. Reputation ruled, with individuals putting their trust in doctors who spent years *earning* their trust. Indeed, part of the rationale for abolishing licensure laws in the nineteenth century was the desire to *protect* quality; as Oliver Wendell Holmes put it, no profession was allowed "to be the best judge of its own men and doctrines."[19] Licensing, in other words, was recognized to be little more than a way to establish an anti-competitive guild system.

But eventually the Argument from Greed took hold and led people to expect that, without government controls, money-hungry quacks would flood the medical industry. They turned to the state, which was ready to intervene. After all, it reasoned, ensuring Americans' "right" to health care involved more than just paying the bills; it involved defining what constituted "suitable" medical care.

Today, you can do virtually nothing in the medical industry without some license or certification. Even many routine medical services must be performed by licensed doctors rather than nurses, paramedics, and physicians' assistants—despite the fact that study after study has shown that the effect on medical outcomes is negligible. Why shouldn't you be free to have your strep throat diagnosed or your broken arm set by a nurse practitioner for a fraction of the cost? No satisfactory answer has ever been given.[20]

The more personnel who have to be licensed, and the more strenuous the licensing process, the worse the results. According to former American Medical Association president William Allan Pusey, "As you increase the cost of the license to practice medicine you increase the price at which the medical service must be sold and you correspondingly decrease the number of people who can afford to buy this medical service."[21] One estimate suggests that medical licensing costs about $6.5 billion a year, $4.7 billion of which ends up as higher incomes for licensed medical professionals.[22]

INSURANCE REGULATION

In a free market, competition leads producers to seek out new and innovative ways to cut costs. But competition and innovation are hard to come by in today's health insurance market. Health insurance companies are some of the most regulated companies in America. (That's no surprise, given our culture's view of selfishness: Since health insurers address some of our most vital concerns, it is critical to protect us from their dangerous "greed.")

Consider each state's laundry list of insurance mandates. We aren't talking about ObamaCare's individual mandate, which forces us to buy insurance whether we want to or not. These state mandates dictate what coverage must be offered in the insurance packages citizens are permitted to buy. Rules vary from state to state, but here are some common mandates:

- Benefit mandates dictate what treatments, procedures, and diagnostic tests an insurance package has to cover. Even if you're young, don't want kids, and don't drink, these mandates can force you to pay top dollar for a package that covers everything from in vitro fertilization, to liver transplants, to alcohol rehab.
- Mandatory guaranteed issue forces insurance companies to insure anyone, regardless of his personal or medical history.

- Guaranteed renewability requires that policies be renewed, even for high-risk customers, so long as their premiums are paid.
- Guaranteed community rating forces insurance companies to insure everyone at the same rate, regardless of crucial differences in things like age, habits, or health. (In most cases, insurance companies today are subject to modified community rating standards, which allow some minor price differentiations.)[23]

Imagine if the same rules applied to car insurance. Imagine if you had to buy an insurance package that covered car washes, window tinting, and hydraulic systems. Imagine if car insurance companies had to cover everyone, charging the same price to you and to the half-blind alcoholic with fifteen DUIs to his name. The net result of this kind of insurance regulation is pretty obvious: higher costs, fewer options, less supply.

To make matters worse, in order to prevent individuals from "getting around" these mandates, health insurance companies are prevented from competing across state lines. If you are a Virginia resident and you want to buy a cheaper health insurance package available to consumers in Delaware, you're out of luck.

To summarize: Government intervention in the name of a "right" to health care drives up costs and cripples quality. Such intervention—not any government *failure* to make health care a right—is the cause of the health care crisis. The reason millions of Americans can't afford insurance, and many more are struggling to pay their bills, isn't because of our free market in health care but because of our *unfree* health care market. Where supply and demand aren't skewed by government intervention, these problems don't exist. Lasik eye surgery, for instance, is wildly popular. Its cost plunged from roughly $2,200 per eye in 1998 to $1,350 in 2004. "Why the price decline in this market and not others?" asks economist Alex Tabarrok.

Could it have something to do with the fact that laser eye surgery is not covered by insurance, not covered by Medicaid or Medicare, and not heavily regulated? Laser eye surgery is one of the few health procedures sold in a free market with price advertising, competition and consumer driven purchases.[24]

If government intervention is the cause of the health care crisis, it doesn't take Dr. House to identify the cure.

THE CURE: TOWARD A FREE MARKET IN HEALTH CARE

There are three crucial steps to ending Big Government: defining clearly the goal (what would a truly free market look like?), defining an agenda for getting there from here (how do we disentangle government from the market?), and waging a powerful defense of that program. How might such an approach work in health care?

If the problem in American health care is government intervention in the name of a "right" to health care, then the solution is economic freedom in recognition that health care must be *earned* through production and trade. And if the goal is to have a system in which rational and productive individuals can best produce and pursue health care, and in which the rights of doctors and patients are consistently protected, then the goal must be a *fully* free market in medicine.

There is a unique difficulty in discussing free market medicine: Medicine as we know it arose at the tail end of America's freer days. Although it was the scientific and technological discoveries made possible by freedom that gave birth to modern medicine, modern medicine did not come into its own in an era of freedom but in

> an era suffused with progressive reformers, socialists, trade unionists, and admirers of Bismarkian social insurance schemes, all unified in their devotion to decidedly murky forms of egalitarian social justice, and their conviction that central planning could cure most human ills.[25]

History can't give us a full sense of what the American health care system would look like absent today's dense web of controls, regulations, and government redistribution programs. And given that unchained markets are centers of innovation, trying to project today's system minus its chains can only approximate a truly free market in medicine. Here, however, is what a free market would *not* look like:

- A free market would not have government-enforced licensing of medical providers, which drives up costs by restricting the supply of medical personnel, with no corresponding benefit to consumers.
- A free market would not have widespread employer-based health insurance, which among other problems keeps people tied to jobs they would otherwise leave.
- A free market would not have perverse incentives for buying insurance that covers regular checkups and low-cost procedures, which is akin to using auto insurance to pay for oil changes.
- A free market would would not prevent people from buying inexpensive insurance that covered only catastrophic medical expenses; there would be no government insurance mandates forcing people to buy expensive packages that cover everything from in-vitro fertilization to massage therapy. Even in today's ultra-regulated, ultra-distorted market, catastrophic plans are available for as low as $29 a month—less than most people pay for their cell phone plans.[26]
- A free market would not have expensive, bureaucratic redistribution programs like Medicare, Medicaid, and SCHIP.
- A free market would not force emergency rooms to treat all comers, regardless of their ability to pay, which imposes tremendous costs on hospitals and has even led many hospitals to close their emergency rooms.
- A free market would not lead to skyrocketing prices and declining quality. As with personal computers, medical services would improve, and prices would decrease.

A free market in health care would look like nothing we're familiar with. Innovation would increase. Instead of costs spiraling out of control, they would tend to steadily decline, as profit seekers found new ways to cut costs without cutting services. Our range of options would explode: We would be able to find insurance packages tailored to our special needs, hospitals with clear pricing policies, competing (voluntary) licensing firms pushing medical standards higher and higher.[27] If you lost your job, you would not have to worry about losing your health care at the same time. Perhaps more important, health care would lose its bureaucratic tinge. We would no longer be numbers; our doctor would be working for us, not for our insurance company, and visiting a hospital would no longer feel like a trip to the DMV. Competition would put the customer back into the driver's seat, and you could count on better, friendlier, more humane service.

If we value medicine and the longer, healthier lives it makes possible, this should be our long-term goal: zero redistribution programs; zero regulations; full freedom of trade and of contract for doctors, hospitals, insurance companies, and patients.

But we can't do it overnight. How can we get there from here? There are many options, but here are some possible steps.

PATIENT PROTECTION AND AFFORDABLE CARE ACT

The Act, better known as ObamaCare, could be repealed totally and immediately.

MEDICARE

People have planned their lives around Medicare, so it's important that it be *phased out* over time. One approach is suggested by House Budget Committee chairman Paul Ryan. Under Ryan's Roadmap for America's Future, people currently over fifty-five would be able to use Medicare as it now exists. Retirees who are currently fifty-five or younger, however, would receive a flat payment they could use to purchase private medical insurance, pocketing any leftover amount or paying out of pocket for any additional costs.[28] Unlike the Ryan plan, however, we would advocate reducing the payment over time. For instance, the first wave of retirees might receive $11,000 a year with which to buy health insurance, with that amount shrinking every two years until it is eliminated.

Another possible reform would be an opt-out provision. Economist Thomas Woods suggests "that upon reaching age sixty-five, people should be given the choice of (1) participating in Social Security and Medicare or (2) for the rest of their lives, be completely exempt from income, gift, and estate taxes."[29] Whether enough people would opt for the latter option to make it workable is an open question.

LICENSING

The government could immediately remove the most irrational licensing restrictions. Patients would be able to elect to have basic procedures performed by trained nonphysicians.[30] The government could begin to allow competition in licensing and to allow the total privatization of licensing services within five years. This adjustment period would give entrepreneurs time to start developing private standards for voluntary medical licensing and would allow consumers to start assessing the reliability of such certification companies (the way we already assess things like car safety today). Consumers who were wary of these new certification companies would remain free to patronize doctors certified by the American Medical Association.

HEALTH INSURANCE

The government could immediately end restrictions on purchasing health insurance across state lines and end the incentive for employer-based health insurance by allowing individuals to purchase health insurance with pretax dollars. At the same time, it could free insurance companies to offer whatever insurance packages they see fit, without expensive and pointless mandates.

MEDICAID

The last reform we advocate would be the abolition of Medicaid. Only once the other reforms start to bring down the cost of health care would it become feasible to do so. Immediate changes, however, are possible. Health care expert John Goodman gives ten suggestions for Medicaid reform, including moving to a block grant system: Instead of the federal government matching states dollar for dollar in Medicaid spending, states would receive a defined contribution toward Medicaid, encouraging thrift.[31]

There are countless options for how to unwind government's grip on health care, and we don't claim that our suggestions are necessarily the best. Our purpose rather is to name what should be the ultimate goal—total freedom in health care and health insurance—and indicate some possible, practical steps for getting there.

CONCLUSION: FREEING THE UNFREE HEALTH CARE MARKET

In mid-2011, the House voted on Representative Ryan's budget. Ryan was the first prominent politician to put forward a serious proposal for dealing with the oncoming entitlement crisis. His plan came under heavy attack, above all for daring to propose changes to the budget-busting Medicare entitlement. The plan is "immoral," insisted critic Michael Tomasky. To support curtailing the entitlement state is to advocate "atrocious treatment of the less fortunate in society."[32] Others denounced "the heartless GOP" and decried Ryan's "war on the weak."[33] "[T]hose in power are morally obliged to preference the needs of the poor," said a group of Catholic academics in a sweeping condemnation of the Ryan budget.[34]

What was the response from the plan's supporters? They sidestepped the moral issue, limply pleading that although it would be ideal to leave entitlements untouched, the deficit just won't allow for it. This played right into the hands of critics, who noted that if balancing the budget was all that was at issue, then it was disingenuous to cut entitlements while taking tax hikes off the table.

> Viewed as an effort to reduce the debt [wrote columnist Jonathan Chait], Ryan's plan makes little sense. Many of its proposals either have nothing to do with reducing deficits (repealing the financial-reform bill loathed by Wall Street) or actually increase deficits (making the Bush tax cuts permanent).[35]

The right had no answer, and the Ryan plan—which wasn't even close to a free market proposal—went down in flames.

What lessons can be drawn from the Ryan bloodbath? Above all, you cannot skirt the moral issue. If altruism is right, and you truly are your brother's keeper, then it *is* wrong—indeed, monstrous—to cut the entitlement state.

To cut health entitlements, and more broadly, to defend a fully free market in health care, you need to be able to overcome four basic challenges:

1. Americans think our current busted system is an essentially free, essentially private market in medicine.
2. They cannot project what a genuine free market system would look like and how it would function.
3. They do not trust doctors, hospitals, and health insurance companies to operate without government controls.
4. They regard it as self-evident that the existence of people with unmet medical needs constitutes a moral and political imperative for others to satisfy those needs.

The mainstream right cannot overcome those challenges: It neither understands nor endorses laissez-faire medicine and could not wage a moral defense of such a program if it did. But a new right—a right inspired and fueled by Ayn Rand's moral defense of capitalism—could.

A new right would be able to explain to Americans what it stood for. It would be able to name the actual causes of today's health care crisis, to explain how a truly free market would end that crisis, and to define a plan (like the one we describe above) for moving us toward that ideal.

A new right would be able to articulate why health care is not, and cannot be, a right. It would be able to make the moral case for a free market in health care. During the debate over ObamaCare, left-wing blogger Ezra Klein asked why the Obama administration was relying on the argument that its plan would save the government money rather than supposedly ethical notions like "equal treatment for everybody." "What happened to the moral case for health-care reform?" he wondered, taking it for granted that a moral debate would work to the advantage of the left.[36] A new right would welcome such a debate.

- It would welcome a debate between those who demand "equal treatment for everybody" (except those who are to be *unequally* taxed to pay for it) and those who demand equal *freedom* for Americans to purchase as much health care as they can afford.
- It would welcome a debate between those who believe it's proper to force some people to pay for the health care needs of others and those who believe that individuals should pay for their own health care or else appeal to private charity.

- It would welcome a debate between those who think doctors should be made into state employees, taking orders from bureaucrats who will decide which tests to perform and which treatments to offer, and those who believe that doctors have a right to offer their services to willing consumers on a free market.
- It would welcome a debate between those who appeal to an entitlement mentality that demands the unearned and those who believe in paying for what they get.

The Free Market Revolution would unleash a self-confident, idealistic movement to liberate American medicine. It would put the interventionists on the defensive. For the first time they would be called on to justify why you are your brother's health care provider.

FOURTEEN
STOPPING THE GROWTH OF THE STATE

I N EARLY 2011, NOBEL LAUREATE AND *NEW YORK TIMES* COL-
umnist Paul Krugman laid out his diagnosis of the basic split in
American politics. America is deeply divided, he said, not over pragmatic
issues—not over the details of this or that policy—but by two fundamentally different *moral* outlooks.

On one side, said Krugman, are those who believe the entitlement state
is morally superior to laissez-faire capitalism. On the other side are those
who believe that individuals have a right to keep the wealth they earn,
and that the entitlement state is the moral equivalent of theft. "There's no
middle ground between these views," Krugman concluded. "[W]hat we're
talking about here is a fundamental disagreement about the proper role
of government."[1]

Krugman was correct in every respect but one. He equated "the other
side" with today's mainstream right. But today's mainstream right shares
the same basic premises of the mainstream left. Both call on government
to use force to control Americans, control the economy, and redistribute wealth in the "public interest." Both are unequivocal supporters of
America's regulatory-entitlement state.

The "other side" Krugman describes is not the political right as it exists but the right as it could be and should be.

WHY ONLY RATIONAL SELFISHNESS WILL DO

Writing in 1980, philosopher Harry Binswanger, a friend and student of
Ayn Rand's, predicted that without a moral footing, the swing to the right

was doomed to fail. Although Americans oppose statism, he observed, they "give their conscious allegiance to . . . altruism"—a moral code that "is patently incompatible with capitalism." He continued:

> To visualize the predicament of America, imagine passengers riding on a train which, they have been told, is taking them to a distant utopia. At first all seems well, but as the train moves closer to its destination, the scene outside the windows becomes ominously bleak. Finally, the passengers catch sight of the destination in the distance. Instead of utopia, they see hungry children, chain gangs, and, in the far distance, the barbed wire and sentry posts of a concentration camp. Frightened, angry, they attempt to negate their forward motion by running back *inside the train*. The attempt, of course, is hopeless; to save themselves, the passengers must get off the train altogether.

The bottom line was that, so long as altruism remained unchallenged, the swing to the right could amount to nothing more than short-term backpedalling.[2]

Binswanger's warning was prescient. The swing to the right, as we've seen, did not stop the growth of the state. The right did not have a clear, pro-capitalist agenda—and it could not defend the agenda it had. As a result, it could not achieve real or lasting success.

Ayn Rand laid out her agenda: She stands for laissez-faire capitalism—built on the foundation of the morality of rational selfishness and its uncompromising defense of the profit motive. Nothing short of this, we have argued, will enable us to change course.

But there are many others who claim to oppose Big Government and who assure us that it is possible to do so without so radical a goal and without challenging conventional moral views.

In the run-up to the 2010 elections, the Republicans produced a document intended to unify the party and provide a plan of action once in power. They called it A Pledge to America.[3] It was an astonishing document—it claimed to call for revolutionary change in government, yet it didn't advocate a single policy that anyone to the right of Michael Moore could find objectionable.

It vowed to cut the size of government—down to *2008*'s record-high levels.

It vowed to fight regulations—by "requiring congressional approval of any new federal regulation that may add to our deficit and make it harder to create jobs."

It vowed not to end or even cut entitlements but to *protect* them.

It did vow to repeal ObamaCare but promised to keep one of its most destructive and unjust measures—the law requiring insurance companies to cover people with preexisting conditions.[4]

With few exceptions, and rhetoric aside, the Republican mainstream has made terms with Big Government. This led one leftist to complain that:

> Progressives routinely denounce their right-wing opponents as "free market fundamentalists." . . . Progressives have to stop doing propaganda service for the right. There are no free market fundamentalists here; everyone recognizes the need for a big role for government in the economy.[5]

Of course it's hardly surprising that politicians are ducking controversy. But what about free market intellectuals? Do they fare any better?

Perhaps the most notable defense of capitalism in recent years is Arthur Brooks's *The Battle,* a book that has received endorsements and accolades from political heavyweights, from Paul Ryan to Newt Gingrich to Karl Rove. *The Battle* has become a battle cry for those seeking to reverse the alarming expansion of government under Obama.

The book has undeniable merits. Brooks recognizes that capitalism requires a moral defense. He recognizes that that moral defense should be grounded in the pursuit of happiness. And he grasps that the pursuit of happiness requires the pursuit of earned success, not unearned loot. But for all its virtues, *The Battle* suffers from two major problems: It doesn't actually advocate capitalism, and it cannot defend the pursuit of happiness.

The Battle claims to be for capitalism, but beyond a few vague generalities ("respects private property, encourages industry, celebrates liberty, limits government, and creates individual opportunity"), it never explains what capitalism is.[6] Elsewhere, however, Brooks makes it clear that whatever he does mean, he does not mean laissez-faire.

> What we must choose is our aspiration, not whether we want to zero out the state. Nobody wants to privatize the Army or take away Grandma's Social Security check. Even Friedrich Hayek in his famous book, "The Road to Serfdom," reminded us that the state has legitimate—and critical—functions, from rectifying market failures to securing some minimum standard of living.[7]

According to Brooks, our choices seem to be anarchy or a regulatory-entitlement state. He doesn't even acknowledge the possibility of another alternative—a fully free, laissez-faire capitalist system. Instead he takes it for granted that we need some regulation, some entitlements, some controls—and says only to keep them small.

It can't be done. The fact is that regulation or wealth redistribution, whatever the amount, counts on a certain justification—and the logic of that justification will determine its ultimate scale.

Why do we need some regulation? *Because we cannot trust greedy profit seekers.*

Why do we need some entitlements? *Because we have a duty to sacrifice for the needs of others.*

Why can't we get rid of the regulatory-entitlement state? *Because that would unleash selfishness.*

We've seen where those ideas lead. It's irrelevant that people like Brooks may genuinely want to keep government small, regulation light, and wealth redistribution to a minimum. The logic of their premises leads irresistibly to a state that restricts selfishness and redistributes wealth more and more.

Brooks sees that government has grown out of control, and he wants to roll it back. But he cannot endorse laissez-faire because that would force him to confront the conflict between the pursuit of happiness and the morality of need. And so he is forced to endorse the very principles that are undermining capitalism.

Brooks's shortcomings aren't unique. Although many intellectuals have understood that freer markets raise men's standard of living, they cannot or will not understand and defend the morality of trying to raise one's own standard of living (i.e., the profit motive). Thus, few of them are true champions of laissez-faire.

Milton Friedman, for instance, declared: "Freedom cannot be absolute. We do live in an interdependent society. Some restrictions on our freedom are necessary to avoid other, still worse, restrictions."[8] Some of these restrictions included wealth redistribution for social goals like unemployment insurance, regulations including anti-monopoly and environmental controls, and government control of the monetary system.[9] Friedman even praised "compassion for the less fortunate . . . through government—provided that . . . it is an expression of a desire to help others."[10] What *wouldn't* that include? Your guess is as good as ours.

F. A. Hayek, meanwhile, insisted that "nothing has done so much harm to the [free market] cause as the wooden insistence . . . on certain rough rules of thumb, above all the principle of laissez faire."[11] Hayek certainly avoided that trap. Like Friedman, he called for government regulation of monopolies and government control of the monetary system, and claimed that a free economy was compatible "with an extensive system of social services."[12]

Intellectuals like these may seek a significant curtailment of illegitimate government programs—but not because they view the capitalist way of life as noble. On the contrary, they regard the profit motive as something to be downplayed and limited insofar as possible, and so they inevitably come to demand that the profit system be limited as well.

Theory, meet practice: Prominent libertarian blogger Megan McArdle recently mused that it may be in the "public interest" for the state to seize your entire estate after you die. The only question that matters, she says, is whether she and other would-be central planners think "the social benefits that inheritance conveys . . . offset its drawbacks."[13]

This kind of outlook cannot ground capitalism. Capitalism does not demand the sacrifice of the individual to the group. It does not allow 51 percent of society to decide that its interests can be achieved by sacrificing the other 49 percent. No one has the power to abolish private property (or confiscate it after you die) in the name of the "public interest." Capitalism leaves each individual free to decide how to make the most of his own life (and it will not stop him if he chooses to make a mess of it).

THE BASIC CONTRADICTION

No one in today's political or intellectual mainstream can end Big Government because no one is willing to challenge today's mainstream moral views. But to fully understand why only rational selfishness will do in the fight against Big Government, we need to go back to the beginning and ask: Why didn't the Founding Fathers' original vision endure?

America is the greatest nation in history. It was the first nation created on the basis of an idea: the sovereign individual's right to exist for his own sake, to live his own life, to pursue his own happiness. But there was a contradiction in the founding.

Although the Founders recognized man's political right to pursue his own happiness, they could not defend man's *moral* right to pursue his own happiness.

Although they created a nation geared toward what would become the capitalist way of life—the rational, productive, selfish pursuit of profit—neither they nor any subsequent philosopher could defend that way of life as the ethical ideal. Jefferson himself declared:

> Self-interest, or rather self-love, or *egoism* . . . is no part of morality. Indeed it is exactly its counterpart. It is the sole antagonist of virtue, leading us constantly by our propensities to self-gratification in violation of our moral duties to others.[14]

This was a lethal contradiction, one that could not be maintained indefinitely. Capitalism is about the selfish pursuit of rewards; altruism is about selfless sacrifices. Capitalism is about profit seeking; altruism is about alms giving. Capitalism is about independence; altruism is about dependence. Capitalism rewards self-reliance, self-assertiveness, and self-esteem; altruism denounces any trace of pride, rewarding instead the poor and the meek. Capitalism is the system that enshrines rationality, productiveness, and trade; altruism enshrines faith, hope, and charity. And capitalism defies altruism's basic principle—your need entitles you to values others have created—by forbidding men from seizing the unearned.

"The signs of the conflict" between altruism and capitalism "and of the toll it was to exact from the distinctively American political approach were evident at the beginning," observes philosopher Leonard Peikoff.

> They were evident in Jefferson's proposal for free public education; in Paine's advocacy of a number of governmental welfare functions; in Franklin's view that an individual has no right to his "superfluous" property, which the public may dispose of as it chooses, "whenever the Welfare of the Publick shall demand such Disposition"; etc.[15]

Altruism was the hole in the dike: It allowed a trickle of government intervention into the Founders' system from the start, and unless the hole was patched—unless altruism was jettisoned completely and laissez-faire introduced—it was inevitable that the trickle would become a torrent.

The defenders of capitalism did not jettison altruism. Instead, in a pattern that persists to this day, they attempted to paper over the contradiction—first by trying to mix altruism and selfishness, then by trying to mix capitalism with state intervention.

Altruism does not demand total self-sacrifice, they said. You can pursue your interests—a little. You can enjoy life—a little. You can make money—a little. Just make sure you're not too healthy, too happy, or too successful—make sure you put the welfare of others above your own *part of the time.* In short, write Austin Hill and Scott Rae, you must distinguish "between self-interest, which [is] legitimate, and selfishness, which [is] evil. . . . There is nothing wrong with pursuing [your] self-interest, as long as it is balanced and within limits."[16]

This defense of a mixed morality leads inexorably to demands for a mixed economy.[17] Capitalism is great, write Hill and Rae—but, *to be sure,* "regulation and capitalism are not fundamentally inconsistent." We must "acknowledge that the market has limits, that forms of regulation are necessary, and that a variety of institutions need to contribute to setting limits on the pursuit of self-interest."[18] Laissez-faire? How decidedly unfair!

But eclecticism is unsustainable over the long run. In the end, consistency wins out. More-consistent altruists seize the moral high ground from less-consistent altruists. More-consistent statists seize the moral high ground from less-consistent statists. *That* is the pattern by which government grows.

Since [writes Rand] both [U.S. political] parties hold altruism as their basic moral principle, both advocate a welfare state or mixed economy as their ultimate goal. Every government control imposed on the economy . . . necessitates the imposition of further controls, to alleviate—momentarily—the disasters created by the first control. Since the Democrats are more consistently committed to the growth of government power, the Republicans are reduced to helpless "me-too'ing," to inept plagiarism of any program initiated by the Democrats, and to the disgraceful confession implied in their claim that they seek to achieve "the same ends" as the Democrats, but by different means.[19]

AYN RAND AND THE FREE MARKET REVOLUTION

What capitalism has lacked since its inception is *moral idealism*.[20] Whatever the defenders of capitalism said, the one thing they would not say was that capitalism is good, great, *noble*. They couldn't say it, since to do so would have required challenging the morality of need and upholding the nobility of rational self-interest and the profit motive.

By their silence [writes Rand]—*by their evasion of the clash between capitalism and altruism*—it is capitalism's alleged champions who are responsible for the fact that capitalism is being destroyed without a hearing, without a trial, without any public knowledge of its principles, its nature, its history, or its moral meaning. It is being destroyed in the manner of a nightmare lynching—as if a blind, despair-crazed mob were burning a straw man, not knowing that the grotesquely deformed bundle of straw is hiding the living body of the ideal.[21]

If there is to be a real movement to stop the growth of the state, it will be one shaped by the ideas of Ayn Rand. Only Rand's morality of rational selfishness can resolve the contradiction at the root of the founding and provide the idealism, the consistency, and the intellectual clarity necessary to end Big Government.

This is the Free Market Revolution. It is a revolution in the way we think about capitalism. It involves completely reconceiving what a free market is, how people function and succeed in one, and how to morally evaluate the capitalist way of life. It's a revolution in the way we think about self-interest, the profit motive, the profit system.

But transforming this intellectual revolution into a viable political movement will not be easy. It will require challenging today's bankrupt mainstream. Americans need to reject the worn-out slogans of altruism, recognize that each of us has a moral right to pursue our own happiness, and demand that our leaders start moving in the direction of complete, unregulated, laissez-faire capitalism.

We will be told that laissez-faire is pie in the sky, utopian, politically unrealistic. We will be told that what America needs are politically feasible solutions to our short-term problems. There is a nugget of truth buried in this objection. We *are* fighting for an ideal—but it is an achievable ideal. But to achieve it will take time. America's regulatory-entitlement state did not come into existence overnight, and it cannot be ended overnight. Our goal should not be to extinguish Big Government tomorrow. But there can be no viable short-term solutions without a long-term program. It's time to define that program.

Our long-term program must be to establish a limited government based on the principle of individual rights, with its economic concomitant, a fully free market. This will require, among other steps:

- The ultimate abolition of all entitlement programs including Social Security, Medicare, Medicaid, and public education
- The abolition of all government controls on business
- The privatization of all property, including public lands, utilities, and roads
- The repeal of all business subsidies and other forms of corporate welfare
- The resurrection of private money (i.e., a gold standard), the abolishment of the Federal Reserve, and the establishment of free banking
- A restoration of freedom of trade and sanctity of contract.

In short, our goal must be the total separation of state and economics.

Achieving these goals will take time. It would be wrong, for instance, to abolish Social Security tomorrow when people have planned their lives around the promise that they will receive government assistance in old age. It may take a generation or two before America can achieve a fully capitalist system.

What immediate steps *should* we advocate? In chapter 13, we laid out a sample program for moving toward freedom in health care. Similar plans need to be developed for every part of the economy and defended with intellectual and moral self-confidence.

Would such a program win widespread acceptance tomorrow? No, it wouldn't. Although many Americans today do not like the direction this country is heading, most still believe that we can return permanently to the policies of 2008, 1998, or 1988. We can't. Those policies led unavoidably to where we are today. The controls bred crises that led to further controls. The cries of "need" only intensified as the entitlement state expanded. As James Madison warned more than two hundred years ago, "[O]ne legislative interference is but the first link in a long chain of repetitions; every subsequent interference being naturally produced by the effects of the preceding."[22] A mixed economy is inherently unstable—it moves either toward complete state control or toward complete capitalism.

Nor should we want to return to the regulatory-entitlement state of the last several decades. Capitalism works. It creates material prosperity and the freedom to make the most of your life. That is what Americans have to be convinced of. We must come to understand what capitalism is, why it is practical, and why it is profoundly moral. Above all, we must grasp that the Argument from Greed and the Argument from Need are fundamentally wrong: They are based on a distorted, incorrect view of selfishness.

The attack on selfishness is an attack on the pursuit of happiness, and it is over the pursuit of happiness that the battle for America's future will be waged. We need to fight for economic freedom not on the grounds that it promotes GDP, or the "public interest," or any other collectivist ideal. We need to fight for it on the grounds that your life belongs to you: Each of us has an inalienable right to act on our own judgment, to produce and trade free from force, for the sole purpose of making our own lives as successful and joyous as they can possibly be. We have to be unequivocal in rejecting the notion that we are a means to the ends of others—or that others are a means to our ends.

The battle for America's future is an *intellectual* battle. It requires fighting for the ideas that freedom depends on. George W. Bush was wrong: Freedom is *not* written on the heart of every human being. To value freedom is a profound intellectual and moral achievement. The man who values freedom is the man willing to take full responsibility for his own life: for his own health care, his own retirement, his own career, his children's education, his own success and happiness. He is the man willing to live independently, by his own productive effort, by his own rational judgment. Remember that freedom arose only during the Enlightenment, when men valued reason, science, individualism, progress, and life on this earth.

The first step to changing this country's direction, then, is to educate yourself. Learn the case for capitalism. Learn its history, its economics, its philosophic foundation. Read the great economists. Read the Founding Fathers. Above all else, read Ayn Rand.

When you know your case, then make it: Speak out, in whatever way and on whatever scale is open to you. Tell people what capitalism is. Tell them how it works (and has worked). Tell them why capitalism is *good*.[23]

That is what's required to change the world.

Stop focusing on the hypocrisy of the left (or the right)—it is not hypocrisy that is destroying our freedom but the moral ideal of sacrifice.

Stop pretending that this country can be saved by lowering taxes, eliminating fraud and waste from government, and a few other inoffensive policies. Lasting change will require fundamental change—it will require rejecting the entire altruist-collectivist-statist framework of the last 120 years.

Stop buying in to the attempts of conservatives to tie capitalism to religion. Capitalism is the system of selfishness—not of selfless service to God. History shows that the greater religion's influence is on a culture, the less free it becomes.

Stop trying to make terms with the mixed economy. When you accept room for a little coercion in human affairs, a little regulation of business, a little welfare for individuals, you concede that self-sacrifice is a virtue, selfishness is an evil, and capitalism—the system of self-interest and the profit motive—is immoral.

Stop demonizing the rich, big business, and the profit motive—and stop defending them on the grounds of the service they render the poor or society. Recognize that growing richer requires no justification other than man's right to make the most of his time on earth. And if you are rich and successful, stop apologizing for your wealth—if you earned it, it is a *moral* achievement.

Stop letting the enemies of capitalism claim the moral high ground. There is nothing noble about altruism, nothing inspiring about the initiation of force, nothing moral about Big Government, nothing compassionate about sacrificing the individual to the collective. Don't be afraid to dismiss those ideas as vicious, unjust attacks on the pursuit of happiness, and self-confidently assert that there is no value higher than the individual's pursuit of his own well-being.

A long line of men, from Aristotle to the Founding Fathers to Adam Smith, made it possible for America, for a few brief, shining decades, to approach the capitalist ideal. Ayn Rand has articulated the exact nature of the capitalist way of life and *why* it is an ideal. She has shown why the profit motive is morally *good*—and that the sacrificial code of altruism, which cannot successfully be reconciled with capitalism, is *wrong*. That is what must be fought for in order to stop the growth of the state.

Is there any hope of victory? At a time when the state is growing out of control and the economic situation is bleak and getting bleaker, many Americans sense that we are on the wrong path. And more and more, they are turning to one thinker. "At the end of the day," said the man whose rant on the floor of the Chicago commodities exchange launched the Tea Parties, "I'm an Ayn Rand-er."[24] Rick Santelli isn't the only one. Today hundreds of thousands of Americans—from high school students to congressmen—are reading Ayn Rand. Her ideas are being discussed and debated everywhere—from the classroom to the Internet to the coffee shop. Not a day goes by that she isn't mentioned in some news story or opinion piece. If there was ever a chance to change Americans' view of capitalism, now is the time.

In 1776, when the Founding Fathers declared their independence from Britain, they were committing themselves to what many thought was an impossible goal: fighting and defeating the mightiest military power on earth. Nevertheless, they believed in their cause, in a nation based on individual rights, and so they pledged their lives, their fortunes, and their sacred honor to that cause.

Today, our odds are slim, but by any objective measure, they are probably better than the odds the Founders faced. The fight won't be easy. It will require the most profound conviction, effort, and integrity. It will require putting everything on the line.

The Founding Fathers were willing to put everything on the line.

We are willing to put everything on the line.

We hope you are, too.

DISCUSSION QUESTIONS

INTRODUCTION

- The authors say they do not like the term "Big Government." Why do you think they nonetheless use the term?
- The authors claim that ending Big Government will require changing the ideas that cause government to grow. Do you think most people agree that ideas determine our political and economic policies? What are other possible explanations for why countries end up with the policies they do?

CHAPTER 1: THE INCREDIBLE UNSHRINKING GOVERNMENT

- The authors offer some evidence that government intervention is increasing. What are other examples and indications of this trend?
- The authors argue that economic freedom is responsible for today's "amazing, amazing world." What are some other possible explanations? How would a critic of capitalism reply to this claim?
- What was the "swing to the right" and why do the authors think it failed to achieve its stated aims? Do you agree?
- The authors pin the blame for the economic problems of the 1970s on government intervention. Are there other possible explanations?
- According to the authors, the Tea Party rebellion "does not know what it stands for or even fully what it is rebelling against." How would you assess the Tea Party?
- Why do you think the authors started the book the way they did? What are other ways they could have started?

CHAPTER 2: WHY GOVERNMENT GROWS

- What, according to the authors, is "the least controversial idea in our culture"? Why is it uncontroversial?
- Do you think that capitalism is a selfish system? Why do most people regard that as a bad thing?
- According to the authors, the Argument from Greed leads to the growth of the regulatory state, and the Argument from Need leads to the growth of the entitlement state. Are there any forms of government intervention that you think don't fall in one of these two categories?

CHAPTER 3: WITH FRIENDS LIKE THESE . . .

- How does the authors' view differ from the commonly heard notion that the "invisible hand" of the marketplace turns individual vice into public virtue?
- Are there thinkers other than Ayn Rand who offer a moral defense of capitalism? What arguments do they make?
- Some argue that capitalism is moral because it inculcates virtue, by teaching men to be, for instance, thrifty, honest, hardworking, and responsible. What do you think of this argument?
- Why do you think so many of those who praise capitalism end up endorsing anticapitalist policies?

CHAPTER 4: THE 2008 HOUSING MELTDOWN: A CRISIS THAT GOVERNMENT BUILT

- Why do the authors say that the financial instruments that played a central role in the crisis were regulated when there were no specific regulations controlling those instruments?
- Given how regulated and controlled markets were during the 2000s, why did people find the claim that "capitalism caused the crisis" plausible?

CHAPTER 5: RETHINKING SELFISHNESS

- The authors claim that Bernie Madoff was unselfish. Why?

- Do you think producers such as Steve Jobs are selfish? Why or why not? How relevant do you think it is that they work to create products and services that other people find valuable?

CHAPTER 6: THE MORALITY OF SUCCESS

- The authors state that "This is not a book about ethics" and do not provide Rand's proof of her ethical code. Why do you think they omitted this? Do you think this undermines their argument?
- How would most people describe "happiness"? How do the authors describe it? How would you describe it?
- Why do so many people think that what makes a person happy is subjective? Why does Ayn Rand think it's objective?
- What, in Rand's view, is a sacrifice? Do you think most people use "sacrifice" in this way?
- Why does Rand say that sacrifice is evil? Why do most people think it's good?
- Some people claim that Rand's critique of altruism is based on a straw man, and that altruism is basically a synonym for kindness. Do you agree? Why or why not?

CHAPTER 7: THE BUSINESS OF BUSINESS

- The authors describe three functions of businessmen: entrepreneurship, management, and finance. Why are each of those roles important? Can you think of any other roles businessmen perform?
- Among businessmen, entrepreneurs tend to be held in the highest regard and capitalists (financiers) tend to be held in the lowest regard. Why is that?
- Why don't more people understand and appreciate the role of businessmen in the economy?

CHAPTER 8: THE NOBILITY OF THE PROFIT MOTIVE

- Why do you think this chapter came after chapter 7? Could the order have been reversed?

- Why are people suspicious of the profit motive?
- The authors argue that adhering to moral principles is crucial for success in business. Can you think of counterexamples? How do you think the authors would respond?
- Can you think of other examples of companies adhering to or violating the principle of rationality, productiveness, or trade? What were the consequences?
- In the final quoted passage, Hank Rearden, a character in Ayn Rand's novel *Atlas Shrugged,* says, "The public good be damned, I will have no part of it!" Why do you think Rearden says this?

CHAPTER 9: SELFISHNESS UNLEASHED

- What are the three pillars of capitalism, according to the authors? Can you give your own examples of the sorts of actions protected by each pillar?
- How do the pillars of capitalism relate to the three principles of rational selfishness discussed in the book?
- The authors say that "Capitalism is the system focused squarely on the individual." Many critics of capitalism, however, point out that we are social creatures who gain many benefits from living in society and so we have an obligation to give something back to society. Do you think that's a convincing argument? If not, how would you answer it?
- Why does Rand hold that only physical force can violate individual rights? Are there any ways people can harm you—even severely harm you—that don't involve force?
- How would you respond to the claim that "A hungry man isn't free"? Without food or an education, how can a person exercise their freedom?
- How would you define laissez-faire capitalism? What are some examples of policies consistent with laissez-faire? What are some examples of policies inconsistent with laissez-faire?

CHAPTER 10: THE DYNAMISM OF THE MARKET

- What do you think the "invisible hand" metaphor is intended to capture? Do you think it's a good metaphor or not?

- Why do the authors claim that the division of labor "is inextricably connected to the institutions of capitalism"? Can this claim be reconciled with the fact that there seems to be a division of labor in controlled economies?
- How does the authors' definition of competition contrast with the idea of "perfect competition"?

CHAPTER 11: THE REGULATORY STATE AND ITS VICTIMS

- How would you define regulation? How would you distinguish it from an objective law?
- The authors argue that a free market without any regulation would lead to safe products. Why do they think so? Do you agree? What is the best argument in favor of safety regulation?
- Some people claim that responsible companies have nothing to fear from regulation. Would you agree?
- What are some arguments in favor of regulation the authors don't address? How do you think they would respond to those arguments?

CHAPTER 12: THE IMMORAL ENTITLEMENT STATE

- The authors argue that entitlements are not only unnecessary, but actually harmful. How might entitlements harm individuals? Are there any ways in which they help?
- Is it ever appropriate to redistribute a relatively small amount of wealth to people who are genuinely unable to support themselves?
- What would happen to the unable in a world without entitlements?

CHAPTER 13: YOU ARE NOT YOUR
BROTHER'S HEALTH CARE PROVIDER

- Two chapters in the book are devoted to concrete issues: the financial crisis (chapter 4) and the health care crisis (chapter 13). Why do you think these issues are such fertile ground for an argument about capitalism?
- What factors do the authors say are primarily responsible for rising costs and declining quality in health care? Can you think of other factors?

- The authors note that a free market in medicine has never existed, but claim that a free market would be superior to today's system. Do you agree with their argument and with the evidence they provide?
- How would Ayn Rand respond to the claim that many foreign countries have government-run medicine, yet have better health outcomes (longer life expectancy, lower infant mortality, etc.) than the United States?

CHAPTER 14: STOPPING THE GROWTH OF THE STATE

- The authors claim that the only way to convince people to embrace capitalism is to change the way they think about morality. Do you agree? Why isn't it enough to show that capitalism makes people better off than any other system?
- Some altruists claim capitalism and altruism *are* consistent: capitalism, after all, makes everyone better off, especially those most in need. Do you think that's a convincing argument? What do you think the authors would say?
- Why do the authors say that "The battle for America's future is an *intellectual* battle"? Can you think of other strategies for fighting for free markets?

NOTES

INTRODUCTION

1. Ayn Rand, "About the Author," *Atlas Shrugged* (New York: Plume, 1999).
2. For instance, Deirdre N. McCloskey, *The Bourgeois Virtues: Ethics for an Age of Commerce* (Chicago: University of Chicago Press, 2006); Arthur C. Brooks, *The Battle: How the Fight Between Free Enterprise and Big Government Will Shape America's Future* (New York: Basic Books, 2010); Jay Richards, *Money, Greed, and God* (New York: HarperOne, 2009); Austin Hill and Scott Rae, *The Virtues of Capitalism: The Moral Case for Free Markets* (Chicago: Northfield, 2010); Steve Forbes and Elizabeth Ames, *How Capitalism Will Save Us* (New York: Crown Business, 2009).
3. McCloskey, *The Bourgeois Virtues*, p. 4.

CHAPTER 1

1. Rick Santelli, "I Want to Set the Record Straight," March 2, 2009, http://www.cnbc.com/id/29471026 (accessed March 21, 2011). We quote liberally from a variety of sources throughout this book. We take it as obvious that we don't necessarily agree with the quoted material in every detail.
2. Mark Murray, "Tea Party Attendance: 268,000-plus?" http://firstread.msnbc.msn.com/_news/2009/04/16/4426422-tea-party-attendance-268000-plus (accessed March 21, 2011).
3. Joe Markman, "Crowd Estimates Vary Wildly for Capitol March," *Los Angeles Times*, September 15, 2009, http://articles.latimes.com/2009/sep/15/nation/na-crowd15 (accessed February 27, 2012).
4. Quoted in Scott Rasmussen and Douglas Schoen, *Mad as Hell* (New York: Harper, 2010), p. 260.
5. Rasmussen and Schoen, *Mad as Hell*, p. 2.
6. David Brooks, "Big Government Ahead," *New York Times*, October 13, 2008, http://www.nytimes.com/2008/10/14/opinion/14brooks.html (accessed March 21, 2011).
7. Karl Rove, "Obama Versus Bush on Spending," *Wall Street Journal*, January 21, 2010, http://online.wsj.com/article/SB10001424052748704320104575015072822042394.html (accessed March 21, 2011); Office of Management and Budget, "Budget of the United States Government: Browse Fiscal Year 2011," http://www.gpoaccess.gov/usbudget/fy11/index.html (accessed February 27, 2012); "The American Recovery and Reinvestment Act of 2009," http://www.cbo.gov/ftpdocs/108xx/doc10871/AppendixA.shtml (accessed October 4, 2011).

8. Christopher Chantrill, "Government Spending Chart in United States 2006–2016," http://www.usgovernmentspending.com/spending_chart_2007_2017USp_XXs1 li111mcn_G0f (accessed March 2, 2012).

9. Brian Riedl, "Obama Budget Raises Taxes and Doubles the National Debt," Heritage Foundation Backgrounder #2382, March 9, 2010, http://www.heritage.org/research /reports/2010/03/obama-budget-raises-taxes-and-doubles-the-national-debt (accessed March 21, 2011).

10. Mary Meeker, *USA, Inc.: A Basic Summary of America's Financial Statements,* February 2011, http://www.kpcb.com/usainc/USA_Inc.pdf (accessed October 3, 2011), p. 247.

11. Breitbart.tv, "Congressman at Town Hall: 'The Federal Government Can Do Most Anything in This Country,'" August 12, 2010, http://www.breitbart.tv/congressman -at-town-hall-the-federal-government-can-do-most-anything-in-this-country/ (accessed March 21, 2011).

12. "Everythings Amazing & Nobodys Happy," YouTube, http://www.youtube.com /watch?v=8r1CZTLk-Gk (accessed April 13, 2011).

13. Fossey John Cobb Hearnshaw, ed., *The Social and Political Ideas of Some Great Thinkers of the Renaissance and the Reformation* (London: Dawsons of Pall Mall, 1967), p. 75.

14. "Maddison Data on Population & GDP," http://sites.google.com/site/econgeodata /maddison-data-on-population-gdp (accessed April 13, 2011).

15. Johan Norberg, *In Defense of Global Capitalism* (Washington, D.C.: Cato Institute, 2003), p. 75.

16. We've only just scratched the surface. For a whirlwind tour of human progress, see Matt Ridley, *The Rational Optimist* (New York: Harper, 2010), especially chapter 1.

17. Terry Miller and Kim R. Holmes, *2011 Index of Economic Freedom,* http://www .heritage.org/Index/pdf/2011/Index2011_Full.pdf (accessed April 13, 2011). These are very rough estimates of economic freedom, and we don't agree with the *Index*'s standards in every respect. However, they do suggest in broad terms the essential link between more freedom and greater prosperity.

18. Terry Miller and Kim R. Holmes, *2009 Index of Economic Freedom,* "Executive Summary," http://www.heritage.org/Index/PDF/2009/Index2009_ExecutiveSumma ry.pdf (accessed April 13, 2011).

19. Kim R. Holmes, Edwin J. Feulner, and Mary Anastasia O'Grady, *2008 Index of Economic Freedom,* http://www.cubasindical.org/docs/Indexofeconomicfreedom2008.pdf (accessed October 14, 2011); Terry Miller and Kim R. Holmes, "United States," http: //www.heritage.org/Index/country/UnitedStates (accessed January 12, 2012).

20. "Dow Jones Industrial Average (1900–Present Monthly)," http://stockcharts.com /freecharts/historical/djia1900.html (accessed October 3, 2011).

21. Edward D. Berkowitz, *Something Happened: A Political and Cultural Overview of the Seventies* (New York: Columbia University Press, 2006), pp. 55–56.

22. Jimmy Carter, "Energy and the National Goals—A Crisis of Confidence," *American Rhetoric,* July 15, 1979, http://www.americanrhetoric.com/speeches/jimmycarter crisisofconfidence.htm (accessed June 13, 2011).

23. John Micklethwait and Adrian Wooldridge, *The Right Nation* (New York: Penguin Books, 2005), p. 88.

24. Ronald Reagan, "First Inaugural Address," January 20, 1981, http://www.bartleby .com/124/pres61.html (accessed October 3, 2011).

25. William Voegeli, *Never Enough: America's Limitless Welfare State* (New York: Encounter Books, 2010), p. 9.

26. Quoted in John Samples, *The Struggle to Limit Government* (Washington, D.C.: Cato Institute, 2010), p. 173.

27. Samples, *The Struggle to Limit Government*, pp. 197–198.
28. Robert Pear, "Hatch Joins Kennedy to Back a Health Program," *New York Times*, March 14, 1997, http://query.nytimes.com/gst/fullpage.html?res=980CE4D81E39F9 37A25750C0A961958260&sec=&spon=&pagewanted=all (accessed June 13, 2011).
29. Richard Stengel, "Campaign '96: Compassion Is Back," *Time*, February 6, 1996, http://www.time.com/time/printout/0,8816,984050,00.html (accessed June 13, 2011).
30. Samples, *The Struggle to Limit Government*, pp. 174–176.
31. Edward H. Crane, "On My Mind: GOP Pussycats," *Cato Institute*, November 13, 2000, http://www.cato.org/pub_display.php?pub_id=4463 (accessed June 13, 2011).
32. George W. Bush, "Commencement Address at the University of Notre Dame in Notre Dame, Indiana," May 20, 2001, American Presidency Project, http://www.presidency.ucsb.edu/ws/index.php?pid=45893 (accessed October 3, 2011).
33. Karl Rove, "Obama's Government Shutdown Gambit," *Wall Street Journal*, April 7, 2011, http://online.wsj.com/article/SB1000142405274870401360457624674090756 5666.html (accessed June 13, 2011).
34. Elspeth Reeve, "Republicans Rethink the Politics of the Ryan Plan," *Atlantic Wire*, May 6, 2011, http://www.theatlanticwire.com/politics/2011/05/republicans-rethink -politics-ryan-plan/37444/ (accessed October 13, 2011).
35. Bob Cesca, "Keep Your Goddamn Government Hands Off My Medicare!" *Huffington Post*, August 5, 2009, http://www.huffingtonpost.com/bob-cesca/get-your-goddamn-governme_b_252326.html (accessed June 13, 2011).
36. Lisa Lerer, "Poll: Tea Party Economic Gloom Fuels Republican Momentum," *Bloomberg*, October 13, 2010, http://www.bloomberg.com/news/2010-10-14/tea -party-s-economic-gloom-fuels-republican-election-momentum-poll-says.html (accessed June 13, 2011).

CHAPTER 2

1. T. R. Reid, *The Healing of America* (New York: Penguin, 2009), p. 182.
2. "Obama's Health Care Speech to Congress," *New York Times*, September 9, 2009, http://www.nytimes.com/2009/09/10/us/politics/10obama.text.html (accessed March 21, 2011).
3. Pete520, "Repeal ObamaCare? Really? How?" Newsvine.com, November 3, 2010, http://sunrisegolf.newsvine.com/_news/2010/11/03/5401452-repeal-obamacare -really-how (accessed March 21, 2011).
4. Quoted in Jeff Muskus, "Pelosi: Health Insurance Companies the Real 'Villains,'" *Huffington Post*, July 30, 2009, http://www.huffingtonpost.com/2009/07/30/pelosi -health-insurance-c_n_247924.html (accessed October 30, 2011).
5. Michael A. Fletcher, "Obama Touts Public Plan at Health Care Town Hall," *Washington Post*, June 11, 2009, http://voices.washingtonpost.com/44/2009/06/11/obama_touts _public_plan_at_hea.html (accessed March 21, 2011).
6. "Obama's Fifth News Conference," *New York Times*, July 22, 2009, http://www .nytimes.com/2009/07/22/us/politics/22obama.transcript.html?pagewanted=11 (accessed March 21, 2011).
7. Morality is not, however, the only relevant factor. There are both deeper philosophic causes (above all, irrationalism and distorted views of human nature) as well as less important contributory factors (such as what economists refer to as "rent seeking" and what Ayn Rand called "pull peddling"). Our claim is not that morality is the sole factor but that it is the central factor.
8. Quoted in Leonard Peikoff, *The Ominous Parallels* (New York: Meridian, 1993), p. 123.

9. Herbert Croly, *The Promise of American Life* (New York: Cosimo, 2005), pp. 415, 422.

10. Theodore Roosevelt, "New Nationalism Speech," 1910, http://teachingamerican history.org/library/index.asp?document=501 (accessed March 21, 2011).

11. William Greider, *The Soul of Capitalism* (New York: Simon and Schuster Paperbacks, 2004), p. 15.

12. Jerry Z. Muller, *The Mind and the Market: Capitalism in Western Thought* (New York: Anchor, 2003), p. 184. See, for instance, Karl Marx, "On the Jewish Question," February 1844, http://www.marxists.org/archive/marx/works/1844/jewish-question / (accessed March 21, 2011).

13. Muller, *The Mind and the Market,* pp. 197–198.

14. Ibid.

15. Daniel Yergin and Joseph Stanislaw, *The Commanding Heights* (New York: Touchstone Books, 2002), pp. 4–6.

16. Franklin Delano Roosevelt, "Annual Message to Congress," January 3, 1936, http://www .presidency.ucsb.edu/ws/index.php?pid=15095#axzz1ncUq9tgf (accessed February 27, 2012).

17. Benito Mussolini, "The Doctrine of Fascism," 1932, http://www.constitution.org/tyr /mussolini.txt (accessed March 21, 2011).

18. Marx, "On the Jewish Question." Emphasis in original.

19. Karl Marx, "Critique of the Gotha Program," 1890–01, http://www.marxists.org /archive/marx/works/1875/gotha/ch01.htm (accessed March 21, 2011).

20. Adolf Hitler, *Mein Kampf,* trans. Ralph Manheim (New York: Houghton Mifflin, 1971), pp. 297–298.

21. Quoted in Eric Fromm, *Escape from Freedom* (New York: Farrar, 1941), p. 233.

22. Barack Obama, "The Audacity of Hope, by Barack Obama: On Principles & Values," http://www.ontheissues.org/Archive/Audacity_of_Hope_Principles_+_Values.htm (accessed March 21, 2011).

23. "Michelle Obama's Commencement Address," *New York Times,* May 16, 2009, http: //www.nytimes.com/2009/05/16/us/politics/16text-michelle.html (accessed March 21, 2011).

24. "Barack Obama's Feb. 12 Speech," *New York Times,* February 12, 2008, http://www .nytimes.com/2008/02/12/us/politics/12text-obama.html (accessed March 21, 2011).

25. Mitt Romney, *No Apology: Believe in America,* http://mittromney.com/sites/default /files/shared/BelieveInAmerica-PlanForJobsAndEconomicGrowth-Full.pdf (accessed October 20, 2011), p. 261.

26. George W. Bush, "First Inaugural Address," January 20, 2001, http://www.bartleby .com/124/pres66.html (accessed March 21, 2011).

27. Deut. 15:11(New International Version).

28. Luke 6:30 (New International Version).

29. Phil. 2:3 (New International Version).

30. Quoted in Thomas Aquinas, *Summa Theologica,* Question 84, Article 2, http://www .newadvent.org/summa/2084.htm (accessed March 21, 2011).

31. Thomas Aquinas, *Summa Theologica,* Question 84, Article 2.

32. See, for instance, Book I of Immanuel Kant, *Religion Within the Limits of Reason Alone* (New York: Harper & Row, 1960).

33. Our former colleague Alex Epstein gets credit for the designations we use for these two arguments. Alex Epstein and Yaron Brook, "Why Conservatives Can't Stop the Growth of the State," in Debi Ghate and Richard E. Ralston, eds., *Why Businessmen Need Philosophy: The Capitalist's Guide to the Ideas Behind Ayn Rand's "Atlas Shrugged"* (New York: New American Library, 2011), pp. 149–168.

34. Clyde Wayne Crews, "Ten Thousand Commandments 2009," Competitive Enterprise Institute, May 28, 2009, http://cei.org/studies-issue-analysis/ten-thousand-comman dments-2009 (accessed March 21, 2011).

35. Veronique de Rugy, "Bush's Regulatory Kiss-Off," *Reason,* January 2009, http://rea son.com/archives/2008/12/10/bushs-regulatory-kiss-off (accessed March 21, 2011).

36. Nicole V. Crain and W. Mark Crain, "The Impact of Regulatory Costs on Small Firms," *Small Business Research Summary,* September 2010, http://www.sba.gov /sites/default/files/rs371.pdf (accessed March 21, 2011).

37. John Allison and Ron Johnson, "Regulations Stifle Economic Growth," *Politico,* October 4, 2011, http://www.politico.com/news/stories/1011/65117.html (accessed October 17, 2011). We discuss the effects of regulation in more detail in chapter 11.

38. Business & Media Institute, "Bad Company: Executive Summary," June 21, 2006, http://www.mrc.org/bmi/reports/2006/Bad_Company_Executive_Summary.html (accessed March 22, 2011).

39. Michael Fumento, "Why Hollywood Hates Business," *Investor's Business Daily,* January 3, 1992, http://www.fumento.com/crime/hollywood.html (accessed March 22, 2011).

40. Diane Coyle, *The Economics of Enough* (Princeton, NJ: Princeton University Press, 2011), p. 33.

41. Thom Hartmann, *Threshold: The Crisis of Western Culture* (New York: Viking, 2009), p. 95.

42. Patt Morrison, "I'd Like My CEO Well-Done, Thanks," *Los Angeles Times,* February 5, 2009, http://www.latimes.com/news/opinion/la-oe-morrison5-2009feb05,0,244 2171.column (accessed March 22, 2011).

43. Maureen Dowd, "Wall Street's Socialist Jet-Setters," *New York Times,* January 27, 2009, http://www.nytimes.com/2009/01/28/opinion/28dowd.html (accessed March 22, 2011).

44. Diana B. Henriques, *The Wizard of Lies* (New York: Times Books, 2011), p. xxiv.

45. Tyler Flynn, "The Great Depression as Moral Failure," http://www.calvin.edu/henry /research/symposiumpapers/Symp09Flynn.pdf (accessed March 22, 2011).

46. "Consumers Believe Greed Is the Reason for Rising Health Care Costs," *AllBusiness,* January 1, 2007, http://www.allbusiness.com/health-care-social-assistance/4014187 -1.html (accessed February 24, 2010).

47. Peter Dreier, "Health Insurance Industry Exposes Its Insatiable Greed," *Huffington Post,* October 12, 2009, http://www.huffingtonpost.com/peter-dreier/health-insur ance-industry_b_318066.html (accessed February 24, 2010).

48. Janet Hook, "'Greed' Inflates Drug Prices, Democrats Say," *Los Angeles Times,* July 17, 2002, http://articles.latimes.com/2002/jul/17/nation/na-drugs17 (accessed February 24, 2010).

49. National Public Radio, "Human Greed Lies at Root of Economic Crisis," September 23, 2008, http://www.npr.org/templates/story/story.php?storyId=94930841 (acces sed March 22, 2011).

50. Coyle, *The Economics of Enough,* p. 54.

51. See chapters 4 and 13. For an overview of the actual facts concerning the Great Depression, see Lawrence W. Reed, "Great Myths of the Great Depression," January 1, 1998, http://www.mackinac.org/4013 (accessed March 22, 2011), and Burton W. Folsom, Jr., *New Deal or Raw Deal? FDR's Economic Legacy Has Damaged America* (New York: Threshold, 2008).

52. Mary Meeker, *USA Inc.: A Basic Summary of America's Financial Statements,* February 2001, http://www.kpcb.com/usainc/USA_Inc.pdf, p. 55 (accessed October 3, 2011).

Note that Meeker's estimate is a little less than 60 percent, as she does not include funding for education.

53. Ibid., p. 74.

54. Robert Rector, "Understanding and Reducing Poverty in America," Heritage Foundation, September 25, 2008, http://www.heritage.org/Research/Welfare/tst 040209b.cfm (accessed March 21, 2011).

55. Quoted in Ron Chernow, *Alexander Hamilton* (New York: Penguin, 2005), p. 300.

56. "US Government Spending as Percent of GDP," http://www.usgovernmentspending .com/us_20th_century_chart.html#usgs302 (accessed November 2, 2010). We are not generally fans of aggregate numbers, which are not fully reflective of reality, but we use them on occasion, for whatever "ballpark value" they provide.

57. Meeker, *USA Inc.*, p. 247.

58. Ibid.

59. Ibid., p. xiii.

60. Terry Gross, "Looking at President Bush, Seeing an 'Impostor,'" *National Public Radio*, February 22, 2006, http://www.npr.org/templates/story/story.php?storyId =5227215 (accessed March 22, 2011).

61. Walter I. Trattner, *From Poor Law to Welfare State: A History of Social Welfare in America* (New York: Free Press, 1994), pp. 296–297.

62. Barack Obama, "Remarks by the President in Commencement Address at the University of Notre Dame," May 17, 2009, http://www.whitehouse.gov/the_press_of fice/Remarks-by-the-President-at-Notre-Dame-Commencement/ (accessed March 22, 2011).

63. *United States v. 12 200-Ft. Reels of Film*, 413 U.S. 123 (1973), http://caselaw.lp.findlaw .com/scripts/getcase.pl?navby=case&court=us&vol=413&invol=123 (accessed March 22, 2011).

CHAPTER 3

1. Irving Kristol, *Two Cheers for Capitalism* (New York: Signet, 1979), p. 80.

2. Michael Novak, "Wealth and Virtue: The Moral Case for Capitalism," *National Review Online*, February 18, 2004, http://www.nationalreview.com/novak/novak 200402180913.asp (accessed March 22, 2011).

3. Rich Karlgaard, "How Moral Is Capitalism?" Forbes.com, February 12, 2007, http: //www.forbes.com/forbes/2007/0212/027.html (accessed March 22, 2011).

4. James L. Doti, "Capitalism and Greed," James L. Doti and Dwight R. Lee, eds., *The Market Economy: A Reader* (Los Angeles: Roxbury, 1991), p. 7.

5. Greg Forster, "Sacred Enterprise," *Claremont Review*, August 12, 2009, http://www .claremont.org/publications/crb/id.1646/article_detail.asp (accessed March 22, 2011).

6. Arthur Brooks and Paul Ryan, "The Size of Government and the Choice This Fall," *Wall Street Journal*, September 13, 2010, http://online.wsj.com/article/SB100014240 52748704358904575478141708959932.html (accessed March 22, 2011).

7. Quoted in Robert H. Bork, *Slouching Towards Gomorrah: Modern Liberalism and American Decline* (New York: Regan, 1997), p. 65.

8. Bork, *Slouching Towards Gomorrah*, p. 56.

9. Rick Santorum, *It Takes a Family: Conservatism and the Common Good* (Wilmington, DE: ISI Books, 2005), p. 44.

10. Adam Smith, *The Theory of Moral Sentiments* (Indianapolis: Liberty Classics, 1976), p. 305.

11. Adam Smith, *The Wealth of Nations* (New York: Bantam, 2003), bk. 5, chap. 1, p. 989.

12. George Gilder, "The Moral Sources of Capitalism," in Douglas A. Jeffrey, ed., *Educating for Liberty: The Best of "Imprimis," 1972–2002* (Hillsdale, MI: Hillsdale College Press, 2002), pp. 130–131, 136.

13. Smith, *The Wealth of Nations,* bk. 4, chap. 2, p. 572.

14. Gilder, "The Moral Sources of Capitalism," pp. 129–139.

15. Stephen Miller, "Adam Smith and the Commercial Republic," *Public Interest* (Fall 1980): 119.

16. F. A. Hayek, *The Road to Serfdom* (Chicago: University of Chicago Press, 1994), p. 41.

17. Kristol, *Two Cheers for Capitalism,* p. 55.

18. David Brooks, "How to Reinvent the GOP," *New York Times Magazine,* August 29, 2004.

19. David Brooks, "A Return to National Greatness: A Manifesto for a Lost Creed," *Weekly Standard,* March 3, 1997.

20. Brooks, "How to Reinvent the GOP."

21. For an analysis of "American Greatness" conservatism, see C. Bradley Thompson with Yaron Brook, *Neoconservatism: An Obituary for an Idea* (Boulder, CO: Paradigm, 2010), chap. 10.

22. David Brooks, "Love the Service around Here," *New York Times,* November 11, 2001.

23. Irving Kristol, "A Conservative Welfare State," *Wall Street Journal,* June 14, 1993.

24. David Frum, "Two Cheers for the Welfare State," *FrumForum,* April 16, 2011, http://www.frumforum.com/two-cheers-for-the-welfare-state (accessed January 10, 2012).

25. Terry Gross, "Looking at President Bush, Seeing an 'Impostor,'" *National Public Radio,* February 22, 2006, http://www.npr.org/templates/story/story.php?storyId=5227215 (accessed March 22, 2011).

26. William McGurn, "After the Welfare State," *Wall Street Journal,* April 5, 2011, http://online.wsj.com/article/SB10001424052748703806304576242960277394774.html (accessed April 13, 2011).

27. Ibid.

28. Quoted in Jacob Weisberg, "The Complete Bushisms," *Slate,* March 20, 2009, http://www.slate.com/id/76886/ (accessed March 22, 2011).

29. Will Bunch, *Tear Down This Myth* (New York: Free Press, 2009), p. 51.

CHAPTER 4

1. Some commentators have noted that early in his life, Greenspan was a friend and student of Ayn Rand, and have drawn the conclusion that his actions as Federal Reserve chairman reflect her philosophy. As will become clear, Greenspan abandoned Rand's philosophy long ago. As just one indication, note that Rand opposed the very existence of the Federal Reserve. Whatever one can say about Greenspan's policies or, more broadly, this country's economic policies over the last thirty years, one cannot plausibly maintain they have anything to do with what Rand advocated.

2. Alan Greenspan, *The Age of Turbulence* (New York: Penguin, 2008), p. 233.

3. Alan Greenspan, "Gold and Economic Freedom," in Ayn Rand, *Capitalism: The Unknown Ideal* (New York: Signet, 1967), p. 105.

4. Steven Horwitz and Peter J. Boettke, *The House that Uncle Sam Built: The Untold Story of the Great Recession of 2008,* http://www.fee.org/doc/the-house-uncle-sam-built (accessed November 2, 2010).

5. Our brief sketch won't come close to cataloging all the ways government intervention distorted the housing and financial markets. For fuller treatments, see Thomas E. Woods, Jr., *Meltdown* (Washington, D.C.: Regnery, 2009); Thomas Sowell, *The*

Housing Boom and Bust (New York: Basic Books, 2009); and Johan Norberg, *Financial Fiasco* (Washington, D.C.: Cato Institute, 2009). See also Yaron Brook, "The Financial Crisis: What Happened and Why," http://arc-tv.com/the-financial-crisis-what -happened-and-why/ (accessed November 2, 2010).

6. Board of Governors of the Federal Reserve System, "The Federal Reserve System: Purposes and Functions," June 2005, http://www.federalreserve.gov/pf/pdf/pf _complete.pdf (accessed April 13, 2011).

7. See, for instance, Woods, *Meltdown*; and George Selgin, William D. Lastrapes, and Lawrence H. White, "Has the Fed Been a Failure?" December 2010, http://www.cato .org/pubs/researchnotes/WorkingPaper-2.pdf (accessed April 13, 2011).

8. Paul Krugman, "Dubya's Double Dip?" *New York Times,* August 2, 2002, http://www .nytimes.com/2002/08/02/opinion/dubya-s-double-dip.html (accessed April 13, 2011).

9. One of the ironies was that, in many cases, government policies, such as "open space" restrictions on building, artificially *increased* the cost of housing. In his book *The Housing Boom and Bust,* Sowell extensively examines the role these policies played in the crises.

10. Jo Becker, Sheryl Gay Stolberg, and Stephen Labaton, "White House Philosophy Stoked Mortgage Bonfire," *New York Times,* December 20, 2008, http://www.nytimes .com/2008/12/21/business/21admin.html (accessed April 13, 2011).

11. Sowell, *The Housing Boom and Bust,* p. 31.

12. James R. Barth, Tong Li, Wenling Lu, Triphon Phumiwasana, and Glenn Yago, *The Rise and Fall of the U.S. Mortgage and Credit Markets: A Comprehensive Analysis of the Meltdown,* Milken Institute, January 2009, http://www.milkeninstitute.org/pdf /Riseandfallexcerpt.pdf (accessed April 13, 2011), p. 18.

13. Fannie Mae, "Understanding America's Homeownership Gaps: 2003 Fannie Mae National Housing Survey," http://www.fanniemae.com/global/pdf/media/survey /survey2003.pdf (accessed April 13, 2011).

14. Russell Roberts, "How Government Stoked the Mania," *Wall Street Journal,* October 3, 2008, http://online.wsj.com/article/SB122298982558700341.html (accessed April 13, 2011).

15. Quoted in Gerald Prante, "Barney Frank on Fannie Mae and Freddie Mac in 2003," Tax Policy Blog, September 17, 2008, http://www.taxfoundation.org/blog /show/23617.html (accessed April 13, 2011).

16. You can find some of the most important ones at *Alphabet Soup,* http://www.bankers online.com/abcsoup/ (accessed October 30, 2011).

17. Horwitz and Boettke, *The House that Uncle Sam Built.* See also Arnold Kling, "Not What They Had in Mind: A History of Policies that Produced the Financial Crisis of 2008," September 2009, http://mercatus.org/publication/not-what-they-had -mind-history-policies-produced-financial-crisis-2008 (accessed October 29, 2011). It should be noted that deregulation does not, in most cases, mean getting rid of regulations completely. Rather it means *re-regulation,* that is, changing the rules from one set to another. In other words, deregulation does not always make things more free.

18. It should be noted that while Lehman Brothers was not bailed out, all other major financial institutions were. And, even in the case of Lehman, its management and many of its creditors believed, to the last minute, that the government would indeed bail them out.

19. George W. Bush, "Remarks at St. Paul AME Church in Atlanta, Georgia," June 17, 2002, http://www.presidency.ucsb.edu/ws/index.php?pid=62687 (accessed April 13, 2011).

20. John McCain, "Press Release—'In Case You Missed It': John McCain on the Financial Markets," September 16, 2008, http://www.presidency.ucsb.edu/ws/index .php?pid=91436#axzz1cHFILV8q (accessed October 30, 2011).

CHAPTER 5

1. Steve Jobs, "Steve Jobs Speaks Out," interview by Betsy Morris, CNN, March 7, 2008, http://money.cnn.com/galleries/2008/fortune/0803/gallery.jobsqna.fortune/index .html (accessed June 8, 2011).
2. Ibid.
3. Andrew Ross Sorkin, "The Mystery of Steve Jobs's Public Giving," *New York Times,* August 29, 2011, http://dealbook.nytimes.com/2011/08/29/the-mystery-of-steve -jobss-public-giving/ (accessed October 3, 2011).
4. Leander Kahney, "Jobs vs. Gates: Who's the Star?" *Wired,* January 25, 2006, http://www .wired.com/gadgets/mac/commentary/cultofmac/2006/01/70072 (accessed October 3, 2011).
5. Quoted in "Jobs vs. Gates: A Thirty Year War," CNN.com, May 25, 1993, http: //money.cnn.com/galleries/2008/fortune/0806/gallery.gates_v_jobs.fortune/2.html (accessed October 3, 2011).
6. Quoted in Walter Isaacson, *Steve Jobs* (New York: Simon and Schuster, 2011), p. 407.
7. Steve Fishman, "The Madoff Tapes," *New York Magazine,* February 27, 2011, http: //nymag.com/print/?/news/features/berniemadoff-2011-3/ (accessed June 7, 2011).
8. Steve Fishman, "Bernie Madoff, Free at Last," *New York Magazine,* June 6, 2010, http://nymag.com/news/crimelaw/66468/ (accessed June 7, 2011).
9. Ayn Rand, "Introduction," *The Virtue of Selfishness* (New York: Signet, 1964).

CHAPTER 6

1. Aristotle, *Nicomachean Ethics,* trans. F. H. Peters (New York: Barnes & Noble, 2004), bk. 4, p. 75.
2. Gen. 22 (New International Version).
3. See Leonard Peikoff, *The Ominous Parallels* (New York: Penguin, 1993), pp. 84–85.
4. In addition to Rand's own works, her moral views have been elucidated in a number of later works. The most important of these is *Objectivism: The Philosophy of Ayn Rand* (New York: Penguin, 1991), a presentation of Rand's full philosophic system, written by her longtime student Leonard Peikoff. Other valuable works include *Ayn Rand's Normative Ethics: The Virtuous Egoist* by Tara Smith (New York: Cambridge University Press, 2006), and her earlier work on the foundations of ethics, *Viable Values* (Lanham, MD: Rowman & Littlefield, 2000). The professional philosophers among you should also see Darryl Wright, "Reasoning about Ends: Life as a Value in Ayn Rand's Ethics," in Allan Gotthelf, ed., and James G. Lennox, assoc. ed., *Metaethics, Egoism, and Virtue: Studies in Ayn Rand's Normative Theory* (Pittsburgh: University of Pittsburgh Press, 2011). One of Rand's most important essays on her moral theory, "The Objectivist Ethics," is available for free online at: http://www .aynrand.org/site/PageServer?pagename=ari_ayn_rand_the_objectivist_ethics.
5. Ayn Rand, *Atlas Shrugged* (New York: Penguin, 1999), p. 1014.
6. Ibid., p. 701.
7. Ibid., p. 1058. For a systematic treatment of the virtue of rationality, see Peikoff, *Objectivism: The Philosophy of Ayn Rand,* pp. 220–229; and Smith, *Ayn Rand's Normative Ethics,* chapter 3.
8. Ayn Rand, "The Objectivist Ethics," *The Virtue of Selfishness* (New York: Signet, 1964).

9. For Ayn Rand's view of the source of emotions and an indication of what it means to understand them, see Peikoff, *Objectivism: The Philosophy of Ayn Rand,* pp. 153–158.

10. David Friedman, *Hidden Order* (New York: Harper, 1997), pp. 3–4.

11. Smith, *Ayn Rand's Normative Ethics,* p. 48. Ayn Rand defined rationality as "man's basic virtue, the source of all his other virtues," in Ayn Rand, *The Virtue of Selfishness* (New York: Signet, 1964), p. 27.

12. Ayn Rand, *Capitalism: The Unknown Ideal* (New York: Signet, 1967), p. 8.

13. For a systematic presentation of the virtue of productiveness, see Peikoff, *Objectivism: The Philosophy of Ayn Rand,* pp. 292–303; and Smith, *Ayn Rand's Normative Ethics,* chapter 8.

14. Austin Hill and Scott Rae, *The Virtues of Capitalism: A Moral Case for Free Markets* (Chicago: Northfield Publishing, 2010), p. 49.

15. Steve Jobs, Commencement Address, Stanford University, Stanford, California, June 12, 2005, http://news.stanford.edu/news/2005/june15/jobs-061505.html (accessed June 8, 2011).

16. For more on Rand's view of money, see Rand, *Atlas Shrugged,* pp. 410–415; and Tara Smith, "Money *Can* Buy Happiness," *Reason Papers* 26, http://www.reasonpapers.com/pdf/26/rp_26_1.pdf (accessed June 8, 2011).

17. Plato, *Republic,* c. 360 BC, 4, Stephanus 550E. Quoted in Jerry Z. Muller, *The Mind and the Market: Capitalism in Modern European Thought* (New York: Anchor Books, 2002), p. 4.

18. Rand, "The Objectivist Ethics," pp. 34–35.

19. Stephen R. Covey, *The 7 Habits of Highly Effective People* (New York: Simon & Schuster, 2004), p. 211.

20. Quoted in John F. Love, *McDonald's: Behind the Arches* (New York: Bantam Books, 1986), p. 64.

21. For an in-depth treatment of this point, see Tara Smith, *Viable Values* (Lanham, MD: Rowman & Littlefield, 2000), pp. 162–182.

22. Rand, *Atlas Shrugged,* p. 1069.

23. Ibid., p. 1028.

24. "The World Mourns the Death of Mother Teresa," Mother Teresa of Calcutta Center, September 5, 1997, http://www.motherteresa.org/10th.html (accessed June 7, 2011).

25. On the question of whether Mother Teresa actually benefited others, see Christopher Hitchens, *The Missionary Position* (London: Verso, 1995).

26. Neil MacFarquhar, "Banks Making Big Profits from Tiny Loans," *New York Times,* April 13, 2010, http://www.nytimes.com/2010/04/14/world/14microfinance.html?pagewanted=print (accessed June 7, 2011).

27. "Yunus Blasts *Compartamos,*" *Bloomberg Businessweek,* December 13, 2007, http://www.businessweek.com/print/magazine/content/07_52/b4064045920958.htm (accessed June 7, 2011).

28. Suicide can sometimes be justified on the basis of rational selfishness, as in cases where a person has a painful, debilitating disease. See Peikoff, *Objectivism: The Philosophy of Ayn Rand,* pp. 247–248.

29. Mark 6:8–9; Matt. 19:20.

30. Marvin Olasky, *The Tragedy of American Compassion* (Washington, D.C.: Regnery, 1992), chapters 10 and 11. We discuss this history in more detail in chapter 12 of this book.

31. Rand, *Atlas Shrugged,* p. 1030.

32. Ibid., p. 1031.

33. David Platt, *Radical* (Colorado Springs, CO: Multnomah, 2010), p. 165. Thanks to Adam Edmonsond for this example.

34. Ayn Rand, *The Fountainhead* (New York: Signet, 1971), p. 637.
35. Deirdre N. McCloskey, *The Bourgeois Virtues: Ethics for an Age of Commerce* (Chicago: University of Chicago Press, 2006), pp. 257–258.

CHAPTER 7

1. Ayn Rand, *Atlas Shrugged* (New York: Penguin, 1999), pp. 29–30.
2. Onkar Ghate, "The Radicalness of *Atlas Shrugged*," *Orange County Register,* May 6, 2007, http://www.aynrand.org/site/News2?page=NewsArticle&id=15491&news_iv _ctrl=2121 (accessed October 3, 2011). Ghate discusses the issue of Rand's view of heroism and its relationship to the case for freedom in "*Atlas Shrugged:* America's Second Declaration of Independence," in Debi Ghate and Richard E. Ralston, eds., *Why Businessmen Need Philosophy: The Capitalist's Guide to the Ideas Behind Ayn Rand's "Atlas Shrugged"* (New York: New American Library, 2011), pp. 253–266.
3. Quoted in Richard S. Tedlow, *Giants of Enterprise* (New York: HarperCollins, 2001), p. 37.
4. Quoted in H. W. Brands, *American Colossus: The Triumph of Capitalism, 1865–1900* (New York: Doubleday, 2010), p. 78.
5. Jean-Baptiste Say, *A Treatise on Political Economy* (New York: Cosimo, 2007), p. 80.
6. Ibid.
7. Ibid.
8. George Reisman, *Capitalism* (Ottawa, IL: Jameson, 1998), p. 475.
9. Josh Kaufman, *The Personal MBA: Master the Art of Business* (New York: Penguin, 2010), pp. 7–8.
10. Credit for looking at the functions of the businessman in terms of the entrepreneur, the manager, and the capitalist goes to Reisman, *Capitalism.*
11. Tony Hsieh, *Delivering Happiness: A Path to Profits, Passion, and Purpose* (New York: Business Plus, 2010), p. 103.
12. Louis V. Gerstner, Jr., *Who Says Elephants Can't Dance?* (New York: HarperBusiness, 2002), p. 23.
13. Ibid., p. 59.
14. Ibid., p. 61.
15. Ibid., p. 31.
16. Ibid., pp. 44–45.
17. Thom Hartmann, *Threshold: The Crisis of Western Culture* (New York: Viking, 2009), p. 95.
18. William J. Bernstein, *The Birth of Plenty* (New York: McGraw-Hill, 2004), p. 125.
19. Ibid., pp. 126–127.
20. Yaron talks about the productive contribution of capitalists at length in "The Morality of Moneylending: A Short History," *Why Businessmen Need Philosophy: The Capitalist's Guide to the Ideas Behind Ayn Rand's "Atlas Shrugged"* (New York: New American Library, 2011); and in his talk "In Defense of Finance," http://www.ayn rand.org/site/PageServer?pagename=reg_ls_defense_finance (accessed November 14, 2011).
21. Scott Adams, "Dilbert," Universal Uclick, http://dilbert.com/strips/comic/1993-10-20/ (accessed June 9, 2011).
22. Thom Hartmann, *Screwed: The Undeclared War Against the Middle Class* (San Francisco: Berrett-Koehler, 2006), p. 63.
23. Deirdre N. McCloskey, *The Bourgeois Virtues: Ethics for an Age of Commerce* (Chicago: University of Chicago Press, 2006), p. 137.
24. Reisman, *Capitalism,* p. 479.

25. See, for instance, Robert P. Murphy, *Lessons for the Young Economist* (Auburn, AL: Ludwig von Mises Institute, 2010), pp. 128–131.

26. Rand, *Atlas Shrugged*, p. 1065. Edgar K. Browning makes a similar point in *Stealing from Each Other* (Westport, CT: Praeger, 2008), pp. 158–159.

27. Charles Platt, "Fly on the Wal," *New York Post*, February 7, 2009, http://www.nypost.com/p/news/opinion/opedcolumnists/item_K8hD47GcZBkh1v3SjNYldI;jsessionid=2C3BED13F51C26DFB78686D10D2E413D (accessed June 9, 2011).

28. Ibid. We should add that we are no fans of Wal-Mart in many respects—above all, their political profiteering in recent years.

29. Ayn Rand, *For the New Intellectual* (New York: Signet, 1963), p. 27.

30. Daniel Bell, "The New Class: A Muddled Concept," *Transaction/Society* 16, no. 2 (January/February 1979): 17; reprinted in Barry Bruce-Briggs, ed., *The New Class?* (New Brunswick, NJ: Transaction Books, 1979).

CHAPTER 8

1. Quoted in Donald L. Luskin and Andrew Greta, *I Am John Galt* (Hoboken, NJ: John Wiley & Sons, 2011), p. 87.

2. Personal interview with John Allison, July 6, 2010.

3. Ibid.

4. Irving Kristol, *Two Cheers for Capitalism* (New York: Basic Books, 1978), p. 83.

5. Gary Hamel, "The Hole in the Soul of Business," *Wall Street Journal*, January 13, 2010, http://blogs.wsj.com/management/2010/01/13/the-hole-in-the-soul-of-business/tab/print/ (accessed June 8, 2011).

6. David Brooks, "The Genteel Nation," *New York Times*, September 9, 2010, http://www.nytimes.com/2010/09/10/opinion/10brooks.html (accessed June 8, 2011).

7. Thomas Sowell, *Basic Economics: A Common Sense Guide to the Economy*, 2nd ed. (New York: Basic Books, 2004), p. 79.

8. Isabel Paterson, *The God of the Machine* (New Brunswick, NJ: Transaction Publishers, 2006), p. 221.

9. Barack Obama, "Presidential Remarks on U.S. Exports and Jobs," July 7, 2010, http://www.c-spanvideo.org/videoLibrary/clip.php?appid=598431426 (accessed October 3, 2011).

10. Here we ignore cases where the government intervenes to create winners and losers, a phenomenon we discuss in chapter 10.

11. Ron Chernow, *The House of Morgan* (New York: Grove Press, 2010), p. 154.

12. Tony Hsieh, *Delivering Happiness* (New York: Business Plus, 2010), p. 184.

13. John Allison, "Using Ayn Rand's Values to Create Competitive Advantage in Business," April 4, 2011 (accessed March 17, 2012).

14. Quoted in Edwin A. Locke, *The Prime Movers* (New York: AMACOM, 2000), p. 44.

15. Quoted in ibid, pp. 44–45.

16. Larry Bossidy and Ram Charan, *Execution: The Discipline of Getting Things Done* (New York: Crown Business, 2002), p. 67.

17. Hsieh, *Delivering Happiness*, p. 179.

18. James C. Collins and Jerry I. Porras, *Built to Last: Successful Habits of Visionary Companies* (New York: HarperBusiness, 1994), pp. 185–186.

19. Louis V. Gerstner, Jr., *Who Says Elephants Can't Dance?: Inside IBM's Historic Turnaround* (New York: HarperBusiness, 2002).

20. Charles Koch, *The Science of Success: How Market-Based Management Built the World's Largest Private Company* (Hoboken, NJ: John Wiley & Sons, 2007).

21. John Allison, introduction to Debi Ghate and Richard E. Ralston, eds., *Why Businessmen Need Philosophy: The Capitalist's Guide to the Ideas Behind Ayn Rand's "Atlas Shrugged"* (New York: New American Library, 2011), p. ix.

22. Andrew S. Grove, *Only the Paranoid Survive* (New York: Currency, 1999), pp. 85–86.

23. Ibid., p. 89.

24. Locke, *The Prime Movers,* p. 44.

25. Sam Walton, *Made in America* (New York: Doubleday, 1992), p. 47.

26. Ibid., p. 56.

27. Ibid., p. 27.

28. Robert Sobel, *When Giants Stumble: Classic Business Blunders and How to Avoid Them* (Paramus, NJ: Prentice Hall, 1999), p. 240.

29. Burton W. Folsom, *The Myth of the Robber Barons* (Herndon, VA: Young America's Foundation, 2003), p. 27; and Michael P. Malone, *James J. Hill: Empire Builder of the Northwest* (Norman, OK: University of Oklahoma Press, 1996), pp. 89–91, 254–255.

30. Folsom, *The Myth of the Robber Barons,* pp. 17–18.

31. Hsieh, *Delivering Happiness,* p. 188.

32. "The 10 Best (and 10 Worst) Companies for Customer Service," *Focus,* September 9, 2009, http://www.focus.com/fyi/10-best-and-10-worst-companies-customer-ser vice/ (accessed November 30, 2011).

33. Moreover, even if a businessman is motivated by "next quarter's stock price," it's still true that *stock prices* are forward looking. In other words, they tend to reflect not so much a company's returns today but its projected returns in the years to come. A businessman driven to increase his stock price today should do so by positioning his company to become more successful in the future.

34. Judith Rehak, "Tylenol Made a Hero of Johnson & Johnson: The Recall that Started It All," *New York Times,* March 23, 2002, http://www.nytimes.com/2002/03/23/your -money/23iht-mjj_ed3_.html (accessed June 9, 2011).

35. Steve Denning, "The Dumbest Idea in the World: Maximizing Shareholder Value," *Forbes.com,* November 28, 2011, http://www.forbes.com/sites/stevedenning/2011/11 /28/maximizing-shareholder-value-the-dumbest-idea-in-the-world/ (accessed January 12, 2012).

36. David F. D'Alessandro, *Brand Warfare: 10 Rules for Building the Killer Brand* (New York: McGraw-Hill, 2001), p. 171.

37. Michael W. Fedo, "How Control Data Turns a Profit on Its Good Works," *New York Times,* January 7, 1979.

38. D'Alessandro, *Brand Warfare,* pp. 171–173.

39. Brian Goldner, "Corporate Social Responsibility," http://www.allyservice.com/en /News.asp?vid=2819.

40. Ibid.

41. It is sometimes claimed that philanthropic activities can bolster a company's bottom line. In some cases, this appears to be true, although it's not clear why—for instance, whether it is because of the philanthropy or the advertising that comes along with it. See, for example, "Corporate Philanthropy Inspires Trust: Does It Also Prompt Higher Profits?" *Knowledge@Wharton,* January 10, 2007, http://knowledge .wharton.upenn.edu/article.cfm?articleid=1638 (accessed January 12, 2012). It also seems likely that to the extent that philanthropy per se helps a corporation's bottom line, that is precisely because of today's widespread animus against the profit motive: If people did not view profit seekers with suspicion, then businessmen would not have to "buy" a new self-image with apparent sacrifices.

42. Ayn Rand, *Atlas Shrugged* (New York: Penguin, 1999), pp. 480–481.

CHAPTER 9

1. Richard S. Tedlow, *Giants of Enterprise* (New York: HarperCollins, 2001), p. 119.
2. Ibid., pp. 125–126.
3. Larry Schweikart and Lynne Pierson Doti, *American Entrepreneur: The Fascinating Stories of the People Who Defined Business in the United States* (New York: AMACOM, 2010), pp. 264–268.
4. Quoted in Lawrence H. White, "The New Deal and Institutionalist Economics," working paper, Mercatus Center, George Mason University, August 2010, http://mercatus.org/sites/default/files/publication/WP1043_The%20New%20Deal%20and%20Institutionalist%20Economies.pdf (accessed October 4, 2011).
5. Ibid.
6. Ibid.
7. "The Confessions and Letters of St. Augustine: Book X. Chapter XXXV—Another Kind of Temptation Is Curiosity, Which Is Stimulated by the Lust of the Eyes," Christian Bookshelf, http://christianbookshelf.org/augustine/the_confessions_and_letters_of_st/chapter_xxxv_another_kind_of_temptation.htm (accessed June 9, 2011).
8. See, for instance, Charles Freeman, *The Closing of the Western Mind* (New York: Vintage Books, 2002).
9. Andrew Bernstein, *The Capitalist Manifesto: The Historic, Economic and Philosophic Case for Laissez-Faire* (Lanham, MD: University Press of America, 2005), pp. 59–62.
10. Gordon S. Wood, *The Radicalism of the American Revolution* (New York: Vintage Books, 1993), p. 90.
11. Of course, as we have indicated in earlier chapters, Smith's defense was incomplete: His brilliant economic case for capitalism was undercut by his relatively conventional approach to morality.
12. Alexis de Tocqueville, *Democracy in America* (New York: Signet, 2001), p. 214.
13. For an in-depth discussion of capitalism's development, see Nathan Rosenberg and L. E. Birdzell, *How the West Grew Rich: The Economic Transformation of the Industrial World* (New York: Basic Books, 1986); and William J. Bernstein, *The Birth of Plenty: How the Prosperity of the Modern World Was Created* (New York: McGraw-Hill, 2004).
14. Wikipedia contributors, "Invictus," *Wikipedia, The Free Encyclopedia,* http://en.wikipedia.org/wiki/Invictus (accessed June 9, 2011).
15. Tedlow, *Giants of Enterprise,* p. 27.
16. Quoted in ibid., p. 28.
17. Joyce Appleby, *The Relentless Revolution: A History of Capitalism* (New York: W. W. Norton & Company, 2010), p. 145.
18. Burton W. Folsom, Jr., *The Myth of the Robber Barons* (Herndon, VA: Young America's Foundation, 2003), pp. 2–3.
19. Leon Trotsky, *The Revolution Betrayed: What Is the Soviet Union and Where Is It Going?,* trans. Max Eastman (Garden City, NY: Doubleday, Doran & Company, 1937), p. 263.
20. Ludwig von Mises, *Human Action* (Auburn, AL: Ludwig von Mises Institute, 2008), p. 283.
21. Ayn Rand, *The Virtue of Selfishness* (New York: Signet, 1964), p. 110.
22. Ayn Rand, *Atlas Shrugged* (New York: Penguin, 1999), p. 1061. See also Ayn Rand, "Man's Rights," in *The Virtue of Selfishness* (New York: Signet, 1964).
23. Ayn Rand, "Collectivized 'Rights,'" in *The Virtue of Selfishness* (New York: Signet, 1964).

24. Leonard Peikoff, *Objectivism: The Philosophy of Ayn Rand* (New York: Penguin, 1991), p. 314. For a systematic treatment of the evil of force, see ibid., pp. 310–323.

25. Steven Reinberg, "Air Bags Dangerous for Tall, Small People: Study," *Washington Post,* May 17, 2007, http://www.washingtonpost.com/wp-dyn/content/article/2007/05/16/AR2007051602381.html (accessed June 9, 2011).

26. Thomas Jefferson, "First Inaugural Address in Washington, D.C.," March 4, 1801, http://www.bartleby.com/124/pres16.html (accessed June 9, 2011).

27. Ayn Rand, "The Nature of Government," in *The Virtue of Selfishness* (New York: Signet, 1964).

28. John Adams in George A. Peek, Jr., ed., *The Political Writings of John Adams: Representative Selections* (Indianapolis, IN: Hackett Publishing, 2003), p. xviii.

29. Ayn Rand, *Voice of Reason: Essays in Objectivist Thought* (New York: Meridian, 1990), pp. 90–91.

30. Ayn Rand, *Capitalism: The Unknown Ideal* (New York: Signet, 1967), p. 11.

31. David Cote, interview by Steve Forbes, "Intelligent Investing: Myth of the Villainous CEO," Forbes.com, March 25, 2011, http://video.forbes.com/fvn/inidaily/honeywell-david-cote-business-heroes (accessed June 9, 2011).

32. H. L. Mencken, "Types of Men," http://www.bizbag.com/mencken/menktypes.htm (accessed October 4, 2011).

33. Cote, "Intelligent Investing."

CHAPTER 10

1. Joseph Stiglitz, "Guided by an Invisible Hand," *New Statesman,* October 16, 2008, http://www.newstatesman.com/business/2008/10/economy-world-crisis-financial (accessed July 12, 2011).

2. Adam Smith, *The Wealth of Nations* (New York: Bantam, 2003), bk. 1, chap. 1, pp. 10–11.

3. Russell Roberts, *The Choice* (Upper Saddle River, NJ: Prentice Hall, 2001), p. 90. For more on this point, see the classic allegory, "I, Pencil," by Leonard Read, available at http://www.econlib.org/library/Essays/rdPncl1.html (accessed October 4, 2011).

4. Quoted in George Reisman, *Capitalism* (Ottawa, IL: Jameson, 1998), p. 137.

5. Prominent conservative George Gilder, for instance, defends this view. See interview with Marvin Olasky, "Server System," *World Magazine,* December 4, 2010, http://www.worldmag.com/articles/17351 (accessed October 4, 2011). A similar suggestion can be found in Ludwig von Mises's concept of consumer sovereignty.

6. Hedrick Smith, *The Russians* (New York: Ballantine Books, 1984), pp. 77–78.

7. Eric Dennis (with Alex Epstein), "HR 1098 and Why Sound Money Is Crucial for Energy," September 26, 2011, http://industrialprogress.net/2011/09/26/hr-1098-and-why-sound-money-is-crucial-for-energy-power-surge-episode-2/ (accessed October 4, 2011).

8. For a witty introduction to this complex subject, see Russell Roberts, *The Price of Everything* (Princeton, NJ: Princeton University Press, 2008), as well as Thomas Sowell, *Basic Economics,* 2nd ed. (New York: Basic Books, 2004).

9. Henry Hazlitt, *Economics in One Lesson* (New York: Three River Press, 1979), p. 161.

10. Ibid., p. 162.

11. "First Cell Phone Was a True 'Brick,'" Associated Press, April 11, 2005, http://www.msnbc.msn.com/id/7432915 (accessed June 10, 2011); "The Evolution of Cell Phone Design Between 1983–2009," *Webdesigner Depot,* May 22, 2011, http://www.webdesignerdepot.com/2009/05/the-evolution-of-cell-phone-design-between-1983

-2009/ (accessed June 10, 2011). We are of course foreshortening: Many, many other phones came on to the market during this time.

12. Ron Chernow, *Titan* (New York: Vintage Books, 1998), pp. 180–181.

13. "CPI Inflation Calculator," U.S. Bureau of Labor Statistics, http://146.142.4.24/cgi-bin/cpicalc.pl (accessed June 15, 2011).

14. Richard S. Tedlow, *Giants of Enterprise* (New York: HarperCollins, 2001), p. 164.

15. See also Ayn Rand, *Atlas Shrugged* (New York: Penguin, 1999), p. 1022; Ayn Rand, "The 'Conflicts' of Men's Interests," in *The Virtue of Selfishness* (New York: Signet, 1964); and Tara Smith, *Viable Values* (Lanham, MD: Rowman & Littlefield, 2000), pp. 174–187.

16. It is worth noting that Microsoft was hobbled by the Justice Department persecuting the company for its success.

17. See also Nathaniel Branden, "Common Fallacies About Capitalism," in Ayn Rand, *Capitalism: The Unknown Ideal* (New York: Signet, 1967), pp. 73–78; and Harry Binswanger, "The Dollar and the Gun," in Debi Ghate and Richard E. Ralston, eds., *Why Businessmen Need Philosophy: The Capitalist's Guide to the Ideas Behind Ayn Rand's "Atlas Shrugged"* (New York: New American Library, 2011), pp. 269–275.

18. Dominick T. Armentano, *Antitrust and Monopoly: Anatomy of a Policy Failure* (Oakland, CA: Independent Institute, 1990), p. 67. See also Alex Epstein, "Vindicating Capitalism: The Real History of the Standard Oil Company," *Objective Standard*, Summer 2008, http://www.theobjectivestandard.com/issues/2008-summer/standard-oil-company.asp (accessed December 3, 2011).

19. Michael Novak, *The Spirit of Democratic Capitalism* (London: IEA Health and Welfare Unit, 1991), p. 38.

20. Joyce Appleby, *The Relentless Revolution: A History of Capitalism* (New York: Norton, 2010).

21. Joseph A. Schumpeter, *Capitalism, Socialism and Democracy* (New York: Harper Perennial Modern Thought, 2008), pp. 82–83.

22. Ibid., p. 83.

23. Rand, *Capitalism: The Unknown Ideal*, pp. 18–19. Emphasis in original.

24. Nathan Rosenberg and L. E. Birdzell, Jr., *How the West Grew Rich* (New York: Basic Books, 1986), pp. 33–34.

25. Russell Roberts, "Obama vs. ATMs: Why Technology Doesn't Destroy Jobs," *Wall Street Journal*, June 22, 2011, http://online.wsj.com/article/SB10001424052702304070104576399704275939640.html (accessed July 13, 2011).

26. Some argue that government can promote innovation, say, by investing in "green energy" schemes. Morally, such efforts are wrong—they involve the government taking people's money and spending it on projects they would not support voluntarily. Economically, they are destructive: Government central planners cannot know where investment would be most productive. See, for instance, Ayn Rand, "Apollo 11," in *The Voice of Reason* (New York: Meridian, 1990), pp. 161–178; and Alex Epstein, "Energy at the Speed of Thought: The Original Alternative Energy Market," *Objective Standard*, Summer 2009, http://www.theobjectivestandard.com/issues/2009-summer/original-alternative-energy-market.asp (accessed January 16, 2012).

27. Nathaniel Branden, "The Divine Right of Stagnation," in Rand, *The Virtue of Selfishness*, p. 146. Emphasis in original.

28. See, for instance, Thomas Sowell, *Basic Economics*, 2nd ed. (New York: Basic Books, 2004), chap. 3.

29. "Shortages: Gas Fever: Happiness Is a Full Tank," *Time*, February 18, 1974, http://www.time.com/time/printout/0,8816,942763,00.html (accessed June 10, 2011).

30. See, for instance, Thomas Sowell's discussion of the effect of the minimum wage on employment among blacks in *Basic Economics*, p. 169.

31. See Barry Ritholtz, *Bailout Nation: How Greed and Easy Money Corrupted Wall Street and Shook the World Economy* (Hoboken, NJ: John Wiley & Sons, 2009).

32. These special cases refer to certain financial institutions in fractional reserve banking systems not backed by gold. When such institutions fail, this can cause a severe deflationary credit contraction, which can devastate an economy. This is one reason that we support freedom in banking and money (i.e., the gold standard); such institutions would never arise.

33. Ayn Rand, "Antitrust: The Rule of Unreason," in *The Voice of Reason* (New York: Meridian, 1990), pp. 254–259.

34. Thomas Catan and Siobhan Hughes, "Google Defends Dominance," *Wall Street Journal*, September 22, 2011, http://online.wsj.com/article/SB1000142405311190379150457658479115583386.html (accessed October 4, 2011).

35. Ayn Rand, "The Money-Making Personality," in Ghate and Ralston, eds., *Why Businessmen Need Philosophy*, p. 68.

36. Andrew Bernstein, *Capitalist Solutions* (New Brunswick, NJ: Transaction, 2011), p. 32.

37. Rand, *Voice of Reason*, p. 91.

38. For a good introduction to the history of capitalism, see Andrew Bernstein, *The Capitalist Manifesto* (Lanham, MD: University Press of America, 2005).

39. "What Was the U.S. GDP Then? Annual Observations in Table and Graphical Format—1790 to Present," http://www.measuringworth.org/usgdp/ (accessed October 4, 2011). Measured in 2000 dollars.

40. "Life Expectancy by Age, 1850–2004," http://www.infoplease.com/ipa/A0005140.html (accessed October 4, 2011).

41. W. Michael Cox and Richard Alm, *Myths of Rich and Poor* (New York: Basic Books, 1999), pp. 43, 57.

CHAPTER 11

1. Helen Jung, "Lemonade Stands Get Reprieve: Multnomah County Chairman Jeff Cogen Apologizes for Health Inspection Shutdown," *Oregon Live Blog*, August 5, 2010, http://blog.oregonlive.com/portland_impact/print.html?entry=/2010/08/lemonade_stands_get_reprieve_m.html (accessed June 10, 2011).

2. For our views on these kinds of controls, see chapter 10.

3. Gabriel Kolko, *The Triumph of Conservatism* (Chicago: Quadrangle Books, 1963), p. 99. See also Lawrence W. Reed, "Ideas and Consequences: Of Meat and Myth," *The Freeman* 44, no. 11 (November 1994), http://www.thefreemanonline.org/columns/ideas-and-consequences-of-meat-and-myth/ (accessed October 4, 2011).

4. "Consumer Probe," *Saturday Night Live Transcripts*, season 2, episode 10, http://snl-transcripts.jt.org/76/76jconsumerprobe.phtml (accessed October 4, 2011).

5. Larry Schweikart, *The Entrepreneurial Adventure: A History of Business in the United States* (Fort Worth, TX: Harcourt College Publishers, 2000), p. 76.

6. Our colleague Thomas Bowden gets credit for this valuable point.

7. Quoted in Russell Roberts, "FDR and FDIC," *Café Hayek*, December 2, 2008, http://cafehayek.com/2008/12/franklin-fannie.html (accessed June 10, 2011).

8. See, for instance, Richard M. Salsman, *The Collapse of Deposit Insurance—and the Case for Abolition* (Great Barrington, MA: American Institute for Economic Research, 1993).

9. Janet Adamy, "Calorie Rules Make Diet a Federal Affair," *Wall Street Journal,* April 2, 2011, http://online.wsj.com/article/SB10001424052748704530204576237203366549 010.html (accessed June 10, 2011).

10. Warren Meyer, "What the Fresh Hell Is This?" Forbes.com, July 8, 2010, http://www .forbes.com/2010/07/08/small-business-owner-regulation-opinions-columnists -warren-meyer_print.html (accessed June 10, 2011).

11. Robert S. Bresalier, Robert S. Sandler, Hui Quan, James A. Bolognese, M. Stat, Bettina Oxenius, Kevin Horgan, Christopher Lines, Robert Riddell, Dion Morton, Angel Lanas, Marvin A. Konstam, and John A. Baron, "Cardiovascular Events Associated with Rofecoxib in a Colorectal Adenoma Chemoprevention Trial," *New England Journal of Medicine* 352 (2011): 1092–1102. http://www.nejm.org/doi/pdf/10.1056 /NEJMoa050493 (accessed June 10, 2011).

12. Todd Zywicki, "Dodd-Frank and the Return of the Loan Shark: In the name of consumer protection, Congress has pushed more Americans outside the traditional banking system," *The Wall Street Journal,* January 4, 2011, http://online.wsj.com /article/SB10001424052748704735304576058211789874804.html (accessed June 10, 2011).

13. M. Peden, K. McGee, and G. Sharma, *The Injury Chart Book: A Graphical Overview of the Global Burden of Injuries* (Geneva, World Health Organization, 2002), http://whqlib doc.who.int/publications/924156220X.pdf (accessed February 27, 2012).

14. Matt Ridley, *The Rational Optimist* (New York: HarperCollins, 2010), p. 219.

15. Deirdre N. McCloskey, *The Bourgeois Virtues: Ethics for an Age of Commerce* (Chicago: University of Chicago Press, 2006), p. 474.

16. Hayek makes a similar observation in "History and Politics," F. A. Hayek, ed., *Capitalism and the Historians* (Chicago: Phoenix, 1963), pp. 15–17.

17. Jerry Z. Muller, *The Mind and the Market* (New York: Anchor, 2002), p. 202.

18. Todd G. Buchholz, *New Ideas from Dead Economists: An Introduction to Modern Economic Thought,* 2nd rev. ed. (New York: Plume, 2007), p. 135.

19. James Rolph Edwards, *Regulation, the Constitution, and the Economy: The Regulatory Road to Serfdom* (New York: University Press of America, 1998), pp. 96–97. Emphasis in original.

20. Michael Bindas, "*L.A. vs. Small Business,*" City Study Series, Institute for Justice, November 2010, http://www.ij.org/images/pdf_folder/city_studies/ij-losangeles_city study.pdf (accessed October 4, 2011).

21. "Whole Foods CEO: Healthy Food Is Affordable Necessity," *USA Today,* September 3, 2010, http://www.usatoday.com/money/industries/food/2010-08-31-wholefoods31 _CV_N.htm (accessed October 4, 2011).

22. Angeljean Chiaramida, "N.H. Fishermen Plead for Changes in Regulations," *Gloucester Times,* May 9, 2011, http://www.gloucestertimes.com/local/x1693503301/N-H-fisher men-plead-for-changes-in-regulations (accessed June 10, 2011).

23. "Federal Team Reviews Effects of Regulations," WMUR.com, May 11, 2011, http: //www.wmur.com/print/27844592/detail.html (accessed June 10, 2011).

24. Ayn Rand, "Choose Your Issues," *Objectivist Newsletter,* January 1962, p. 1.

CHAPTER 12

1. This quote, and next quote, from Ayn Rand, *Atlas Shrugged* (New York: Penguin, 1999), pp. 660–670.

2. Thomas A. Bowden, "What's America's Moral Ideal?" *Voices for Reason* (blog), Ayn Rand Institute, December 23, 2010, http://blog.aynrandcenter.org/whats-americas -moral-ideal/ (accessed June 10, 2011).

3. Gary M. Walton and Hugh Rockoff, *History of the American Economy*, 9th ed. (Toronto: Thomson Learning, 2002), p. 233.

4. Ibid., p. 392.

5. W. Michael Cox and Richard Alm, *Myths of Rich and Poor: Why We're Better Off Than We Think* (New York: Basic Books, 1999), p. 55.

6. Ibid., p. 43.

7. New York State Government Report, http://www.poorhousestory.com/YATES _REPORT_ENTIRE.htm#940 (accessed December 12, 2011).

8. "New York: 2000: Population and Housing Units Counts," U.S. Census Bureau report, September 2003, http://www.census.gov/prod/cen2000/phc-3-34.pdf (accessed June 10, 2011).

9. Charles Richmond Henderson, *Modern Methods of Charity* (New York: Macmillan, 1904), p. 447.

10. Walter I. Trattner, *From Poor Law to Welfare State: A History of Social Welfare in America* (New York: Free Press, 1994), pp. 92–93.

11. Marvin Olasky, *The Tragedy of American Compassion* (Washington, D.C.: Regnery, 1992), p. 153.

12. David T. Beito, *From Mutual Aid to the Welfare State: Fraternal Societies and Social Services, 1890–1967* (Chapel Hill: University of North Carolina Press, 2000), p. 219.

13. Ibid., p. 204.

14. Quoted in ibid., pp. 12–14.

15. Cox and Alm, *Myths of Rich and Poor*, p. 15.

16. Quoted in Jonah Goldberg, *Liberal Fascism* (New York: Doubleday, 2007), pp. 86–87.

17. Ibid.

18. Olasky, *The Tragedy of American Compassion*, p. 119.

19. Ibid., p. 140.

20. Ibid., p. 76.

21. Ibid., p. 121.

22. Edward Bellamy, *Looking Backward: 2000–1887*, Project Gutenberg, Historical Section, Shawmut College, Boston, August 3, 2008, http://www.gutenberg.org /files/624/624-h/624-h.htm (accessed June 10, 2011).

23. Olasky, *The Tragedy of American Compassion*, p. 136.

24. William Voegeli, *Never Enough: America's Limitless Welfare State* (New York: Encounter Books, 2010), pp. 69–93.

25. As Milton Friedman points out, the fact that Social Security was hard to sell to Americans is further evidence that most were able to thrive without an entitlement state. See "Milton Friedman—Social Security Myth," YouTube, http://www.youtube .com/watch?v=rCdgv7n9xCY (accessed December 8, 2011).

26. Charlotte A. Twight, *Dependent on DC: The Rise of Federal Control Over the Lives of Ordinary Americans* (New York: Palgrave, 2002), pp. 63–71; and Olasky, *The Tragedy of American Compassion*, pp. 157–158.

27. Voegeli, *Never Enough*, p. 91. See also pp. 149–150.

28. Edgar K. Browning, *Stealing from Each Other: How the Welfare State Robs Americans of Money and Spirit* (Westport, CT: Praeger, 2008), p. 91.

29. The exact cost to the individual is impossible to calculate, but some estimates are available. See, for instance, *USA Inc.: A Basic Summary of America's Financial Statements*, Kleiner Perkins Caufield & Byers, February 2011, www.kpcb.com /usainc/USA_Inc.pdf (accessed June 10, 2011); and Browning, *Stealing from Each Other*.

30. Theodore Dalrymple, *Life at the Bottom: The Worldview that Makes the Underclass* (Chicago: Ivan R. Dee, 2001), p. 158.

31. See, for instance, Walter E. Williams, *Up from the Projects: An Autobiography* (Stanford, CA: Hoover Institution Press, 2010), especially pp. 4–9.

32. Charles Murray discusses this phenomenon in *Losing Ground* (New York: Basic Books, 1994), pp. 186–191.

33. See, for instance, George Reisman, *Capitalism* (Ottawa, IL: Jameson, 1998), pp. 588–590, 658–661, and 938–942.

34. Ayn Rand, "Collectivized Ethics," in *The Virtue of Selfishness* (New York: Signet, 1964).

35. Ayn Rand, *Capitalism: The Unknown Ideal* (New York: Signet, 1967), p. 19. Emphasis in original.

36. Quoted in Pope Paul VI, "On the Development of Peoples," *Catholic Social Teaching*, March 26, 1967, http://www.vatican.va/holy_father/paul_vi/encyclicals/documents/hf_p-vi_enc_26031967_populorum_en.html (accessed December 12, 2011).

37. Quoted in Voegeli, *Never Enough*, p.123.

38. Olasky, *The Tragedy of American Compassion*, p. 152.

39. Ibid., p. 154.

40. Ibid., p. 165.

41. Ibid., pp.168–169.

42. Ibid., pp. 182–183.

43. Angelo M. Codevilla discusses the development of the entitlement mentality in America in *The Character of Nations* (New York: Basic Books, 1997), chap. 11.

44. Mark Steyn, *America Alone* (Washington, D.C.: Regnery, 2006), p. xi.

45. Ronald Regan, "Acceptance of the Presidential Nomination," 1980 Republican Convention, July 17, 1980, http://www.nationalcenter.org/ReaganConvention1980.html (accessed June 10, 2011).

46. Voegeli, *Never Enough*, p. 216.

47. Ibid., p. 217.

48. Dean Alfange, "Respectfully Quoted: A Dictionary of Quotations. 1989," Bartleby.com, http://www.bartleby.com/73/71.html (accessed February 27, 2012).

CHAPTER 13

1. Quoted in Robert Pear and David M. Herszenhorn, "Obama Hails Vote on Health Care as Answering 'the Call of History,'" *New York Times*, March 21, 2010, http://www.nytimes.com/2010/03/22/health/policy/22health.html (accessed December 8, 2011).

2. George Silver, "Health Care: Beyond Markets," *Washington Post*, November 11, 2004, http://www.washingtonpost.com/wp-dyn/articles/A41307-2004Nov10.html (accessed October 4, 2011).

3. This is a necessarily brief sketch. For fuller treatments, see Paul Starr, *The Social Transformation of American Medicine* (New York: Basic Books, 1982); John C. Goodman and Gerald L. Musgrave, *Patient Power* (Washington, D.C.: Cato Institute, 1993); John C. Goodman, Gerald L. Musgrave, and Devon M. Herrick, *Lives at Risk* (New York: Rowman & Littlefield, 2004); Michael F. Cannon and Michael D. Tanner, *Healthy Competition*, 2nd ed. (Washington, D.C.: Cato Institute, 2007).

4. Cannon and Tanner, *Healthy Competition*, p. 52.

5. Quoted in John Samples, *The Struggle to Limit Government* (Washington, D.C.: Cato Institute, 2010), p. 24.

6. "U.S. Health Plans Have History of Cost Overruns," *Washington Times*, November 18, 2009, http://www.washingtontimes.com/news/2009/nov/18/health-programs-have-history-of-cost-overruns/ (accessed October 4, 2011).

7. Meeker, *USA Inc.*, February 2011, http://www.kpcb.com/usainc/USA_Inc.pdf, p. x (accessed October 3, 2011).

8. Ibid.

9. Overall, the average American receives about *three times* as much care as he pays for during his working years—just one more piece of evidence that Medicare is not "insurance," as its supporters claim. Ricardo Alonso-Zaldivar, "Analysis Illustrates Big Gap between Medicare Taxes and Benefits," *Washington Post,* January 3, 2011, http://www.washingtonpost.com/wp-dyn/content/article/2011/01/02/AR2011010203213.html (accessed December 11, 2011).

10. "The Cost of Dying: End-of-Life Care," CBSNews.com, August 6, 2010, http://www.cbsnews.com/stories/2010/08/05/60minutes/main6747002.shtml (accessed October 4, 2011).

11. Carol Raphael, Joann Ahrens, and Nicole Fowler, "Financing End-of-Life Care in the USA," *Journal of the Royal Society of Medicine* 94, no. 9 (September 2001): 458–464, http://www.ncbi.nlm.nih.gov/pmc/articles/PMC1282187/ (accessed December 12, 2011).

12. "The Cost of Dying: End-of-Life Care."

13. Robert M. Ball, "Perspectives on Medicare: What Medicare's Architects Had in Mind," *Health Affairs* 14, no. 4 (1995): 62–72, http://content.healthaffairs.org/cgi/reprint/14/4/62.pdf (accessed October 4, 2011).

14. Goodman and Musgrave, *Patient Power,* pp. 302–304.

15. Ayn Rand, *Atlas Shrugged* (New York: Penguin, 1999), p. 744.

16. Cannon and Tanner, *Healthy Competition,* p. 55.

17. Ibid., p. 54.

18. Ronald Hamowy, "The Early Development of Medical Licensing Laws in the United States, 1875–1900," *Journal of Libertarian Studies* 3, no. 1, http://mises.org/journals/jls/3_1/3_1_5.pdf (accessed December 12, 2011).

19. Quoted in Starr, *The Social Transformation of American Medicine,* p. 30.

20. Goodman and Musgrave, *Patient Power,* p. 150.

21. Quoted in Starr, *The Social Transformation of American Medicine,* p. 126.

22. Christopher J. Conover, "Health Care Regulation: A $169 Billion Hidden Tax," *Policy Analysis,* no. 527, October 4, 2004, http://www.cato.org/pub_display.php?pub_id=2466 (accessed October 4, 2011).

23. Lin Zinser and Paul Hsieh, "Moral Health Care vs. 'Universal Health Care,'" *Objective Standard* 2, no. 4 (Winter 2007–2008), http://www.theobjectivestandard.com/issues/2007-winter/moral-vs-universal-health-care.asp (accessed October 4, 2011).

24. Alex Tabarrok, "Seeing Is Believing (in the Free Market)," *Marginal Revolution* (blog), November 23, 2004, http://marginalrevolution.com/marginalrevolution/2004/11/seeing_is_belie.html (accessed October 4, 2011).

25. Linda Gorman, "The History of Health Care Costs and Health Insurance," Wisconsin Policy Research Institute, October 2006, http://westandfirm.org/docs/Gorman-01.pdf (accessed October 4, 2011).

26. "How Much Do Catastrophic Health Plans Cost?" http://www.catastrophic-health-insurance.org/costs-of-catastrophic-health.php (accessed October 4, 2011).

27. Recall our discussion of private certification and licensing in chapter 11.

28. Paul Ryan, "The Roadmap Plan," http://www.roadmap.republicans.budget.house.gov/plan/#Healthsecurity (accessed October 4, 2011).

29. Thomas E. Woods, Jr., *Rollback* (Washington, D.C.: Regnery, 2011), p. 175.

30. According to Goodman and Musgrave, *Patient Power,* p. 150, "Numerous studies in the 1970s established that nonphysicians can safely perform many routine medical tasks. . . . Studies also showed that when trained nonphysicians were used innovatively

under the direction of physicians, the costs of medical treatment could be substantially reduced."

31. John C. Goodman, Michael Bond, Devon M. Herrick, Gerald L. Musgrave, Pamela Villarreal, and Joe Barnett, "Ten Steps to Reforming Medicaid," July 1, 2008, http://www.heartland.org/healthpolicy-news.org/article/23437/Ten_Steps_to_Reforming_Medicaid.html (accessed October 4, 2011).

32. Michael Tomasky, "Ayn Rand: The GOP's Favorite Bonkers Demagogue," *The Daily Beast,* June 6, 2011, http://www.thedailybeast.com/articles/2011/06/06/ayn-rand-the-gop-s-favorite-bonkers-demagogue.html (accessed October 4, 2011).

33. Eric Sapp, "GOP Must Choose: Ayn Rand or Jesus," *Huffington Post,* May 27, 2011, http://www.huffingtonpost.com/eric-sapp/ayn-rand-and-republicans_b_866097.html (accessed October 4, 2011); Jonathan Chait, "War on the Weak," *The Daily Beast,* April 10, 2011, http://www.thedailybeast.com/newsweek/2011/04/10/war-on-the-weak.html (accessed October 4, 2011).

34. Michael Sean Winters, "Catholic Academics Challenge Boehner," *National Catholic Reporter,* May 11, 2011, http://ncronline.org/blogs/distinctly-catholic/breaking-news-catholic-academics-challenge-boehner (accessed October 4, 2011).

35. Chait, "War on the Weak."

36. Ezra Klein, "What Happened to the Moral Case for Health-Care Reform?" *Wonkbook* (blog), *Washington Post,* July 27, 2009, http://voices.washingtonpost.com/ezra-klein/2009/07/what_happened_to_the_moral_cas.html (accessed October 4, 2011).

CHAPTER 14

1. Paul Krugman, "A Tale of Two Moralities," *New York Times,* January 13, 2011, http://www.nytimes.com/2011/01/14/opinion/14krugman.html (accessed June 14, 2011).

2. Harry Binswanger, *Objectivist Forum,* February 1980.

3. "A Pledge to America," GOP.gov, http://pledge.gop.gov/ (accessed October 4, 2011).

4. On this point, see our Forbes.com series, http://blogs.forbes.com/objectivist/2011/02/10/the-road-to-socialized-medicine-is-paved-with-pre-existing-conditions/, http://blogs.forbes.com/objectivist/2011/03/10/the-road-to-socialized-medicine-is-paved-with-preexisting-conditions-part-2/, http://blogs.forbes.com/objectivist/2011/04/06/the-road-to-socialized-medicine-is-paved-with-preexisting-conditions-part-3/.

5. Dean Baker, "'Free Market Fundamentalism' Is an Invention of Progressives," *Huffington Post* Business, June 14, 2010, http://www.huffingtonpost.com/dean-baker/free-market-fundamentalis_b_611659.html?view=print (accessed June 13, 2011).

6. Arthur C. Brooks, *The Battle: How the Fight between Free Enterprise and Big Government Will Shape America's Future* (New York: Basic Books, 2010), p. 3.

7. Arthur C. Brooks and Paul Ryan, "The Size of Government and the Choice This Fall," *Wall Street Journal,* September 13, 2010, http://online.wsj.com/article/SB10001424052748704358904575478141708959932.html (accessed June 13, 2011).

8. Milton Friedman and Rose Friedman, *Free to Choose: A Personal Statement* (New York: Harcourt Brace Jovanovich, 1980), p. 69.

9. Ibid., pp. 44, 133, 214, 270.

10. Ibid., p. 140.

11. F. A. Hayek, *The Road to Serfdom* (Chicago: University of Chicago Press, 1994), p. 21.

12. Ibid., pp. 22, 43. We should add that Friedman and Hayek were not consistent in the policies they opposed and supported.

13. Megan McArdle, "Why Do We Allow Inheritance at All?" *Atlantic,* June 6, 2011, http://www.theatlantic.com/business/archive/2011/06/why-do-we-allow-inheritance-at-all/240004/ (accessed June 8, 2011).

14. Thomas Jefferson to Thomas Law, "The Moral Sense," June 13, 1814, Teaching AmericanHistory.org, http://teachingamericanhistory.org/library/index.asp?document=1506 (accessed June 14, 2011).

15. Leonard Peikoff, *The Ominous Parallels: The End of Freedom in America* (New York: Meridian, 1993), p. 115.

16. Austin Hill and Scott Rae, *The Virtues of Capitalism: A Moral Case for Free Markets* (Chicago: Northfield Publishing, 2010), p. 62.

17. Credit for this helpful point goes to Onkar Ghate.

18. Hill and Rae, *The Virtues of Capitalism,* p. 138.

19. Ayn Rand, "The Anatomy of Compromise," in Debi Ghate and Richard E. Ralston, eds., *Why Businessmen Need Philosophy: The Capitalist's Guide to the Ideas of Behind Ayn Rand's "Atlas Shrugged"* (New York: New American Library, 2011), p. 229.

20. See on this point Onkar Ghate, "*Atlas Shrugged:* America's Second Declaration of Independence," in Ghate and Ralston, *Why Businessmen Need Philosophy,* pp. 253–266.

21. Ayn Rand, *Capitalism: The Unknown Ideal* (New York: Signet, 1967), p. viii.

22. James Madison, "No. 44," *The Federalist Papers,* January 25, 1788, http://press-pubs.uchicago.edu/founders/documents/a1_10_1s5.html (accessed June 14, 2011).

23. For more on this point, see Ayn Rand, "What Can One Do?" in *Philosophy: Who Needs It* (New York: Signet, 1984), as well as Yaron Brook's talk, "Defending Capitalism," http://arc-tv.com/defending-capitalism-2/ (accessed October 4, 2011).

24. Jeff Poor, "CNBC's Santelli Explains His Anti-Obamanomics Call for Revolt," Business and Media Institute, February 19, 2009, http://newsbusters.org/blogs/jeff-poor/2009/02/19/cnbcs-santelli-explains-his-anti-obamanomics-call-revolt (accessed February 27, 2012).

INDEX

ABOUT THE AUTHORS

YARON BROOK

Yaron Brook is president of the Ayn Rand Institute. He is a columnist for Forbes.com, coauthor of *Neoconservatism: An Obituary for an Idea,* and a contributor to *Why Businessmen Need Philosophy: The Capitalist's Guide to the Ideas Behind Ayn Rand's "Atlas Shrugged."* Dr. Brook is an internationally sought-after speaker on such topics as the causes of the financial crisis, the morality of capitalism, and U.S. foreign policy. He blogs at www.laissezfaireblog.com.

DON WATKINS

Don Watkins is a fellow at the Ayn Rand Institute. He is a columnist for Forbes.com, and his op-eds have appeared in such venues as *Investor's Business Daily, The Christian Science Monitor,* and *Forbes.* He appears frequently on radio and television, and is a regular guest on PJTV's *Front Page with Allen Barton.* He blogs at www.laissezfaireblog.com.

AYN RAND INSTITUTE

The Ayn Rand Institute, a nonprofit educational organization, was established in 1985 to serve as the center for the advancement of Objectivism. The institute brings Ayn Rand's ideas to the attention of students, scholars, business professionals, and the general public. Its Objectivist Academic Center provides university-level training in Objectivist philosophy and sponsors writing grants, fellowships, and scholarly publications. The institute's other programs include essay contests for high school and college students, a network of campus Objectivist clubs, and a campus speakers' bureau. For more information about the activities of the institute, please visit www.aynrand.org.